RAMLE REMADE

Danna Piroyansky

RAMLE REMADE

The Israelisation of an Arab Town
1948–1967

Pardes Publishing

PARDES PUBLISHING
1 Palmer Gate St., Haifa 3133602, Israel

Copyright © 2014 by Pardes Publishing

Copy-editor: Ami Asher

First published 2014

Printed in Israel

Danna, Piroyanski.
Ramle Remade: The Israelisation of an Arab Town 1948–1967
262 p. 15x23 cm.
Includes bibliographical references and index.
ISBN 978-1-61838-113-2 (paperback)
1. Israel.   2. Palestine.   3. I. Title

ISBN 978-1-61838-113-2 Paperback

To my grandparents,
Maria Cecilia Brawn-Wroclawski
and Mauricio Wroclawski

Contents

Acknowledgments. *9*

Introduction *11*

Chapter One
*Property and Ownership: Expropriation and
Reallocation in an Urban Setting* *23*

Chapter Two
Asset Appropriation: The Non-Free Market *61*

Chapter Three
On Men and Trees: The Town's Green Areas *99*

Chapter Four
*Walking the City: Communal Processions as
Spatial Performance.* *133*

Chapter Five
*The Old and the New City: Segregation,
Incorporation and Expansion* *167*

Epilogue
*Return Visits and the Uncertain Futures of an
Open-Ended City.* *205*

Appendix
An Abridged Historical Introduction. *217*

Bibliography *237*

Acknowledgments

An international research project supported by a grant from the GIF, the German-Israel Foundation for Scientific Research and Development, in 2005–2008 ('Out of Place: Ethnic Migration, Nation State formation and Property Regimes in Poland, Czechoslovakia and Palestine/Israel'), served as the womb in which this study was conceived. The book's conceptualisation and writing were accordingly framed and inspired by ongoing comparative discourse among project members (in workshops, conferences and personal correspondence), who subscribed to various disciplines—law, geography, sociology, and history—and whose work focused on several countries and cities. It is both a pleasure and an honour to thank all of the project's members and friends who contributed greatly to the design of this book—to Dieter Gosewinkel, Claudia Kraft, Sandy Kedar, Geremy Forman, Philipp Ther, Ana Moskal, Iris Engemann, Gal Oron, Anat Stern, and Rona Sela. Yfaat Weiss, who introduced me to the project and to modern history more generally, has become both a role model and a friend; reading several drafts of this manuscript she was ever happy to share her knowledge and insights with me, always doing it wisely and kindly. Daniel Monterescu is another project-member made friend who read and commented extensively throughout. The manuscript's anonymous and less anonymous readers offered their input and contributed to the book's final version, as did Ami Asher who edited the text, Orna Landman who proof-read, and Hila Malihi who helped in translating from the Arabic. This is also an opportunity to express my gratitude to

David Gottesmann and to Pardes Publishing House for helping this book see daylight.

Shmulik Kulishevsky, Yigal Sitri and Shimon Gat enabled access to valuable sources in Ramla's city archive, museum and historical landscape respectively, and were helpful in linking me with others to whom Ramla is dear—Hila Keren-Steinmatz and Bothaina Dabit among others. Ramla's past and present residents interviewed throughout this study deserve my special gratitude: Yonatan Tubali, Baruch Kamil, Michael Fanus, Tzipi Puter, Samir Dabit, Yona Sirius, Ehud Zaxenberg, Shmulik Partush, Ilana Elchalal, Yossi Gold, and the late Mouhhamad Taji. I am grateful also to Esther Jawitz, Shay Jawitz and Ruti Blumenfeld.

Helena and Galia at the Israel State Archives were always helpful and kind, as was Aviad Doron at the Israel Defense Forces and Defense Establishment Archives. Ramla Municipality Archive and Ramla's Museum, the Central Zionist Archives, Pinhas Lavon Institute for Labour Movement Research and the Haganah History Archive are likewise to be thanked, as are the libraries of the Hebrew University, Tel Aviv University and Beit Ariela library's newspapers archive.

Sharon Livne, Shira Philosof and Viola Rautenberg—my bright and beautiful friends—shared willingly good advice and contributed informed comments and sense of camaraderie, and I am ever grateful for their support.

On 6 June 1971 my grandparents first arrived in Ramla. Leaving Buenos Aires behind them on their way to resettle in a new homeland, they were sent by the Jewish Agency to reside in one of the town's new neighbourhoods. They stayed to live in Ramla for only two years howbeit this period has become deeply engraved in my family's past, an inseparable component of its intimate memories. My greatest appreciation and love is therefore to my family, to my mother Ana, and above all to my beloved triumvirate—Avi, Idan and Or Stokholm—who help me live fully every moment of the present while studying the past.

Introduction

The violent riots that erupted on the streets of Ramla on 22–23 August 1965 shook the country. They were reported and condemned in Israel's leading dailies, and denounced by Prime Minister Levi Eshkol; in their aftermath, there were even some who referred to them as 'pogrom', whose victims were the town's Arab minority, attacked by young Jewish men.[1] At the same time, a call was heard to found a committee that will inquire into their causes.[2] On this 'Black Sunday'[3] and the following Monday, brutal aggression and deep hostility were directed toward Ramla's Arab population. An inflamed crowd blocked the town's main road (connecting Jerusalem and Tel Aviv); another group stormed the Arab neighbourhood, stoning houses and injuring several Arab passers-by; smaller groups attacked other symbols of 'Arabness': a gas station employing several Arabs, the local Communist Party

---

1 The incidents were referred to in Maariv, Haaretz, Al Hamishmar, Kol Haam, Haolam Haze and The Jerusalem Times; Eshkol's denunciation was reported in *Haaretz*, 25 August, 1965; For the term 'pogrom' and description see *Haaretz*, 24 August, 1965; *Haolam Haze*, 25 August and 1 September, 1965; *Kol Haam*, 24 August and 25 August 1965; Ramla Town Council Minutes, 27 August, 1965; ISA 50//3195/7–gimel.

2 Ramla Town Council Minutes, 27 August, 1965, ISA 50//3195/7–gimel; *Kol Haam*, 29 August, 1965.

3 A term used by Kol Haam's reporter, 27 August, 1965. 'Black Sunday' has been used throughout the twentieth century to describe harsh events caused by man and nature alike. One 'Black Sunday' that Kol Haam's reporter may have had in mind when writing was 14 November 1937, the day Etzel initiated a series of violent attacks against Arab civilians (as retaliation for Arab attacks on Jews in Jerusalem).

club, and a café owned by an Arab next to the main street. The police was scattered around town, preventing further bloodshed and mayhem. At the end of the two days of tension, seven people were injured and another twenty-two arrested.[4]

It was the death of Yitzhak Darazi, a seventeen-year-old Jewish motorcyclist hit by an Arab taxi driver named Mahmood Fauzi Al-Huri on 20 August 1965, which triggered the riots. The Arab driver was blamed by some for killing Darazi deliberately, and violence erupted immediately after Darazi's funeral.[5] One call that was repeatedly shouted during the event was '[we] don't want Arabs'.[6] The reasons for this hostility, as some locals explained, varied: the town's Arabs seemed to be too self-assured and insolent, they harassed young Jewish women, and they earned a lot of money.[7] Other, more general circumstances such as the upcoming elections (2 November 1965) also seemed to have played into the timing and intensity of the events.[8] Whatever the root causes, the rioters' message was clear: the town should be exclusively Jewish; Arab residents were not wanted. In a way, these events were just another act in an ongoing play—the attempt to turn the formerly Arab Ramle (i.e., pre-1948) into an Israeli and Jewish Ramla. This process of Israelisation,[9] begun after the 1948 War and continued during the 1950s and 1960s, stands at the heart of this book.

* * *

4   *Maariv*, 23 August, 1965.
5   *Ibid.*
6   *Lo rotzim 'aravim*: *Kol Haam*, 23 and 27 August, 1965; *Maariv* reported that the call was 'kill'em all' (*lirtzoach et kulam*), *Maariv*, 23 August, 1965; *Al Hamishmar*, 27 August, 1965.
7   *Maariv*, 24 August 1965; *Kol Haam*, 27 August 1965; *Al Hamishmar*, 27 August 1965.
8   *Maariv*, 24 August, 1965; *Kol Haam*, 27 August, 1965.
9   Several former writers, among them Ghazi Falah, Oren Yiftachel, Haim Yacobi, Alexandre Kedar and Benny Morris, aiming to depict this process referred to it as one of 'Judaisation'. I prefer using the term 'Israelisation', which articulates better, in my opinion, the heterogenic nature of 'Israeliness' as joining together Jewish, Zionist and Hebraic aspects.

Ramle's Israelisation, as that of other formerly-Arab and mixed towns, has been part of a project aimed at creating a new society in the framework of the Israeli state. The town's Israelisation has been therefore the process of remaking Arab Ramle into a 'new' town, with typical 'Israeli' traits—Jewish hegemony, Hebrew language and culture, as well as control over urban space and planning. These were reflected in shifting ownerships—real and symbolic—and in transformed landscapes.

Anthropologist Virginia R. Domínguez writes on contemporary Israeliness (*yisraeliyut*), stressing in her analysis what she calls peoplehood or oneness—so obvious and vague at the same time that one tends to miss it and see pluralisation and fragmentation instead. Creation of this collective identity, as Domínguez shows, is achieved through various means, ritual being one of them; Benedict Anderson interpreted the process of Israeli nation building as 'an alchemic change from wandering devotee to local patriot'.[10] This 'magical' transformation is the process of Israelisation, the traces of which the following study aims to reveal using Ramla as a case study.

The process of Ramle's Israelisation has been often a lingering, ongoing endeavour, as well as an indeterminate and open one. In British maps and guidebooks predating 1948, the town's name is transcribed as 'Ramle', 'Er-Ramle' or 'Ramleh'. In later maps and documents published by Israeli authorities or institutions, it appears as 'Ramla'.[11] A different pronunciation, stressing the last syllable rather than the first, was another important feature of the name's Hebraisation. No doubt, this seemingly minor difference

---

10 Virginia R. Domínguez, *People as Subject, People as Object: Selfhood and Peoplehood in Contemporary Israel* (Madison, Wis., 1989), esp. p. 11; Benedict Anderson, *Imagined Communities* (London, 1991)[1983], p. 149, note 16.

11 For example, AA 'Er Ramle' [1] 135–145.7 1931 (plan I, II, III, IV); 'Er Ramle' AD 900A—[1] 13/14 1941; 'Ramle' AA 45 1947 (1:2500) sheet 1 and 2; AA 'Er Ramle' [1] 135–145.7 1931 (plan I, II, III, IV); Maisler and Yeivin, *Palestine Guide*, p. 195; G. Olaf Matson, *The American Colony Palestine Guide* (Jerusalem, 1930), p. 206; 'Ramle/Ramla' AD900A [4] 13–14 1945 (this is a topo-cadestrial map drawn by Z. Lifshitz, in which the name of the city appears in Latin transcription as Ramle and in Hebrew transcription as Ramla.)

in vowels and accent was of great importance to the town's new leadership: a series of leaflets published by the town's municipality in the mid-1950s distinctly vowelised the town's name as 'Ramla'.[12]

The process of creating a Hebrew map of the country and replacing Palestinian place-names with Zionist (and often biblical) ones constituted, as Meron Benvenisti claimed, 'a declaration of exclusive proprietorship' and 'the essence of nationalism'.[13] Ramle's renaming as Ramla was therefore an assertion of the town's new identity and ownership. The names Ramle and Ramla will be therefore used throughout the book as follows: the pre-1948 Arab town will be referred to as 'Ramle'; the post-1948 predominantly Jewish town will be called 'Ramla'.

Not only the town's new name, but also its ostensibly innocuous new municipal symbol was pregnant with meaning. The emblem selected by the predominantly Jewish municipality in 1952 combined a vertical olive branch with a smaller cogwheel situated to its right and a Star of David to its left. It represented 'a Hebrew city, industry and labour, and agriculture'.[14] The Star of David clearly marked the city's orientation as Jewish, while marginalising the other religious communities in town; the cogwheel signified the industrial character to which the city was predisposed after 1948. Finally, the olive branch was a reminder of the area's olive trees and latter-day thriving oil and soap industries; in this case, it did not represent, as we might have expected from a town

---

12 *Mehana'asa Ba'ir* 3 (1954), 4 (1957), 5 (1957). Regretfully, I did not manage to discover when and how exactly it was decided to refer to the city as Ramlā, but, as with other names of formerly Arab settlements, there was some deliberation concerning the manner the city's name needs to be pronounced and written. See, for example, letter from the Ministry of Transport to the Department of Antiquities, 13 June 1949, concerning names of Arab settlements (including that of Ramle/Ramla) written by three different methods of transcription. ISA,72//968/1—pe. See also Rashid Khalidi on naming practices of and in Jerusalem. Rashid Khalidi, *Palestinian Identity: The Construction of Modern National Consciousness* (NY, 1997), pp. 14–16.

13 M. Benvenisti, *Sacred Landscape: The Buried History of the Holy Land since 1948*, trans. M. Kaufman-Lacusta (Berkeley, 2000), p. 47.

14 Minutes of Municipal Meeting, 2 September 1952, ISA, 59//13616/9—gimel lamed.

inhabited by both Jews and Arabs, a symbol of peace.[15] Much like the town's renaming, this emblem was meant to represent Ramla's new Israeli-Jewish identity and ownership, and the symbolic and material appropriation of its formerly Arab past, assets and landscape.

Ramle's Israelisation in 1950s was carried out by individuals who were themselves new immigrants in the process of self-Israelisation, and were often not quite sure what being Israeli exactly meant.[16] To a certain degree, some institutional tolerance did exist at this period towards local minorities, in the form of freedom of religion and education, or the use of Arabic (as on street ads, next to the binding Hebrew lettering).[17]

Since 1948, Ramla has been considered a mixed town. As such, it encapsulates a twofold socio-demographic reality that includes both Arab and Jewish residents, which breaks into subtler

15 This is the explanation of the symbol according to the website of Ramla's municipality: http://www.ramla.muni.il/index.asp?id=1097 (quoting from a miscellaneous publications record number 633, 13 November 1958), accessed on 16 July 2013.

16 An anecdote and accompanying caricature published in the *Palestine Post* (22 December 1949) illustrate this confusion and uncertainness underlying the ongoing practice of becoming an Israeli: 'We have been told of a sabra who was driving his car toward Ramleh when he had a breakdown. In addition to his knowledge of Hebrew, he also knew a little German and some English. He tried speaking Hebrew to the first man he saw in the vicinity, but the fellow only knew Bulgarian. With difficulty, he stuttered some form of Yiddish-German and recommended a near-by garage. The driver finally located the mechanic's establishment and tried to explain his motor problem to several garagemen. However, his Hebrew was incomprehensible to them. He couldn't make himself understood with the little German he knew. Finally, the garage owner called in the only worker who understood Hebrew. Sure enough, he was an Arab.' The two main protagonists in this story—the sabra (a native albeit not a local) and the Arab (apparently both local and native) represent here, in a way, 'true' Israeliness, since they share knowledge of the local (Hebrew) language. In between them are those still in the process of acquiring a sense of belonging—new immigrants who live in town, walk its streets and work there, yet still struggle with mastering the language and becoming 'proper' Israelis. This narrative is unique in allowing the 'Arab' to be part and parcel of Israeliness (although his knowledge of the language is presented as the story's punch line).

17 *Ramla Bevinyana Uvehitpatchuta*, p. 18; Ramla Town Council Minutes, 23 January 1958, ISA, 50//2024/26–gimel.

categories of ethnic communities and religious denominations. In the framework of the mixed town, different modes and degrees of neighbourly relations are retained: financial activity, governmental and municipal services, leisure and entertainment, and housing. However, it is difficult to define the town as mixed in the sense of 'a shared locus of memory, affiliation and self-identification'.[18] In this sense, Ramla, as other Israeli 'mixed' cities, is more divided than mixed.[19] Frederick Boal classified divided cities into five categories: the first is a city characterised by assimilation, in which heterogeneity is replaced by homogeneity and social and spatial boundaries dissolve; the second type of city is typified by pluralism, where a degree of ethnic distinctiveness is rendered, while collective institutions and attitudes are shared. A third type of divided city is the segmented one, presenting sharper socio-spatial boundaries than those typical of the pluralised city, whereas a fourth category offered by Boal distinguishes the divided city characterised by polarisation, caused by unresolved ethno-national conflict and articulated by non-consensual government. The fifth and last category is of a cleansed city, in which an absolute ethnic homogeneity was achieved at the expense of other ethnic groups, through their flight, expulsion, or even extermination.[20] Following this classification, Ramla may be considered as both a segmented town, with a tendency for separation (blurred in certain contact zones, where space is contested), and a polarised one, severed along ethno-national boundaries. At least during the 1950s and 1960s, these boundaries were often dynamic; yet Ramla's levels of segregation, as those of other mixed cities such as Haifa, Jaffa

18 D. Rabinowitz and D. Monterescu, 'Introduction: The Transformation of Urban Mix in Palestine/Israel in the Modern Era', in *Mixed Towns, Trapped Communities: Historical Narratives, Spatial Dynamics, Gender Relations and Cultural Encounters in Palestinian-Israeli Towns*, D. Monterescu and D. Rabinowitz (eds.) (Aldershot, 2007), pp. 1–34 (p. 3).

19 For the strategies through which Israeli authorities attempt separation of Jews and Arabs in mixed cities see Yitzhak Schnell, 'New Approaches to the Study of Mixed Cities: The Case of Israel', in *Together But Apart: Mixed Cities in Israel*, Elie Rekhes (ed.)(Tel Aviv, 2007)[in Hebrew], pp. 19–26 (pp. 19–20).

20 F.W. Boal, 'From Undivided Cities to Undivided Cities: Assimilation to Ethnic Cleansing', *Housing Studies* 14:5 (1999), pp. 585–600.

and Lydda, increased over time, especially between 1961 and the 1980s.[21]

As in Christine Boyer's City of Collective Memory, Ramla could have represented 'the collective expression of architecture'; it could have carried 'in the weaving and unravelling of its fabric the memory traces of earlier architectural forms, city plans, and public monuments.'[22] But whereas some of the town's features survived throughout the ages, others were reshaped, renamed, slowly deteriorated or purposely destroyed.

* * *

Ownership and space are the two main aspects of Ramle's process of Israelisation discussed in this book, in which the material and symbolic appropriation of the formerly-Arab town, and its spatial manifestations, were central. The story of Ramle's Israelisation is narrated here mainly from the predominant Israeli-Jewish perspective, representing the gradual marginalisation of Israel's Arab minority also in terms of history-writing, documents archiving and linguistic domination. Since for the most part, fiction and research literature, as well as oral history representing the Palestinian perspective, have been published in Arabic, these were inaccessible to me. Likewise, much of the documental material relating to the pre-*Nakba* Arab community is limited in scope and difficult to locate.[23] Nor is Israeli historiography too helpful in regards to urban life in Ramle prior to 1948: research conducted until recently deals mainly with the town's medieval

---

21 Ghazi Falah, 'Living Together Apart: Residential Segregation in Mixed Arab-Jewish Cities in Israel', *Urban Studies* 33:6 (1996), pp. 823–857 (esp. p. 833).

22 Christine Boyer, *The City of Collective Memory: Its Historical Imagery and Architectural Entertainments* (Cambridge, Mass., 1994), p. 31.

23 As are, for example, documents relating to pre-1948 *waqf* property in Ramle, according to Muhammad Taji, former head of *waqf* in town. Interview, 25 June 2007.

past, particularly from an archaeological perspective.[24] Otherwise, scholars touched briefly on the matter of Ramle only in the context of British Mandate.[25] While in general, Israeli-Jewish scholars showed little to no interest in exploring Ramla's not-so-distant past, in recent years, with the opening of archives, it has been studied as part of the research into the 1948 War and its immediate aftermath.[26]

Documental evidence—military administration reports, town council minutes, municipality leaflets, committee proceedings, national press reports, minutes of cabinet discussions, police records, and several surveys which were conducted in town— provided most of the primary written sources used. Regrettably, the nature of these sources was somewhat eclectic: Ramla's municipal archive contained only few documents dating to the relevant period and whereas the IDF archive provided much information on the town's military administration period, relevant documents in the State Archive were usually scattered in a variety of files. The same was true for photographs of Ramla's inhabitants in their daily lives—an inconsistent though rich and important source contributing in painting the reality of daily life in Ramla with more vivid colours. Maps, on the other hand, consistently depicted the slow changes in the town's cartographic matrix along the years. Finally, printed and video-recorded narratives of former residents (Arabs and Jews) were used as primary sources, as were oral interviews with some of Ramla's past and present inhabitants; these helped to illuminate certain issues that surfaced during research.

---

24 See, for example, the various articles published along the years in the journal *Chadashot Archeologiyot* (Archaeological News); also Luz, N., 'Umayyad Ramle', *Cathedra* 79 (1996), pp. 22–52; M. Rosen-Ayalon, 'The First Mosaic Discovered in Ramla', *Israel Exploration Journal* 26 (1976), pp. 104–119; M. Rosen-Ayalon, 'The First Century of Ramla', *Arabica* 43 (1996), pp. 251–263.

25 For example, Gideon Biger, *An Empire in the Holy Land: Historical Geography of the British Administration in Palestine 1917–1929* (Jerusalem, 1994).

26 In the works of Morris, *The Birth*; Golan, 'Lydda and Ramle'; Golan, *Wartime Spatial Changes*; Kadish et al., *The Occupation*. Also Spiro Munayyer and Walid Khalidi, 'The Fall of Lydda'.

Despite being firmly rooted in the historical discipline, an interdisciplinary approach was adopted in the researching and writing of this book. Legal, geographical, anthropological, sociological and architectural perspectives and terminologies were incorporated while attempting to combine a theoretical approach with empirical research. *Ramle Remade* is therefore a study of Ramla's post-1948 cultural history as investigated through different contexts, and whereas each of its chapters can stand as an independent research on its own, it is rather their ingathering that provide this book with a synergetic appeal. The image of the Israelised Ramle, as developed throughout the following chapters, is in that sense more complete than if examined using one research prism only.

Three theoretical perspectives are combined in this book: property and repossession, post-war transformation and urban spatial practices. It portrays a long and complex process of change found also in other formerly Arab towns in Israel, as, more generally, in countries which experienced different forms of colonisation throughout the ages. The case presented here—the remaking of Arab Ramle into Israeli Ramla—aims to reconstruct the town's story of Israelisation by examining its post-war urban history. At the same time, it also serves as another example of many histories in which one national ethos is pushed aside and marginalised in favour of another national ethos.

The following five chapters therefore aim to portray the gradual Israeli-Jewish appropriation of Ramle's assets and urban space, that of radios, houses, agricultural land, public gardens, marketplace, cafés, neighbourhoods, and street names. At the same time, they attempt to depict the chronological progression of this ongoing appropriation, advancing from the town's conquest in July 1948 to the return visits of its former Arab residents in 1967. Chapter one examines acts of expropriation by military, national and local authorities as well as by individuals, during and after the war, raising questions concerning their legality and legitimacy. It also analyzes the mechanisms behind them, encountering many institutional conflicts in the process, and sets these in a wider international framework. Chapter two investigates commercial appropriation and cultural takeover through the examination of two important institutions—those of the local market, which was gradually Israelised in a long process, and the town's cafés, that changed ownership in the early 1950s—sold by Arabs to Iraqi Jews. Through this discussion, the chapter also depicts and interprets the consolidation of national and urban hierarchies, in which Ashkenazi (European) Jews acquired the most powerful status, whereas the weaker Mizrachi (African and Asian) Jews established their supremacy over an even more oppressed Arab population. Chapter three discusses the town's groves and public gardens, and investigates how urban landscape was redesigned in pursuit of municipal and national ideologies as well as pragmatic goals. It deals with both Palestinian and Zionist attitudes to nature, expanding on the role of the olive tree as a contested symbol of the two peoples; it also elaborates on three particular public gardens which function as useful case studies in the attempt to chronicle and understand the transformation of the town's landscape. Chapter four analyses the performance of three types of civic processions— the military parade of 1954, May Day parades and the processions to Nabi Salah's tomb—and the spatial appropriation of the urban surrounding they symbolised. Chapter five deals with segregation and inclusion in this 'mixed town' by examining Ramla's overall planning, and particularly the juxtaposition of the derelict Old City and newly built neighbourhoods; this chapter also discusses the founding history and later annexation of the Arab village of Jawarish, and of resulting tensions. A different perspective on the debate on segregation/inclusion in Ramla is offered through the study of the town's changing street names. The Epilogue explores the phenomenon of return visits to the Palestinian-made-Israeli houses and towns, and delves into one particular visit to Ramla, which took place in 1967, whereas the book concludes with several general remarks on the current situation in Ramla.

A final note must refer to the sensitive issue of terminology usage throughout the book. Whereas the term 'new immigrants' always refers to Jews from other countries coming to Israel, with their nationality of origin emphasised by linking religious and national identifiers (as in 'Iraqi-Jews'), the use of 'Israelis' (i.e. post-1948 residents of the State of Israel) is more complicated in the sense that it combines current alternating nationalities; consequently, the slightly exhausting use of Israeli-Jews or Israeli-Arabs is practiced. Terminology linked to Arab and Palestinian identities is even more elaborate, and so the term 'Palestinians' is used when discussing issues of more national nature, whereas 'Arabs' employed when treating either pan-Arab matters (related to the Arab world more broadly), or, alternatively, when treating local issues, linked to Ramle/Ramla more specifically. In paragraphs in which religious identity was of significance, religious denomination was also marked (as in 'Christian Arab'). Finally, whenever primary sources were quoted, either directly or indirectly, terminology was kept as in the origin.[27]

27 On the complexity of Palestinian identities see Khalidi's important study *Palestinian Identity*. On the Hebrew terminology see D. Rabinowitz,, 'Oriental Nostalgia: How the Palestinians Became "Israel's Arabs"', *Theory and Criticism* 4 (1993), pp. 141–152 [in Hebrew].

CHAPTER ONE

Property and Ownership: Expropriation and Reallocation in an Urban Setting

The study of reparations politics, which has expanded in the last decades, covers 'retribution, reparation, remembering, recording, [and] reconciliation'.[1] It deals not only with acknowledging acts of conquest, ethnic displacement and dispossession, but also, occasionally, with financial restitution of dispossessed individuals, groups and ethnic entities. The struggle of several groups for recognition of and compensation for past sufferings proved successful in some cases, the funds set up by the German, Austrian, and Swiss governments to compensate victims of Nazism being a case in point. Other claims for compensation, such as those by African slave descendants, have subsided.[2] As part of the attempt at reconciliation with the past, the political and public reparation discourse have contributed to the emergence of academic writing

---

1 Charles S. Maier, 'Overcoming the Past? Narrative and Negotiation, Remembering, and Reparation: Issues at the Interface of History and the Law', in *Politics and the Past: On Repairing Historical Injustices*, John Torpey (ed.) (Lanham, Md., 2003), pp. 295–304 (p. 295).
2 John Torpey, *Making Whole What Has Been Smashed: On Reparations Politics* (Cambridge, Mass., 2006), p. 3.

on and analysis of the past, from different perspectives and aspects than the ones employed until recently.[3]

Research into the Israeli-Palestinian conflict and its consequences, especially the spatial, legal, economic and symbolic dimensions of the Israeli-Jewish conquest of the land of Israel/ Palestine has likewise intensified in recent decades. Although rarely intended to contribute directly to the discourse on financial compensation or repatriation of Palestinian refugees, in searching the archives and continually uncovering new source material, and in re-interpreting known documents, academic writing on various aspects of the Israeli-Palestinian conflict has been part of the attempt to redress the country's past (the other aspect of the matter, as we shall see in Chapter two, has been the political issue of linking any reparation to Palestinian refugees with the Jewish property left behind and/or nationalised in Arab countries such as Iraq and Egypt).[4] The complex picture that arises from this versatile body of work depicts an abundance of legal, spatial, financial and symbolic ways in which national and local institutions, as well as individuals, gained control over Palestinian landscape and property during and after the war, whether deliberately or as a response to unfolding circumstances.

The scope and value of the Palestinian assets left behind and appropriated by the new Jewish state has been (and still is) debated between both governments and scholars.[5] In the book *All*

---

3   For studies on reparations politics see also Elazar Barkan, *The Guilt of Nations: Restitution and Negotiating Historical Injustices* (Baltimore, 2000); *Taking Wrongs Seriously: Apologies and Reconciliation*, Elazar Barkan and Alexander Karn (eds.) (Stanford, Calf., 2006); *Restitution and Memory: Material Restoration in Europe*, Dan Diner and Gotthard Wunberg (eds.)(NY, 2007); *Robbery and Restitution: The Conflict Over Jewish Property in Europe*, Martin Dean, Constantin Goschler and Philipp Ther (eds.)(NY,2007); Regula Ludi, *Reparations for Nazi Victims in Postwar Europe* (Cambridge, 2012); Shahira Samy, *Reparations to Palestinian Refugees: A Comparative Perspective* (London and NY, 2010).

4   See, for example, works by Arnon Golan, Yfaat Weiss, Tamir Goren, Haim Yacobi, Michael R. Fischbach, Benny Morris, Alexandre Kedar, Geremy Forman, Tamar Berger, Oren Yiftachel, and the controversial Ilan Pappe.

5   Michael R. Fischbach, *Records of Dispossession: Palestinian Refugee Property and the Arab-Israeli Conflict* (NY, 2003), p. xxii, and Appendix 1 (Comparison of Studies on Scope and Value of Refugee Property).

That Remains, commemorating Palestinian villages depopulated in 1948, historian Walid Khalidi mentions also Palestine's urban centres—the cities of Haifa, Jerusalem and Jaffa and the towns Acre, Beersheba, Baysan, Lydda, Majdal, Nazareth, Ramle, Safad and Tiberias—and the appropriation of their inhabitants' property:

> Their immovable assets—commercial centres, residential quarters, schools, banks, parks and utilities, all passed en bloc into the possession of the citizens of the nascent State of Israel. Also appropriated intact by Israelis were the personal movable assets: furniture, silver, pictures, carpets, libraries, and heirlooms—all the accoutrements of middle class life of the erstwhile Palestinian residents.[6]

This vast property lost by Palestinians, as Michael R. Fischbach points out, only worsened their position: not only had they experienced a political, social and demographic catastrophe, they became destitute refugees as well (fig. 1). Palestinian villagers were even worse off than town people: not only were they forced to leave their lands behind them, they often had no liquid capital to take with them into exile.[7]

Questions of Legality and Legitimacy

The terminology used to describe acts of dispossession and appropriation of Arab property in Ramla during and in the immediate aftermath of the 1948 war is revealing. Overall, as we shall see, the fledgling Israeli state adopted a legal and ethical system of justifying the appropriation of formerly Palestinian assets. However, a careful reading in the various documents can

6 *All That Remains: The Palestinian Villages Occupied and Depopulated by Israel in 1948*, Walid Khalidi (ed.)(Washington, D.C., 1992), p. xxxii.
7 Fischbach, *Records of Dispossession*, p. xxii.

expose the different ways in which attitudes towards dispossession of Arab property shifted according to various factors: writer and agenda, appropriator and purpose, property involved, and period. At different times and for different people, assets that had once been owned by Ramle's Arabs were taken, confiscated, plundered, or simply robbed. Where does the fine line between an innocent 'taking' (*lekicha*)[8] and criminal robbery pass? Who was authorised to define the difference between legitimate and illegitimate repossession, and on what grounds? More crucially, who were the victims of illegitimate and/or illegal appropriation?

Fig. 1: Arab Refugees on Ramle's Highstreet, July 1948 (Courtesy of the Israel Defense Forces and Defense Establishment Archives).

8   See below for the use of this term by a soldier carrying a radio set.

Whereas legality is constituted and enforced through civil and martial law, legitimacy is a much wider, fluid and fuzzy concept linked to morals and mores, that was used in national, military and private spheres. Questions of legality and legitimacy manifested themselves in two discourses that evolved almost simultaneously from the onset of occupation. Both operated among Israeli-Jews, mostly government officials, and it is their perspective that will be therefore predominantly used here to inquire into matters of property and ownership in post-war Ramla.

In the first discourse, the original Arab owners were perceived as the original and thus legitimate owners of the property in question. They were the ones dispossessed, and the legitimacy and legality of this act were debated. In the other discourse, the State of Israel—the new property holder and the implicitly legitimate owner—was considered the one potentially harmed and dispossessed were it not to fully control the property now in its possession; the legitimacy and legality of *this* potential act of dispossession were also questioned. Occasionally, these two discourses fused. As time elapsed, and as the Jewish State grew stronger, the first was gradually marginalised in Israeli officialdom, and the second discourse gained dominance in its stead; the Jewish State acquired the power not only to appropriate Arab assets, but also to authorise or prohibit it, both legally and in terms of endowing it with legitimacy.

The Army

The first to take hold of goods and movables in the deserted or semi-deserted Arab towns, including Ramla, was the army. Arab weapons, vehicles and ammunition were thus confiscated and used for and by the newly established IDF.[9] This kind of confiscation was a customary wartime practice, viewed as legitimate and legal.

9   A. Kadish, A. Sela and A. Golan, *The Occupation of Lydda 1948* (Tel Aviv, 2000)[in Hebrew], pp. 51–2.

According to the Hague Regulations, signed in 1899 and 1907, the only legitimate wartime confiscation was that justified by military necessity. Article 53 established that

> An army of occupation can only take possession of cash, funds, and realisable securities which are strictly the possession of the State, depots of arms, means of transport, stores and supplies, and generally, all movable property belonging to the State which may be used for military operation[...][10]

At the same time, albeit, these Regulations allowed for the confiscation of civilian enemy property, under the preface that it could be used toward the funding of the war effort.[11]

The Israeli military legal system attempted to follow these international wartime norms and ethics, but it was not always clear when was confiscation carried out for military needs and when was it practiced for personal benefit. Tel Aviv District military Attorney General, Ezra Reichart, commented on this issue in June 1948:

> If cars with refrigerators and carpets come out of Jaffa for the battalions, it is difficult to know later what of this [property] reaches the commander himself. So one can not distinguish between robbery (*shod*) for military needs and personal robbery. In which case is it robbery and in which case is it confiscation (*hachrama*)? It is all just names [...].[12]

In Hebrew, the spoils of war (*shlal milchama*) can denote legitimate booty, as in Deuteronomy 20:14 ('But the women, and the little

---

10 Michael Kagan, 'Destructive Ambiguity: Enemy Nationals and the Legal Enabling of Ethnic Conflict in the Middle East', *Columbia Human Rights Law Review* 38 (2007), pp. 263–319 (quoted in p. 271).
11 Kagan, 'Destructive Ambiguity', pp. 272–273.
12 Quoted in Zvi Inbar, *The Scales of Justice and the Sword*, 2 vols.(Tel Aviv, 2005) [in Hebrew], vol. I, p. 403.

ones, and the cattle, and all that is in the city, even all the spoil thereof, shalt thou take unto thyself; and thou shalt eat the spoil of thine enemies, which the Lord thy God hath given thee'),[13] but it is also seen as a serious crime, as in Joshua 7:1 ('But the children of Israel committed a trespass in the accursed thing: for Achan [...] of the tribe of Judah, took of the accursed thing: and the anger of the Lord was kindled against the children of Israel').

In the immediate aftermath of occupation there were many soldiers who felt entitled to the abandoned property they found; pillage has become one of the most severe phenomena to surface during the war.[14] The partisan and poet Abba Kovner, who was during the war Giv'ati Brigade's officer in charge of culture, warned soldiers in a leaflet (dated 5 November 1948) not to touch the enemy's property, 'not to open any door and house without an order; not to rummage in the yards.' Whoever will not follow these guidelines, he threatened, will be deemed a traitor, not fit to be included among the brigade's fighters. He ended his message with the call: 'Giv'ati men will not soil their belligerent tradition!'[15]

Plunder was therefore seen to be immoral, illegitimate, and also illegal. The IDF attempted to fight this spreading problem through investigations and trials, not too successfully. Reasons for this incompetence varied: culprits received cover; special conditions existed within the fighting units and often made looting (of food supplies, for example) a necessity; shortage of people existed in military and civil police forces; lack of understanding prevailed as to the role of the IDF's General Attorney Office's position; and finally, also obscurity and misunderstanding in regards to the legal definition of looting abided.[16] When in November 1948 a list was compiled of the trials of soldiers who had held in their possession

---

13 All Biblical quotes throughout the book are from the King James Bible version.
14 Inbar, *The Scales*, vol. I, p. 400.
15 This document was reproduced in Dov Doron, 'Ha'ayara Majdal VeSvivata BeMilchemet HaKomemiyut', in *Ashkelon—4,000 Ve'od Arba'im Shana*, ed. Naftali Arbel (Ashkelon[?], 1990), pp. 26–35 (p. 35).
16 Inbar, *The Scales*, vol. I, pp. 401, 402.

abandoned property, it consisted of 175 cases.[17] Punishment
for looting ranged from several days of imprisonment to mere
reprimand; some cases were dropped for lack of evidence, whereas
others were closed following a general amnesty.[18] Many other acts
of pillage probably went unnoticed. A blind eye was often turned
when the property taken was of marginal value—a ring, a *kafiya*
or a necklace—commonly regarded as wartime mementos.

When Yitzhak Gvirtz of the Department for Arab Property[19]
visited Ramle the day it was occupied he saw a soldier carrying
a radio set on the main street. When he tried to inquire as to
its origin, the soldier said he had taken it from 'some Arab's flat
in Ramle' and was carrying it to his unit. The soldier's direct
commander later backed him up, taking responsibility for the act
and refusing to return the radio set.[20] The military administration
of Ramla was the address for complaints of plundering committed
by soldiers in town. Two such incidents were reported to Zusman
Jawitz, the military governor of Ramla and Lydda, in the beginning
of December 1948: soldiers had been caught loading mattresses,
blankets, a radio set and other goods on a truck; another vehicle,
similarly loaded, managed to escape despite several shots fired in
the air.[21] This kind of conduct was also criticised in higher circles.
IDF Chief of General Staff Yaacov Dori chastised Yigal Alon
(commander of Operation Dani) for the plundering of Ramle and
Lydda by soldiers of Yiftach and Har'el brigades (both Palmach
brigades), testifying that he, personally, witnessed several such
incidents. On this occasion, Dori used harsh terminology: he
ordered an immediate end to 'plunder', demanding an investigation
into this issue, and punishment of those responsible. David Ben-

---

17   *Ibid.*, vol. I, p. 404.
18   *Ibid.*, vol. II, examples in pp. 612–613, 668, 708, 712.
19   *Machlaka Lenechasim Araviyim*. This department was founded by the Haganah
     in March 1948, and after the establishment of the temporary government
     started operating as part of the Ministry of Minorities Affairs. It was later
     replaced by the Custodian of Abandoned (later Absentees) Property Office.
     Dov Shafrir, *Arugat Chaim* (Tel Aviv, 1974/75), p. 223.
20   Gvirtz to Kiryati, 13 July 1948, ISA, 49//297/2–gimel
21   Dated 7 December 1948, IDF Archive, 1860/50/31.

Gurion was also appalled to discover that a commander in the Fifth Palmach Regiment demanded that his soldiers go to Ramle and rob the city.[22] The army attempted to deal as decisively as possible with these cases and soldiers were tried for acts involving looting even months after the town's occupation.[23]

It is not always clear under whose commands soldiers were operating when 'taking' property, and how aware were they of the legitimacy and legality of their acts: was the 'taking' of property for personal use illegal, but expropriation for their units legitimate? Was expropriation for the army always legal? We cannot be sure, for example, under whose command operated the Jewish officer who came with members of the Arab Ramla Committee to the house of Abdullah Zidan in December 1948, and took, according to his complaint, 'all that [he] had': barley, wheat, coffee, rice, lentils, kerosene, mattresses, beds, a wooden cupboard, sewing machine, gold rings and 180 Israeli pennies.[24] Likewise, it was not clear who stood behind the 'great movement of confiscation of property, especially furniture' in Ramla, mentioned in an intelligence report of early September 1948. Was it orchestrated by the Custodian of Abandoned Property (see below), or were these sporadic acts by individual soldiers? [25]

Attempts were gradually made to regulate and organise asset confiscation to prevent illegal dispossession. From January 1949, for instance, goods could not pass through checkpoints surrounding Ramla after 15:30 o'clock, and in any case had to be weighed and fully registered before transported to the CAP

---

22 Letter classified 'personal', 16 July 1948, IDF Archive, 6122/49/115; David Ben-Gurion, *Yoman ha-Milchama* ([Tel Aviv], 1984), vol. II, entry 15 July 1948.

23 B. Morris, *The Birth of the Palestinian Refugee Problem Revisited* (Cambridge, 2004), p. 428; for other cases, not all of which ended with trial or even the pressing of charges, see Inbar, *The Sclaes*, vol. II, pp. 750, 754, 766, 775.

24 Letter from Abdullah Zidan to the Military Governor, 2 January 1949, ISA, 85//2276/32–gimel.

25 Intelligence Report, 3 September 1948, signed by Sharl Sasson, IDF Archive, 50/863/365.

Jaffa warehouse.[26] By March, though, the checkpoints were dismantled.[27]

Civilians

Pillage of what has been termed 'abandoned property' in the recently occupied Palestinian towns and villages was committed not only by soldiers, but by civilians too.[28] Confusion as to the right of military courts to judge civilians who had been caught stealing Arab assets in towns under military administration persisted until the summer of 1948. In Safad, for example, civilians caught looting were 'conscripted' and then tried before military courts, whereas in Jerusalem they were exempted due to the military court's lack of authority over them.[29]

Since Jews did not reside in Ramle prior to the war and new Jewish immigrants arrived there only in November 1948, civilian looting in this town was rarer than in other places. In one incident a certain lady from the town of Netanya, active in the local soldiers club, asked a commander in the Alexandroni Brigade to help organise enemy property furniture for the club. This commander provided the club manager (whose name appears in the document as Y.P.), with a letter to the military commander of Ramla-Lydda. The club manager arrived in Ramla on 18 July 1948 (less than a week after its occupation), but since the military governor could not be found, he decided to collect the furniture himself, and was aided in the process by several soldiers. These were stopped in

---

26 'Report on the Activities of the Military Administration in Ramla-Lydda for January 1949', 10 February 1949, IDF Archive, 1860/50/31.

27 'Report on the Activities of the Military Administration in Ramle and Lydda for February 1949', 20 March 1949, IDF Archive 1860/50/31; compare to the situation in Haifa, Tamir Goren, *Mitlut Lehishtaltut* (Haifa, 1996), p. 74.

28 Anat Stern, 'Is the Army Authorized to Prosecute Civilians? Trial of Civilian Looting by the IDF in 1948', in *Citizens at War: Studies on the Civilian Society During the Israeli War of Independence*, M. Bar-On and M. Chazan (eds.) (Jerusalem, 2010)[in Hebrew], pp. 465–493.

29 *Ibid.*, p. 473.

mid action by the deputy of Ramla's military governor; due to the particular circumstances, all involved were merely reprimanded.[30] In this case no personal benefit could be gained, only a collective one (for the visitors in Netanya's soldiers club), yet, it nevertheless proves to illustrate the easiness with which normative civilians assumed the taking of enemy property to be legitimate.

Looting was deemed illegitimate and illegal, harmful to the state and its interests (moral and economic alike), but individuals and families also aided the state's mechanism of expropriation and contributed to the redesign of the Israeli landscape—particularly the urban one—in this period, as well as to the ongoing discourse linked to questions of legality and legitimacy.[31] This was especially the case with the settling of Israeli-Jews in abandoned Arab houses, a practice carried out in order to prevent their Arab residents' possible return on the one hand, and offer accommodation to the many newcomers who needed it on the other hand.[32]

When new Jewish immigrants were settled in Ramla, from November 1948, they were encouraged to find a house or were provided with one. Dov Friberg and his friends from Kibbutz Mishmarot, for instance, had heard on the ways through which individuals gained flats and stores in Ramla; they found out that they better look for available accommodation on the town's side streets, and then try to 'establish facts' on the ground.[33]

However, ambivalence and unease were also occasionally expressed by the Jewish settlers as their new houses retained their previous owners' characteristics. In his autobiographical war memoir Yoram Kaniuk remembered how he had found in the deserted Arab houses of Ramle tables set for meals, and food that had dried on the plates.[34] The mundane practice of having a meal in one's house has evolved into a symbol of the Palestinian hurried

---

30 Inbar, *The Scales*, vol. II, p. 708.
31 A. Golan, *Wartime Spatial Changes: Former Arab Territories Within the State of Israel, 1948-1950* (Beer Sheva, 2001)[in Hebrew], p. 265.
32 Morris, *The Birth*, Chapter 6; Golan, *Wartime Spatial Changes*, p. 260.
33 Dov Friberg, *To Be Like Anyone Else* (Ramla, 1966)[in Hebrew], p. 69.
34 Yoram Kaniuk, *1948* (Tel Aviv, 2010), p. 172.

flight from a warzone, an alarming and often uncomfortable reminder to the house's new Jewish inhabitants of its former dwellers and their fate.[35] Micko and Loti, a couple who had arrived in Ramla from Bulgaria, described years later how they went into a house they had found vacant, only to be shocked by a baby's cot, dummy, and diapers left there by the previous dwellers.[36] The fictitious essay, written by the seventh-grader Rina Yitzhak for the tenth anniversary of 'The Hebrew Ramla' (in 1958), however, describes best this emotionally charged 'encounter' between the old Arab residents who had left their house, and the Jewish newcomers. Yitzhak started by narrating how, upon her family's arrival in Ramla, her parents were asked to 'choose [...] one of the houses we would fancy'. She eloquently depicted the empty, silent streets, the abandoned houses, and the entrance to one of the houses they liked:

> [B]ut when we went in, our bodies shuddered and our hearts were beating hard, a terrible spectacle was revealed before our eyes. Blood spilt on the floor, bones and skeletons scattered here and there, and I was a little girl and could not stand the fear and started crying[.] My mother comforted me and told me it was the blood of the Arabs, and the bones and skeletons—theirs. And I asked my parents not to live in a house where blood had been spilt.

Eventually Rina's family managed to find a 'small and nice house'.[37] All this happened, according to the young author, in 1950. Unless Rina indicated a wrong date, these could not have

35 See also, for example, Golda Meir's comment after visiting Haifa (on 6 May 1948) on the coffee and pita bread left on the tables in Arab houses (that made her think of Jewish towns where food was assumingly similarly left). Yfaat Weiss, *A Confiscated Memory: Wadi Salib and Haifa's Lost Heritage*, trans. Avner Greenberg (NY, 2011), p. 27.

36 R. Bidas, A. Moshe, R. al-Nablusi and Y. Tamari, *Zochrot et al-Ramle* ([?], 2004), p. 8.

37 *Yediot Ramla* (Ramla, 1958), p. 15.

been real memories: by 1950, there were hardly any vacant houses left in Ramla,[38] certainly not ones with blood and skeletons scattered in them. Rina was probably describing not an event she had experienced herself, but mere fiction. Yet the description nevertheless illustrates the power of the collective narrative of post-war events, which was one of duality: on the one hand, uneasiness with settling in houses whose owners had been recently forced out, on the other hand the joy of finding a home in the new homeland.[39] Although this process was deemed legal, in the eyes of (at least some of) the town's new Jewish settlers, its moral legitimacy was doubted.

Questions of legitimacy dogged the process of redistribution of Arab property by its self-legitimised new owner, the State of Israel. They were related also to the discourse of the state as potentially dispossessed. A certain phenomenon that troubled officials was the squatting of individuals and families in vacant rooms or flats. In some of Jaffa's neighbourhoods, for instance, new immigrants squatted with the encouragement of the JA's Absorption Department that was dissatisfied with the number of flats allocated for new immigrants in town; some squatting soldiers were cajoled by the army, struggling with ensuring accommodation for families of conscripts. There were in Jaffa also individuals who sought to profit from squatting, by taking control over more

---

38 Already at the beginning of 1949 there was a shortage of housing for new immigrants. Golan, *Wartime Spatial Changes*, p. 155.

39 When this essay was reprinted in a municipal leaflet eight years later (in 1966), the paragraph quoted above was omitted. The gory experience of entering the house was not mentioned at all; rather, the 'small and nice house' into which the family had decided to move, became the only house Rina's family inspected upon arrival. *Yediot Ramla* (Ramla, 1958), p. 15; *Ramla: Bit'on 'Iryat Ramla* 1 (Ramla, 1966), p. 12.

than one flat and charging 'key money' from their tenants.[40] In Jerusalem the police refused to deal with soldiers who, for lack of accommodation, squatted in flats allocated for government personnel and offices.[41] In Wadi Nisnas in Haifa, set aside for the resettling of the town's Arab residents, Jewish squatters attempted to take over flats; often, squatting there took place under the direct or indirect approval of the army, as happened in April 1949, when about two hundred soldiers, among them officers, invaded into seventeen houses in Wadi Nisnas and on 'Abbas street.[42]

Ramla too witnessed similar incidents of squatting. The most alarming episode that occurred there, which deteriorated into violence, took place on 17–19 June 1949, when about twenty-five war veteran families entered the *sakne* (Ramla's Arab neighbourhood), then still an enclosed military perimeter. Believing they had license from the Ministry of Defence to enter the flats, they were joined at a later stage by about fifty more new immigrant families. When the Military Governor's deputy asked them to leave, he was verbally abused and threatened with violence; the squatters were also 'impudent towards the Military Governor, cursing the military administration and the army under its command'. The army and military and civil police were duly summoned, concluding with a 'battle', as the daily press later called it, which ensued for over an hour; violence was used towards both men and women. The deputy reported that 'resistance was very

---

40 Golan, *Wartime Spatial Changes*, pp. 98–100. The practice of paying 'key money' (dmey mafteach) was regularised in a 1958 law, codifying the common custom in which the new tenant entering a protected property paid money to the leaving tenant (who shared it with the actual owner). 'Key money' thus embodied the right to reside in a protected property, and be made immune from escalating rent and possible eviction. According to the law, when a protected tenant wished to leave the flat he had two options: one was to 'sell' his right for protected tenancy to a new tenant of his choice, the other was to 'sell' it back to the 'real' owner, in our case the Development Authority.

41 *Ibid.*, p. 57.

42 Weiss, *Confiscated Memory*, p. 76.

hard', but the vacation order was carried out.[43] At times, however, as we have seen in the examples cited above, soldiers themselves were a source of disorder. Similar incidents occurred in Ramla too: a house in town, claimed to be in possession of a certain military transportation company, was invaded by members of that unit before it was due to be vacated and handed over to another military unit as planned.[44]

Squatting, or 'invasion' (*plisha*), as the authorities called it, was viewed as illegal and illegitimate, since it subverted their power in two ways: by defying orders, and by eroding the authorities' holding over appropriated assets. The press was often in favour of the invaders, as was the case in Ramla. It responded to the voices from the street, which perceived the act of entering vacant Arab property as legitimate.

Squatting had other results, too, first and foremost unfair distribution. *Davar* daily reported in April 1951 that many in Ramla 'lived in unusual comfort' in three and even four-bedroom flats; moreover, there were cases of 'disgraceful abuse' of flats belonging to the public, as when a family of two or three lived in a house of five or even six rooms. In this situation, claimed the writer, real estate profiteering was prospering. Surveying all the flats in town, he opined, will result in returning the vacant flats to public ownership, opening the city to families of professionals, much needed in Ramla and its area.[45] In the process of housing Ramla's new inhabitants—in effect, the redistribution of Arab property—the perceived victims were not the original owners, but rather the Jewish-Israeli collective: Ramla's (Jewish) citizens and the country at large.

43 'Report on the Removal of an Organised Invasion to Ramla's "sakne"', dated June 1949 (exact date illegible). IDF Archive, 1860/50/31; *Al Hamishmar*, 21 June 1949; *Kol Haam*, 22 June 1949, p. 4.
44 Letter from army base commander Captain Aryeh Katz to Storage Base 561, 13 April 1949, IDF Archive, 68/53/240.
45 *Davar*, 25 April 1951, p. 4.

The State

The need to clarify questions of legality and legitimacy in regards to repossession of Arab property was keenly felt with the emergence of the State of Israel as the internationally recognised power sovereign in the country. Declaring independence obliged the nascent state and its leaders to comply with international standards of ethical conduct. Semi-legal or illegal practices that may have been legitimate for a defiant Yishuv confronting British dictates and facing an Arab threat were less acceptable now. The new Israeli state was therefore faced with the need to use law as a means of normalising the war's outcome: the expropriation and later nationalisation of conquered Arab lands, as well as movable and immovable property.[46]

The use of legislation in times of ethnic or national conflict or in its aftermath as a means to legitimise and provide legality to the dispossession of civilians, has not been a new phenomenon.[47] One example of many is the legislation enacted in Germany and Nazi-occupied countries during the Second World War, initially nationalising Jewish assets through decrees and then privatising them, turning all profits from its management and liquidation to contribute the Nazi war effort.[48] Another example is the Polish post-war legislation aimed at dispossession of German citizens or people of German descent in the process of their expulsion from Poland.[49] Other cases, involving the Arab states of Iraq and Egypt, and the legislation enacted by their governments in order

---

46 G. Forman and A. Kedar, 'From Arab Land to "Israel Lands": The Legal Dispossession of the Palestinians Displaced by Israel in the Wake of 1948', *Environment and Planning D: Society and Space* 22 (2004), pp. 809–830 (p. 810).

47 For a brief outline of relevant examples, see Forman and Kedar, 'From Arab Land', p. 810.

48 Götz Aly, *Hitler's Beneficiaries: Plunder, Racial War, and the Nazi Welfare State*, trans. J. Chase (NY, 2006)[2005], Chapter 7.

49 Dieter Gosewinkel and Stefan Meyer, 'Citizenship, Property Rights and Dispossession in Postwar Poland (1918 and 1945), *European Review of History* 16:4 (2009), pp. 575–595.

to dispossess Jewish communities and bring about their prompt emigration will be discussed in Chapter two.

In twelve years (1948–1960) the State of Israel managed to bring under its control most of the country's Palestinian land; Geremy Forman and Alexandre (Sandy) Kedar identified this as a four-phased process, that was first and foremost legislative, but also administrative and law-courts based.[50] The first phase evolved as a response to the illegal ad-hoc seizure of property during the war. In June 1948 two general ordinances were passed, one concerning Abandoned Property, the other Abandoned Areas; these authorised a government minister to issue regulations related to Palestinian property in recently occupied ('abandoned') areas. Emergency Regulations Regarding the Cultivation of Fallow Lands and Unexploited Water Sources from October that year empowered the Minister of Agriculture to authorise retroactively seizure and reallocation of lands that had already taken place. These regulations, however, did not guarantee the long-term goals of securing Jewish cultivation and development. A more extensive law was therefore formulated, passing in December 1948, regulating expropriation of Arab assets through the foundation of the office of Custodian of Absentees Property (CAP). This regulation gave the already operating Custodian of Abandoned Property (see below for more on the office's foundation in July 1948) a legal status and a new emphasis, no longer focusing on abandoned property, but rather on the status of its owners as 'absentees' (*nifkadim*). This terminology came to refer to all Palestinians displaced during the war, whether or not they returned at a later stage. As a result, tens of thousands of Arab citizens were also classified as 'present absentees' (*nochachim nifkadim*). The expropriation made legal by this particular Emergency Regulation was not permanent; it did prohibit selling the land or leasing it for more than five years,

---

50 The following paragraph is based on Forman and Kedar, 'From Arab Land'; also Fischbach, *Records of Dispossession*, Chapter 1.

yet, as Forman and Kedar comment, 'absentee property was now treated by the administration as state property.'[51]

It has been argued that acceptance of international norms of behaviour in interstate conflict (in the form of treatises, mainly the regulations agreed upon in Hague and Geneva), and especially of the distinction between combatants and civilians, did not necessarily mean their straightforward implementation. More applicable by the Israeli government in its post-war legislation, rather, was the doctrine of enemy nationals, according to which, in times of conflict, a person can be considered potentially dangerous based on his or her nationality only. Michael Kagan states:

> [...] international law has often been ignored in the course of the Arab-Israeli conflict. But neither Israel nor the Arab states broke the law without restraint; they framed their policies in a conscious effort to make them appear at least plausibly legitimate.[52]

Here too we find an interplay between legitimacy and legality, when deliberate ambiguity in use of the enemy nationals doctrine as a theoretical platform for legislation appears to provide an

---

51   *Ibid.*, p. 815. The second phase saw legislation transferring Emergency Regulation (Absentees' Property) into a more permanent system. According to the Absentees' Property Law of March 1950 and the Development Authority (Transfer of Property) Law of July 1950 the CAP could now sell—not only lease—land to one buyer only: the Development Authority. In the third phase, present-absentees claimers of property were offered compensation in the framework of the Land Acquisition (Validation of Acts and Compensation) Bill of March 1953, according to which lands could not be returned to its owners due to needs of security and essential development. In the fourth and last phase in the legislation securing dominance and ownership of Arab lands, the state was forbidden to transfer the ownership of agricultural lands to anyone except the JNF, Development Authority or a local authority (State Property Law, 1951). Forman and Kedar, 'From Arab Land'.
52   Kagan, 'Destructive Ambiguity', p. 316.

international veneer of legitimacy, while used in fact to cover for internationally illegal policies.[53]

The Israeli government, as seen briefly above, was not alone in applying legislative mechanisms to provide legitimacy to overall illegal practices. The institution of the CAP, to which we now turn, was also not an Israeli invention. Implemented during both First and Second World War, Britain's British Enemy (Amendment) Act of 1914 created a special custodian of enemy property who collected revenues on German property; also in 1939 Poland the Nazi-occupied General Government founded a Trust Office, authorised to confiscate property that had become ownerless because of the war, and in fact dispossessed Jews and other 'enemies'.[54] The trustee's official role in all these cases—of acting on behalf of the legitimate owners and in their interest— was in practice a means for taking hold of enemy property.

The establishment of the CAP in Israel was closely linked to the occupation of Ramle and Lydda. Prior to mid-July 1948, Minister of Finance Eliezer Kaplan had offered the appointment to Dov Shafrir, a Ukrainian-born Zionist who was head of the Neve Oved company that provided housing for agricultural workers,[55] but it was only on the morning of 15 July that Shafrir was urgently asked to start operating, instructing him to 'go at once to both towns [i.e. Ramle and Lydda] and determine the arrangements required to protect the property against looting and thefts'. The official appointment, authorising Shafrir to administer the abandoned property in the country on behalf of the Finance Ministry, was given only after he returned to Tel Aviv.[56] The timing of Shafrir's appointment was thus linked to the situation enfolding in Ramla and the rest of the country. In a sense, Ramla highlighted the growing urgency in establishing formal responsibility for assets expropriated in conquered Arab settlements, which kept accumulating, and required protection as the IDF advanced.

---

53 *Ibid.*, p. 316.
54 Kagan, 'Destructive Ambiguity', p. 273; Aly, *Hitler's Beneficiaries*, pp. 184–185.
55 Shafrir, *Arugat Chaim*, pp. 11, 15 and Chapter 8.
56 I=*bid.*, pp. 222-23.

Shafrir saw himself responsible for collecting the movables which tempted the 'evil inclination and weakness of mind' of many. On several occasions he referred to the moral consequences of looting and theft, which, as he saw it in retrospect, overshadowed the young state's impressive accomplishments.[57] Ethical questions linked to the formal act of expropriation did not particularly preoccupy Shafrir, who considered the property he was responsible for to be abandoned by its fleeing owners, its expropriation therefore being both legal and morally legitimate.[58] Rather, Shafrir perceived his office as designed to protect the State of Israel against becoming a victim of massive individual plundering. On the face of it, we see here the coexistence of the two discourses: protection of property for the benefit of its (former) Arab owners *and* for the benefit of the state. Yet the definition of the property as 'abandoned' and later as belonging to 'absentees' ensured the priority of the state as the new owner and, at the end of the day, the rule maker.

Under Shafrir's guidance Ramle's confiscated property was stored in special warehouses secured against larceny. By January 1949, only part of it was still stored in the CAP's depots in Ramla; most was by then transported to the Jaffa depot or sold.[59] A month later, in February 1949, the CAP's office in Ramla received the military governor's permission to enter the Arab neighbourhoods of both Ramla and Lydda, and recover any absentee property.[60] Fearing complaints by some of the original owners it was agreed around this time that goods claimed by their alleged original non-

---

57 *Ibid.*, pp. 225, 242–3.
58 *Ibid.*, pp. 222–3.
59 'Ramla', report dated 2 January 1949, signed by Shlomo Asherov (Ministry of Minorities Affairs), ISA, 49//297/5–gimel.
60 Iron, tin, wood and machine parts were expropriated on that occasion; food, which its confiscation had become a point of disagreement between the institutions operating in Ramla, was not expropriated on this occasion, at least according to the CAP's representative in town. Letter from Asherov to Machnes, 14 February 1949, ISA, 49//297/5–gimel; also letter from Yochananof to Shafrir, 24 February 1949, ISA, 49//297/2–gimel; letter from Shafrir to Machnes and Avner, 10 March 1949, ISA, 49//297/2–gimel.

absentee owners will be 'frozen', and their status decided by the Military Governor.[61]

Already at the beginning of February 1949, the CAP seemed to be set on inquiring into the legal status of property, mainly real estate, in Ramla. Informing the ministries of the Interior, Justice, Minorities Affairs and Police, that his office wished to review official mandatory and municipal documents found in Ramla for that purpose, Shafrir invited representatives from these ministries to be present while the sacks containing documentation were opened.[62] It is not clear whether it was a genuine attempt at settling the legal status of certain assets or a smokescreen designed to facilitate and legitimise the ongoing expropriation of property from the *sakne*.

Even when claims to non-absentees property held by the CAP were backed by valid documentation, it was not always easy to retrieve the assets in question. At times, the CAP representative in Ramla was notably sluggish in dealing with such requests. The deceased Nicola Azar al–Wahab's family, for instance, tried in vain from 1949 to 1952 to retrieve its assets in town. 'Despite our various applications and the many promises given to us', his heirs protested to the district officer, 'the file [on the property] has not yet been sent to the CAP's office in Jaffa, to release the property'. Al Wahab's relatives ended their letter with a plea for the district officer's help in mediating with the CAP.[63]

The CAP's dealings with such claims were no doubt influenced by the applicants' status and connections. Religious institutions were particularly privileged in that sense. Whereas al–Wahab's heirs struggled to get their assets back, all real estate owned by the Greek Orthodox Church in Ramla was released by July 1951.[64]

---

61 Letter from Yochananof to Shafrir, 24 February 1949, ISA, 49//297/2–gimel.
62 Letter from Shafrir to the Ministries of the Interior, Justice, Minorities Affairs and Police, 1 February 1949, ISA, 49//297/4–gimel.
63 Plots 59, 60, 61 and 62, in block no. 4348. Letter dated 30 January 1952, ISA, 85//2276/32–gimel.
64 Letter from the representative of the Greek Orthodox Patriarch to the head of Ramla's municipality, 4 July 1951, ISA, 85//2276/32–gimel.

In any case, the CAP was reluctant to release buildings and lands that could be used for its own profit. When the Fanus family, for example, claimed back (in 1949 and again in 1952) tenure over several plots (including four semi-built stores), the CAP declined, despite the fact that the family had never left the country. The family also protested against the uprooting of olive trees as part of preparations to build on these plots (see also Chapter five), and it is probable that a link existed between such building prospects and the sluggish treatment of their ownership claim, even in the face of Eliya Fanus' involvement in municipal activity.[65]

In the discourse emphasising Arab dispossession by the state, the Ministry of Minorities Affairs, which until its abolishment in July 1949 did strive to protect Arab rights, was more persuasive than the CAP in the sincerity of its intentions.[66] In October 1948, when tension erupted in Ramla around the important issue of supplying food to the remaining Arab population, the ministry's representative in town was trying to protect this population's interests. 'One can not strike twice', wrote the representative, Moshe Erem, to the CAP, 'both to expropriate property and to refuse allocating some of this property for the support of inhabitants, from whom all had been taken […].'[67] This comment is a clear manifestation of the first discourse, the one which saw Israel's Arab residents as dispossessed victims. Parts of Israeli officialdom seemed to view the state's legitimacy in expropriating Arab property not as clear-cut and obvious, but rather as questionable.

65 Letter from Isaac Ben-Ishai, Advocate, to the Minister of the Interior, 9 November 1952, ISA, 50//1966/80–gimel; Letter from Eliya Fanus to person in charge of absentees' property in Ramla, 26 September 1949, ISA 85//2276/32–gimel.

66 On the short period of the Minorities Office activity and the reasons for its dissolution see Alina Korn, 'Good Intentions: The short History of the Minority Affairs Ministry, 14 May 1948—1 July 1949', *Cathedra* 127 (2008), pp. 141–168 [in Hebrew].

67 Letter from M. Erem to the CAP, 12 October 1948, ISA, 49//297/7–gimel.

Conflict and Criticism

The post-war process of redesigning the Israeli landscape was highly conflictual. Civil and military institutions, governmental offices, local authorities and individuals—both new immigrants and old settlers—were involved in the appropriation and redistribution of assets which had been formerly possessed by the country's Arabs, to varying degrees and with different levels of legitimacy, power and responsibility. This tapestry of stakeholders was not fixed; rather, it kept changing throughout the first months and years after the war, occasionally becoming a veritable institutional battlefield: while some of these stakeholders gradually acquired power and influence, others weakened or even disappeared, the Ministry of Minorities Affairs being an obvious example.

Ramla's native inhabitants who remained or returned to town lived only in the designated Arab neighbourhood under military rule and were therefore hardly in a position to confront the newcomers or dispute their presence. The municipality was not a factor in the first two years after occupation since it was founded only in mid-1950 and for quite a while thereafter was fragile and dependent on central government, although it gained some power over the following years. Unlike other places, where military needs occasionally conflicted with civil interests, in Ramla relations were more harmonious: in Majdal, for instance, soldiers opened fire in June 1949 on an official in charge of abandoned property, following his attempt to collect Arab property that had been confiscated by that military unit from Arab infiltrators; in Haifa, decision on the concentration of the town's remaining Arab inhabitants was made by military elements without consulting civilian authorities, even before the British had left town (30 June 1948).[68] In Ramla, rather, Military Governor Zusman Jawitz seems to have been cooperative with both local and national civil authorities. Born

68 Dov Doron, 'Tkufa Yisraelit Chadasha', in *Ashkelon—4,000 Ve'od Arba'im Shana*, Naftali Arbel (ed.) (Ashkelon[?], 1990), pp. 36–50 (p. 40); Weiss, *Confiscated Memory*, p. 73.

in Łódź (Poland), Jawitz had been the fifth Haganah commander in Tel Aviv (in 1931), and was made Ramla and Lydda's Military Governor after their occupation.[69] Apparently age, experience and character contributed to Jawitz's emergence as a balancing force between various elements in town:[70] he occasionally mediated between the Arab population and the CAP, as between the CAP and the Ministry of Minorities Affairs.

The CAP and the Ministry of Minorities Affairs

From the foundation of the CAP in July 1948 until the abolishment of the Ministry of Minorities Affairs a year later, the latter was gradually stripped of its responsibilities in favour of the Finance Ministry (within which the CAP operated) and the Ministry of Agriculture.[71] This process mirrored the development of the state's attitude towards the Arab minority within its borders: priority was given to the appropriation of its assets, rather than to its compensation through the returning of property to its original owners.

In what was becoming a pattern, the Ministry of Minorities Affairs would criticise the CAP's conduct, while the latter, in response, would avoid direct confrontation and brush aside any criticism. The October 1948 dispute around the important issue of food supply for Ramla's Arab population (still enclosed) may have sparked the conflict that was to last for the next months. Was the CAP, who expropriated the property of Ramle's inhabitants (including the granary) and stored it in its depots, responsible for feeding the Arab population, or was it the ministry's responsibility? In a meeting on 7 October 1948, it was agreed that the CAP would allow the Military Governor to provide for the population

---

69 Mussa Brener, *Asara Mi Yode'a? (Aseret Mefakdey HaHaganah Shel Ha'ir Tel Aviv)* (Private publisher, 1987/8), pp. 52–53.
70 His wife Esther Jawitz, daughter Ruti Blumenfeld and son Shay Jawitz emphasised the good relations Zusman kept for years to come with Arabs and Jews from Ramla. Interview dated 6 February 2008.
71 Forman and Kedar, 'From Arab Land', p. 813.

from its warehouses, on condition that distribution would be supervised, and food provided only to those incapable of working.[72] This compromise did not completely satisfy the ministry, while the CAP coolly refused to accept any responsibility for feeding the town's Arab inhabitants. Since it had not been instructed by the Ministry of Finance to distribute basic provisions for free, its letter stated, the ministry that was supposed to cover these expenses (i.e., the Ministry of Minorities Affairs) was also required to pay for the food, if it were to be supplied from the CAP depots.[73]

Following this dispute a ministry official criticised the CAP for confiscating possessions from the Arab population of Ramla without making the proper distinction between present and absentee residents; the town 'was thoroughly emptied', its representative complained, initially by the army and later by the CAP.[74] General concern was also voiced by the ministry in January 1949 since the CAP operated in Ramla without any supervision, neither by the Military Governor, nor by the ministry: in the five months following Ramla's occupation the CAP had 'cleaned' (*nika*) it of almost any valuables.[75] By mid-February 1949, the conflict seemed unavoidable, at least in the eyes of the local ministry representative, who recommended to his superior to launch a 'heavy and difficult campaign' against the CAP.[76] Shafrir responded rather aloofly by implying, following another accusation voiced against his office, that someone seemed to be slandering it.[77] The ideological *raison d'etre* behind the two authorities was different, if

---

72 IDF Archive, 1860/50/31.
73 Letter from M. Erem to the CAP, 12 October 1948, ISA, 49//297/7–gimel; Letter, 19 October 1948, ISA, 49//297/7–gimel.
74 Letter, 12 October 1948, ISA, 49//297/7–gimel; Letter from Shafrir to Erem, 19 October 1948, ISA, 49//297/7–gimel. See also letter from Asherov to Machnes, stating that ateliers and workshops owned by Arabs were 'totally emptied' by the CAP, the army and individuals. Dated 14 February 1949, ISA, 49//297/5–gimel.
75 'Ramla', report dated 2 January 1949, signed by Shlomo Asherov (Ministry of Minorities Affairs), ISA, 49//297/5–gimel.
76 Letter from Asherov to Machnes, 14 February 1949, ISA, 49//297/5–gimel.
77 Letter from Shafrir to Machnes and Avner, 10 March 1949, ISA, 49//297/2–gimel.

not contradictory: whereas one attempted to protect the needs of the minority population, the other was promoting state interests, at the expense of that very group.

The CAP, the Jewish Agency, and Jewish individuals

In July 1949, things changed in Ramla: firstly, the governmental office of the Ministry of Minorities Affairs was closed down; secondly, martial law was over. These developments ushered in a new phase in the redistribution of Arab property. The issue of housing became a bone of contention between institutions and individuals in town, as was also the case in other cities: in Jaffa, for example, conflicts linked to housing erupted between national and local authorities as soon as June 1948, whereas in Jerusalem housing conflicts developed between the establishment (the JA's Absorption Department or the Army's welfare authorities), on the one hand, and private people—war refugees, veteran residents or new immigrants—on the other hand.[78]

Until July 1949, a clear division of labour existed in Ramla between the JA, Military Governor and the CAP;[79] afterwards, housing responsibilities in town needed some clarification. Whether this new ambiguity was due to mere confusion, or to aspirations of certain institutions to seize the opportunity and achieve greater influence, is not clear.[80] The JA's authority to distribute flats in Ramla and Lydda was contested by the CAP, which claimed that the vacant flats in Ramla were under its authority, having the power to rent them out. Conflict was always lurking in the background with so many groups of interest operating in such a restricted space: war veterans were allocated flats by the

---

78 Golan, *Wartime Spatial Changes*, pp. 90, 55.
79 A. Golan, 'Lydda and Ramle: From Palestinian-Arab to Israeli Towns, 1948–67', *Middle Eastern Studies* 39 (2003), pp. 121–139 (p. 127).
80 'Housing in Ramla and Lydda', letter from Ramla's District Officer to the Police Officer of Ramla, 12 July 1949, ISA, 56//2210/61–gimel; Letter from Shafrir to Chayun, District Officer, 25 July 1949, ISA, 85//2277/1–gimel.

Department for Soldier Rehabilitation; new immigrants were housed according to recommendations by the JA's Department of Absorption; buildings for public use were earmarked by the municipality; and assets intended for government institutions were distributed by the housing officer in charge.[81] Yet, as shown above, this conflict occasionally erupted away from the relatively safe environment of formal correspondence and committee debates; sometimes it became downright violent. Veterans or new immigrants would kick older or weaker dwellers (both Jews and Arabs) out of their flats, or squat in vacant ones. Rabbi Yisrael Glazer, for example, complained to Ramla's military governor that 'a family with two or three children' invaded a building using as a synagogue, allocated to the congregation by the JA in January 1949, preventing worship there; a more severe case was that of an old and blind Arab woman claimed to have been attacked and then expelled from her room by a Jewish man, without the police's intervention.[82] Such incidents, however, were relatively rare.

The State and Arab Individuals and Institutions

Ramla's Military Governor Jawitz was seen by the city's Arab inhabitants as a potential mediator with state authorities. During October-November 1948, they submitted applications for compensation for crops confiscated by the CAP; in early January 1949, Jawitz was still receiving applications for help in retrieving lost property.[83] Yet the Ministry of Minorities Affairs was a more popular address for complaints. In January 1949, the ministry's local representative reported:

81 Letter from Shafrir to the District Officer, 25 July 1949, ISA, 85//2277/1–gimel.
82 Letter from Yisrael Glazzer to the Military Governor, 23 March 1949, IDF Archive, 1860/50/32; Meeting of the Subcommittee on Ramla Affairs, 11 August 1952, ISA, 60//89/15–kaf.
83 'Report on the Activities of the Military Administration in Ramla and Lydda for the period 10 October—15 November 1948', IDF Archive, 1860/50/3; Letter dated 2 January 1949, ISA, 85//2276/32–gimel.

[T]he population complains bitterly that all the property of the residents who had been expelled from their houses and enclosed in the neighbourhood was robbed by individuals or taken in an organised manner by the Custodian for Abandoned Property, without giving any time or opportunity for the population which had stayed to stand and defend its property.[84]

When Minister Shitrit visited Ramla himself ten months later (on 11 November 1949, formerly the head of the Ministry of Minorities Affairs and now the Minister of Police), he was similarly approached with requests and supplications.[85] On the same visit, Shitrit also heard (perhaps read, it is not clear) ten appeals by Isma'il al-Nachas, on his own and on the town's people's behalf. Although Nachas was a member of the Arab Committee of Ramla, he represented Ramla's Muslim inhabitants, or at least some of them. In his petition he referred mainly to the issue of dispossessed property, noting that the town had surrendered on condition that the population's property and life—in this order—will not be harmed. Nachas requested, among other things, to enable orchard owners or their representatives and relatives to cultivate their lands; to enforce rent payment when houses and lands were used by someone other than their owners; to cease the demolition of inhabitants' property; and to make it easier for them to prove ownership after damage to their property or after losing relevant documentation.[86] Nachas was right to point out that in leaflets distributed before Ramle's surrender the inhabitants' life and property were guaranteed.[87] In the surrender document, however, no mention was made of property. A discrepancy existed, therefore, between what the Arab population might have come to

---

84 'Ramla', report by Shlomo Asherov, 2 January 1949, ISA, 49//297/5–gimel.
85 'Speech of the Head of the City of Ramla's Committee, Mr. Eliya Fanus...', ISA, 49//297/5–gimel.
86 Untitled and undated, signed by Ismail al-Nachas, ISA, 49//299/75–gimel.
87 'We have no intention of harming life or property'; 'your leaders will be held responsible for your spilt blood and destroyed property', in 'Announcement', 10 July 1948, IDF Archive, 6400/49/46. For a detailed account of the town's surrender see the Appendix.

expect, the actual surrender signed by the town's representatives, and what ultimately happened.[88]

Another way for Ramla's Arab population to regain their assets was by co-operating with the Committee of Inquiry into Property Claims in Ramla and Lydda. This committee, whose membership included representatives of the Military Administration, the CAP, and the Ministries of Agriculture and Minorities Affairs, convened several times between March and May 1949. The claimants had to provide proofs—written or oral—of their rights to the land in question, and also to prove that they had not been considered absentees.[89] In each session, the committee decided on two to five cases,[90] decisions that then had to be approved by the CAP. Even in the rare cases when Arab ownership was acknowledged, the land remained under the CAP's guardianship, while the owners were only allowed to cultivate it and profit from its product. This consent was not given if more than half the co-owners of a certain parcel were absentees, even if the claimant himself could prove partial ownership; in such cases, the land was considered absentee property.[91]

As time went by, protesting voices grew impatient. This was especially the case, it seems, when claimants were backed by powerful institutions or by their own capital. For example, Rev.

88 According to Dr. Shimon Gat, a member of Kibbutz Na'an and a historian of medieval Ramle, the handwritten surrender document was improvised on the spot, after the town's delegation arrived to the Kibbutz. Due to this hastiness the document was not translated from Hebrew into Arabic so that those who signed it did not know what exactly they agreed to; for the same reason, surrender terms included in it were not related to promises which had been given during earlier stages of fighting in town. Personal email correspondence, 22 July 2007.

89 On the committee's membership and procedures, see 'Minutes from a Meeting on 3 March 1949', ISA, 49//297/2–gimel; also ISA, 85//2276/36–gimel; 'Minutes of the First Meeting of the Committee of Inquiry into Property Claims in Ramla and Lydda', 6 March 1949, ISA, 85//2276/36–gimel; 'Announcement', undated, ISA, 85//2276/36–gimel; the other committee minutes appear in the same file in the ISA.

90 Except for the seventh and last session of the committee, which lasted for a week (2–9 September 1949) and discussed eighteen cases.

91 See minutes of committee meetings 1 to 7 in ISA, 85//2276/36–gimel.

Khalil Jamal, Secretary of the Council of the Arab Evangelical Episcopal Community in Palestine and Transjordan, informed the Military Governor in March 1949 that, despite an agreement to pay rent for the use of a school building belonging to the Anglican Church as a military hospital, 'no rent has in fact been paid so far'. Jamal urged Jawitz to 'take the necessary steps to settle all outstanding accounts and pay future monthly rents regularly.'[92] Eliya Fanus wrote directly to the CAP's local representative after having been informed of its intention to complete construction work on a building belonging to Fanus himself, and then rent out the property. He and he only, Fanus insisted, was the legal owner of this building, and had all documentation to prove it.[93] In a later case in which Fanus properties were involved, the matter took an altogether graver tone and a lawyer was hired. A letter sent on 9 November 1952 from the lawyer's office on behalf of the Fanus family, claimed ownership over several lots in town. This step followed acts on the ground to which the CAP was held accountable: the uprooting of olive trees and other preparations for construction (see Chapter five). In the letter, the Minister of the Interior was informed that already two years earlier the Fanus family had demanded tenure over six lots. The CAP, so the letter stated, had so far refused to return tenure over the land despite the fact that the Fanus family never left Ramla, and despite their Israeli citizenship. A claim for the return of tenure was accordingly filed in a Tel Aviv court, stating that any action taken in the meantime would be considered illegal.[94] Another individual claimant was Abed al-Rauf, the Imam of the al-Zaytuna mosque who, by July 1953, had not yet received tenure over his house despite an earlier application to the committee. Like Fanus, he was willing to take the matter to court. 'Since I have no more strength to wait, and also since I cannot afford the expenses of submitting applications anymore', he informed the Head of the Department of Minorities

---

92 Letter dated 28 March 1949, ISA, 85//2276/32–gimel.
93 Letter dated 26 September 1949, ISA, 85//2276/32–gimel.
94 ISA, 50//1966/80–gimel.

(by then part of the Ministry of the Interior), 'I await the committee's response.... If my request is denied, I intend to file a lawsuit against the CAP at the High Court of Justice'.[95] In this phrasing al-Rauf expressed obvious exasperation after his former applications to the committee had been overruled and denied. His intent to approach the High Court of Justice testifies to his frustration with the sluggish treatment and often unreasoned decisions of the Committee of Inquiry into Property Claims.[96]

Arab population throughout the country was becoming disgruntled in view of the failure to be acknowledged as owners of their property through co-operation with the establishment through committees and law-courts. Claims of present-absentees and non-absentees were submitted soon after the seizure of their assets, yet the state was reluctant to release the property which was usually already in use by others.[97] The legal solution reached at by the Israeli government was the Land Acquisition (Validation of Acts and Compensation) Bill of 1953, according to which compensation was offered to non-absentees and present-absentees owners, for lands that were claimed to be used for essential development, settlement or security purposes by the Israeli state. Many Arab owners, however, refused to apply for compensation, seeing it as legal and moral recognition of state appropriation.[98] This was not an offer at restitution that 'acts as a means of remembrance'[99]; not enough time elapsed between the act of confiscation and the offer at financial restitution for dispossessed land. From the owners' perspective it was rather an attempt at giving a final stamp of approval to an ongoing act of pillage.

---

95 Letter from Abed al-Rauf al-Jabali to head of the Minorities Department, 5 July 1953, ISA, 85//2276/32–gimel.
96 I did not manage to discover any court discussions or rulings related to this case.
97 Forman and Kedar, 'From Arab Land', p. 819.
98 *Ibid.*, pp. 821–822.
99 Dan Diner, 'Memory and Restitution: The Second World War as a Foundational Event in a Uniting Europe', in *Restitution and Memory: Material Restoration in Europe*, D. Diner and G. Wunberg (eds.)(NY, 2007), pp. 9–23 (p. 15).

Defiance was practiced in other ways too. A different approach was taken by some of the refugees who were considered by the State of Israel as absentees with no rights to property. Israel went into great lengths to check what it called 'infiltration' (*histanenut*)— attempts by refugees to cross the border into Israel. Peaking in 1952, between 1948 and 1956 thousands of Palestinian Arabs crossed the borders every year, mainly to collect crops left behind and visit relatives. Whereas some came to rob, others only wanted to gaze at their old houses from afar. Overall, 'infiltration' was driven by socio-economic rather than political factors, and it was usually neither organised nor armed.[100] Interestingly, as Fatma Kassem shows, while the word *mistanen* (infiltrator) has been used in Hebrew to dehumanise those Palestinians attempting to come back home and depict them as dangerous terrorists, its use by Palestinian women today emphasises instead these people's heroism and defiance in the face of danger.[101]

In the Ramla area, most 'infiltrators' were former residents now living in Ramallah, some of them returning, at times repeatedly, to recover former possessions. This was yet another way of dealing with the fact that abandoned property of any kind would probably not reunite with its original owners. Traffic between Ramallah and Ramla was mainly aimed, as shown by testimonials taken by the police, at recovering money and other valuables, sometimes from relatives who had never left, in order to support refugee families not allowed to return.[102] The fifteen-and-half-year-old Eliya Bishara who, according to his father's petition to the local police station, 'got carried away from the fleeing crowd' (presumably while leaving Ramle in mid July 1948), 'infiltrated' in April 1950 from Transjordan in order to be reunited with his family in Ramla. Another sixteen-year-old Arab-Christian who

---

100 B. Morris, *Israel's Border Wars, 1949–1956: Arab Infiltration, Israeli Retaliation and the Countdown to the Suez War* (Tel Aviv, 1996)[in Hebrew], Chapter 2.
101 Fatmeh Kassem, 'Language, History and Women: Palestinian Women in Israel Describe the *Nakba*', *Theory and Criticism* 29 (2006), pp. 59–80 [in Hebrew] (pp. 76–77).
102 ISA, 79//39/11–lamed; 79//6/26–lamed; 79//189/7–lamed.

had crossed the border from Ramallah in January 1951 (and was caught by police) testified that he came in order to ask for money from his aunt (whose husband was the owner of a local café in Ramla), 'since we have nothing to live from in Ramallah.'[103]

Whereas institutions, people with connections, or individuals who could finance legal counselling could reclaim ownership more convincingly, others had to settle for what the Israeli authorities were willing to give. Those at the bottom of Ramle's Arab society—the refugees in Ramallah—resorted to 'infiltration'. Attitudes also changed with time: whereas early on many of Ramle's Arabs still believed they could recover their property, by the end of 1949 they realised this was far from probable.

Municipality and State

While flats considered absentee property were continuously rented out or leased to Ramla's Jewish inhabitants, their legal status was seldom clear. The post-1948 history of Ramla is fraught with difficulties establishing ownership of certain plots and buildings. Already in the beginning of February 1949, the CAP was inquiring into the assets in the area;[104] some of these inquiries have not been satisfactorily resolved to this day.

Ramla's new municipality was as keen to inquire into property in town, especially that which belonged to the former Arab municipality or to its head (*mukhtar*), which it considered its own. Around 1954, therefore, the appropriate records were consulted in Britain, and an asset list compiled.[105] Now this information needed to be communicated to proper state authorities, approved, and duly recorded. Regretfully, the municipality was not always successful in following this process through: in a report by the

---

103 Letter to Police Officer Ramla, 1 May 1950, ISA 79//7/9–lamed; Testimony dated 21 January 1951, ISA 79//7/5–lamed.
104 On this see above; ISA, 49//297/4–gimel.
105 'Minutes in the Office of Ramla Municipality', 18–19 October 1959, ISA, 59//13610/2–gimel.

State Comptroller (*Mevaker Hamedina*) on Ramla's municipality
(for the fiscal period 1954/55–1957/58), the latter was criticised
for not keeping its land records straight. It stated the original
mandatory land records of the Ramle district, which were by then
outside the country, listing 174 lots belonging to the former Arab
municipality; the new municipality had failed to register all of
them under its own name. There were other problems too: firstly,
the Israeli municipality's assets identified as formerly owned by the
Arab municipality, as well as new buildings erected by 1957/58,
were not yet registered in the land registry; secondly, those which
had been registered lacked information as to the type of land,
mode of acquisition, and changes made thereto. The Comptroller
highlighted the importance of complete and updated records
of a local authority's real estate, particularly in formerly Arab
municipalities. He also warned against sloppy registration; in such
cases, there was reason to fear the non-registered assets 'might fall
out of the local authority's hands'. It is clear who would lose from
such a development; it is not entirely clear, however, who would
benefit—the state or the original Arab owners.[106]

A case in point is that of today's Ramla Municipal Museum
on 112 Herzl Blvd. This impressive stone building was erected
in 1922 as the Arab municipality. During British Mandate,
it was indeed used as the municipality building and, some of
the time, as a post office too.[107] Following the 1948 war, it was
declared absentee property and used for various municipal and
administrative purposes. A 1966 photograph (fig. 2) shows the
two-story edifice, its arched windows a clear marker of Arab
architecture, with a sign hanging from the building that reads:
'State of Israel/ Finance [Ministry]/ Income Tax Dept./ Ramla
Assessor's Office'; it is written in Hebrew only.

---

106 ISA, 50//3255/72–gimel; State Comptroller's Report 9 for the year 1957/58, p.
342.
107 In a map from 1931 the building was identified as post office and municipality;
in one from 1947 it proved to be municipality only. N. Bar Nisan, 'Ramla's
Museum', work submitted to the Department of Geography at the Hebrew
University (2004), pp. 11–12.

Fig. 2: Moshe Pridan, Ramle›s Municipality turned Income Tax Building, 1 December 1966 (Courtesy of the GPO).

The building's ownership was at issue already by the end of 1949, and is still contested. The police, which had initially been based in this building, relocated its headquarters around this time, and was asked by the municipality to ensure the building would be handed over 'in good and organised state to the municipality of Ramla that is the owner of the building'. The police, however, had no intention of giving it up: even after moving out, the police placed guards on the spot, claiming to still require it, probably for the purpose of housing police officers.[108] It was not clear what the municipality intended to do with the asset—turn it into a maternity hospital or use it again as a post office.[109] Be that as it may, two and a half months later the building was still not vacated by the police, which was now using it as an atelier.[110]

The local dispute surrounding this building turned national in August 1950. Presumably in an attempt to gain support Ramla's Mayor Meir Melamed applied to the Ministry of Finance's Department of State Assets. He stated that the building had been owned and used in the past by Ramle's Arab municipality, and was therefore legally owned by the municipality he was now heading, which was the Arab one's successor. In reply, Melamed was informed that the land on which the disputed building stood was in fact registered on the name of the former British High Commissioner, as state property. It was admitted that the former municipality had used the edifice, albeit without any written agreement with the government. There was some good news

---

108 Letter from M. Melamed, Ramla's Mayor, to Police HQ, 8 December 1949, ISA, 79//2151/6–lamed; letter from the local District Officer to the Tel Aviv District Officer, 27 December 1949, ISA, 85//2277/1–gimel.

109 Letter from the Postal Authority's Economy Department Manager to the District Supervisor at Central Police HQ, 13 December 1949, ISA, 79//2151/6–lamed; another letter dated 27 December 1949, ISA, 85//2277/1–gimel.

110 Letter from District Officer to Housing Committee Chairman, 16 February 1950, ISA, 85//2277/1–gimel.

too: the department was willing to lease out the building to the municipality, as soon as the police vacated it.[111]

By 1953, the building was still used by the police as an atelier, a fact that possibly prompted the municipality to keep inquiring into the matter of legal ownership even if it had by now accepted that the land was considered state property. When the State Comptroller asked Ramla's municipality to explain how it had determined which assets belonged to its predecessor, it replied that inquiries had been made through both the appropriate institutions (without specifying these) and Ramla's Arab inhabitants. In these inquiries it found out, quite cryptically, that 'Ramle's Arab municipality had no assets whatsoever, except for the municipality's previous building, using these days as an atelier for the police, over which the Arab inhabitants have no certainty as to who had been the owner.'[112] When the municipality's lawyer was instructed in 1954/55 to look into assets owned by the former Arab municipality, the building was not included in his list.[113]

The building's ownership was contested even as late as the year 2000. Correspondence from that year between the Israel Lands Administration (founded in 1960) and the Municipality of Ramla shows that the legal status of the lots on which the building stands (*halich hesder karka'ot*, a legal procedure in which the lots are mapped and registered) had already begun. While ownership of the disputed lots was still claimed by the state, Ramla's municipality insisted that since the building was initially built to house the municipality it should own it today as well.[114]

---

111 Letter dated 10 September 1950, ISA, 59//13616/1–gimel-lamed; letter from Head of District Housing Committee to Ramla's District Officer, 4 August 1950, ISA, 85//2277/1–gimel; list of state assets composed in November 1950 by the State Assets Department in the Finance Ministry and sent to the Mayor of Ramla, ISA, 85//2276/38–gimel.

112 Letter from inspection party to secretary of Ramla's municipality, 18 May 1953, ISA, 59//13616/1–gimel lamed.

113 'Minutes in the Office of Ramla Municipality', 18–19 October 1959, ISA, 59//13610/2–gimel.

114 N. Bar Nisan, 'Ramla's Museum', Appendix 2.

* * *

Moral and ethical doubts triggered by the occupation of Ramle and the urgent need to secure the new *status quo* both legally and in practice shaped prevailing attitudes towards Arab property. Many individuals and institutions took part in redesigning Ramla's spatial landscape in the period discussed above, representing a variety of interests, both public and private. Not only in the immediate aftermath of occupation, but also in the following months and years to come, conflict erupted among them, especially over the process of housing. Much like the actual act of expropriation, the redistribution of Arab assets was not an easy task; rather, it was fraught with ambiguities, doubts and disputes.

Legal definitions and processes were used to legitimise the appropriation of Palestinian property. The state enacted legislative formulations and decided what was considered legitimate, and in the process invalidated the claims of smaller and weaker entities— individuals and small groups, first Arabs and later Jews. A double standard marked the authorities' position as to Arab property and its post-war use: as long as the state's agenda was satisfied, legality and legitimacy were guaranteed; when any action defying its authority for the purpose of individual gain at its expense was carried out, it was declared illicit and illegitimate. In this processes the original Arab owners were marginalised; the only perceived injured party was the Jewish collective.

Moreover, the two discourses presented in this chapter and the ongoing tension between them shed light on the broader issue of the treatment of Israel's Arab citizens. Whereas one discourse, no doubt the dominant one, privileged the Jewish ethnos and its needs, excluding non-Jewish residents in the process, the other was more inclusive, seeking to treat minorities as equals and to defend their interests. However, during the formative years of 1948–1950, 'Hebrew Ramla' tried to sound and appear more Israeli and Jewish than Arab and managed to do so, among other things, by marginalising the needs and rights of its remaining Arab inhabitants.

CHAPTER TWO

Asset Appropriation:
The Non-Free Market

It has become a truism that consumption practices 'work as a mirror of our relationships and of the larger social structure and its ideologies, while offering a terrain where models of relations, social structures and ideologies are played out, transformed and brought into question'.[1] Devious and dispersed, consumption—as Michel de Certeau commented—'sinuates itself everywhere, silently and almost invisibly, because it does not manifest itself through its own products, but rather through its *ways of using* the products imposed by a dominant economic order'.[2] Consumption is therefore another means of imposing cultural hegemony and dominion, as in Nazi Germany's consumption-culture; at the same time, however, consumer practices can also function as occasions for popular resistance, as in the marketplaces of Ghandi's India.[3] It is especially at times of conflict or transition, as Deborah Bernstein and Badi Hasisi have shown in the case of Mandate Palestine, that

---

1   Roberta Sassatelli, *Consumer Culture: History, Theory and Politics* (London, 2007), p. 55.

2   Michel de Certeau, *The Practice of Everyday Life*, trans. S. Rendall (Berkeley and LA, 1984)[orign. 1980], pp. xii-xiii.

3   *Ibid.*, p. xix; Sassatelli, *Consumer Culture*, p. 81; S. Jonathan Wiesen, *Creating the Nazi Marketplace: Commerce and Consumption in the Third Reich* (Cambridge, 2011); Anand A. Yang, *Bazaar India: Markets, Society, and the Colonial State in Gangetic Bihar* (Berkeley and LA, 1998), Chapter 4.

consumerism highlights a complex interplay between nationalism and class formation.[4]

After the initial legitimacy the state of Israel had provided for the expropriation of houses, lands and movables—mainly, but not only, through legislation—in the immediate post-war years, appropriation turned to focus on the commercial milieu in Ramla, through two forms of Jewish economic takeover that dominated consumption in the 1950s: one was orchestrated and organised by the municipality, and involved the gradual transformation of the town's market in the first half of the 1950s, when the traditional Arab *suq* was made into an Israeli bazaar in terms of sellers, buyers, goods on sale, and overall appearance and design. Another form of Jewish economic takeover was initiated and transacted by and between individuals, and concerned Arab businesses sold to Jews: from 1950 to 1956, many of Ramla's Arab cafés changed hands in a way that transformed the town's socio-economic map.

The process of economic and commercial transfers and transformations is significant for several reasons. To begin with, it allows for a further exploration into the discourses of legality and legitimacy in the period following Ramle's occupation, and to an evaluation of the continuity and changes therein. Secondly, since these changes carried not only economic but also ethnic, social, national and symbolic implications, they contributed to the creation and remake of identities in town. Finally, in the particular case of Ramla's cafés, the process was associated with fears and discussions of broader significance, thus linking local events with national and international circumstances, and shedding important light on the reconstruction of the formerly Arab urban landscape into an Israeli-Jewish one.

4   D. Bernstein and B. Hasisi, '"Buy and Promote the National Cause": Consumption, Class Formation and Nationalism in Mandate Palestinian Society', *Nations and Nationalism* 14:1 (2008), pp. 127–150.

The Town's Marketplace: From Suq to Shuk

Since Cliford Geertz's seminal publication on the *suq* (Arabic for market) in Moroccan Sefrou, many anthropologists, sociologists and historians have written on marketplaces worldwide.[5] Whether in Tokyo, Tehran, Balta or Damascus, most of the scholars writing today on marketplaces refer to them as units of economic, social, cultural and political organisation.[6] While emphasising the articulation of power relations within these marketplaces, many writers have also highlighted their spatial dimensions.[7] Ramla's marketplace, therefore, enables an examination of the shifts and turns of the twentieth century, especially on the backdrop of national and social conflicts current at the time. Writing on the town's marketplace, however, is not an easy task: scarcity and the eclectic nature of primary sources (municipal records, pictures, personal narratives and the daily press) pose a great challenge, imposing a careful reconstruction made of various clues and hints relating to the market and its daily operation both before and after 1948.

Ramle's markets were famous throughout the high and late Middle Ages, and it is possible that the town's medieval fruit market, located on Ramle's central thoroughfare (leading from Lydda to Gaza, and crosscutting the road between Jerusalem and Jaffa), has evolved into the *shuk* (Hebrew for market) we are

5 Clifford Geertz, 'Suq: The Bazaar Economy in Sefrou', in *Meaning and Order in Moroccan Society: Three Essays in Cultural Analysis* (Cambridge, 1979), pp. 123–313. For some recent publications on marketplaces see, for example, Theodore C. Bestor, *Tsukiji: The Fish Market at the Center of the World* (Berkeley and LA, 2004); Arang Keshavarzian, *Bazaar and State in Iran: The Policies of Tehran Marketplace* (Cambridge, 2007); Y. Petrovsky-Shtern, 'The Marketplace in Balta: Aspects of Economic and Cultural Life', *East European Jewish Affairs* 37:3 (2007), pp. 277–298; Faedah M. Totah, 'Return to the Origin: Negotiating the Modern and the Unmodern in the Old City of Damascus', *City & Society* 21:1 (2009), pp. 58–81.
6 Yang, *Bazaar India*, p. 166;
7 Keshavarzin, *Bazaar and State*, pp. 71–72.

familiar with today.[8] During Ottoman rule and British Mandate period Ramle's *suq* retained its centrality and importance, and even today the market's various architectural layers are still visible: in the western side of the market street, adjacent to the Armenian Church compound, are found long and narrow shops, as well as other, more ancient, buildings going back to Mandate and Ottoman rule, perhaps as old as the eleventh century; the street's eastern side, on the other hand, has a more provisional character, with improvised tin shacks and similar makeshift constructions added to late nineteenth and early twentieth century buildings. The northern part of the street's eastern side is visibly newer and dates to after 1948: during British Mandate the adjacent municipal garden (discussed extensively in Chapter Three) was larger; after the town's occupation by the Israeli forces the market gradually crawled towards the garden, expanding at its expense.[9] Situated next to the town's Great Mosque, the market's location testifies to its significance as one of the core elements typical of the Middle Eastern Muslim town.[10] After 1922, when Ramle's municipal building was erected on the market's margins, the area has become not only a centre of devotional and commercial lives, but also of civic activity.

Geertz treated Sefrou's *suq* as an amalgam of several 'realms': a fixed market, a temporary one, as well as other nearby businesses.[11] Ramle's *suq* in the first half the twentieth century was similarly constructed: shops in the street market operated throughout the week on Omar Ibn Abed al-Khatab Steet (called after a companion of Prophet Muhammad), and was apparently much wider than

8   S. Gat, 'The City of Ramla in the Middle Ages' (PhD thesis, Bar Ilan University, 2003)[in Hebrew], pp. 164–166; Hila Keren-Steinmetz, 'The Location and Place of Ramle's Old Market' (work submitted to Geography Department, Bar Ilan University, 2010)[in Hebrew], p. 16.

9   Keren-Steinmetz, 'The Location and Place of Ramle's Old Market', p. 8.

10   Besim Selim Hakim, *Arabic-Islamic Cities: Building and Planning Principles* (London, 1986), pp. 169–170; see also Janet L. Abu-Lughod, 'The Islamic City—Historic Myth, Islamic Essence, and Contemporary Relevance', *International Journal of Middle East Studies* 19:2 (1987), pp. 155–176.

11   Geertz, 'Suq', p. 126.

it is today; according to Muhammad Taji, the now deceased former head of *waqf* in town,[12] animals burdened with goods could walk within the street market and unpack their cargo.[13] At the margins of the Great Mosque a little peddlers' market was located, where small industry craftsmen operated, the local knives sharpener, for instance. Wednesday was an extended market day, with merchants coming from further afield to offer their goods in stalls, and village men and women bartering agricultural products from baskets.[14] Ramle's market was therefore a meeting place for the region's people—the town's residents but also neigbouring villagers and traders from other Palestinians cities and towns. During this period various goods were sold and bartered at the *suq*—fruit, vegetables, herbs, cheese, spices and poultry, as well as fabrics (silk from Syria, linen from Egypt, and cotton from Gaza) and dyes for the traditional embroidery.[15]

The town's occupation in mid July 1948 triggered a series of changes and transformations that contributed to Ramle's gradual metamorphosis from an Arab town into an Israeli one.[16] Thousands of Jewish immigrants arriving in town from November 1948 onwards populated the mostly-emptied town. This drastic change was articulated also in the marketplace, with many of its former Arab shop owners and sellers now gone, and Jewish buyers cramming it in search of foodstuff, fabric and clothing, as well as other necessities. Yet, it seems that, at least initially, the marketplace

---

12 *Waqf* being a religious endowment of a building or plot of land made for charitable purposes.
13 Muhammad Taji, cited in Keren-Steinmetz, 'The Location and Place of Ramle's Old Market', p. 21.
14 *Ibid.*, idem.
15 Sandy Tolan, *The Lemon Tree: A Jew, An Arab, and the Heart of the Middle East* (NY, 2006), p. 16; Interviews with Fawzi al-Basoumi (dated 30 March 2005); Maliha al-Khayri (dated 18 March 2005); Abdel Rahman Abu Hamdeh (dated 30 August 2003). All interviewed as part of the Oral History Project of the Palestine Remembered website (http://www.palestineremembered.com/OralHistory/Interviews-Listing/Story1151.html#al-Ramla).
16 Ze'ev Vilna'i, *Ramla: Hove Ve'avar* (Ramla, 1961), pp. 15, 88; Hagit Chovav, *Ramla—Hair Ha'atika: Seker Chevrati* (1968), p. 70; 'Ramle', 2 January 1949, ISA, 297/5–gimel. See also Appendix.

remained an Arab territory, bordering with the Arab 'ghetto' and populated by Arab sellers.[17] A photograph taken on 5 September 1949 by Hugo Mendelson, who had immigrated to Israel from Berlin in 1934, is a fascinating remnant of the market in this transformative period (fig. 3),[18] showing a mundane transaction taking place in the *shuk* between Etka Berman, a forty-year-old new immigrant from Poland, and the fifty-five-year-old Anton Afif (his place of origin was not indicated by Mendelson, who may have known or assumed that he is local).

In a series of intervention acts Ramla's municipality shifted gradually the nature of the *suk* and appropriated it. Sometime before September 1950 it was announced that the problem of 'peddlers and vegetable sellers in the streets, who made the centre of town dirty' was solved; a new and organised peddlers market in the town centre offered facilities for a more sanitary operation. Anton Afif may have been one of those vegetable sellers referred to here as 'a problem in itself'.[19] Apparently, this did not help much the crowdedness and hygienic conditions of the streetmarket, now on Jabotinsky St. (named after the Zionist Revisionist leader). Ramla's municipality published therefore in mid-April 1954 a tender calling for the construction of an urban market in town:[20] the municipality was planning to invest 70,000 Israeli Pounds in order to turn the unsanitary and crammed marketplace into a modern market with 59 shops and 12 open stalls; these were to be connected to electricity, water and sewage systems. Public phone, police station, public lavatories and a paved road were likewise planned.[21] Construction was to be accomplished

---

17   Tolan, *The Lemon Tree*, pp. 111–112; Bilha Toren, *Sdom Vehamora: Sipurim—Lo Liyladim!* (Tel Aviv, 2004), p. 19.

18   Between 1943 and the early 1950s Mendelson worked with International Press agency, visiting as photographer countries such as Jordan, Cypress and Egypt. In the early 1950s he quit professional photography. Guy Raz, *Photographers of Palestine: Eretz Israel/ Israel (1855–2000)*(Tel Aviv, 2003)[in Hebrew], p. 122.

19   *Iryat Ramla: Sikum Pe'ulot Ha'irya* (Ramla, 1950), p. 22; *Ramla Bevinyana Uvehitpatchuta* (Ramla, 1952), p. 24.

20   *Davar*, 14 April 1954.

21   *Mehanaasa Ba'ir: Igeret Le'ezrachey Ramla 1* (Ramla, August 1954), p. 6.

Fig. 3: Hugo Mendelson, Etka Berman and Anton Afif in Ramla›s Market, 5 September 1949 (Courtesy of the GPO).

within a year, and the new marketplace's cornerstone was to be laid during Independence Day celebrations (see Chapter Four for Independence Day celebrations of 1954).[22] Ramla's municipality attempted to retain some of the characteristics of the Middle Eastern market yet modernise it; as late as 1967, however, the market was still perceived as a social and sanitary nuisance.[23]

A more general Jewish urge to modernise the traditional Arab *suq* has been voiced already from the 1930s. Alfred Bonné, a German professor of economics who immigrated to Palestine in 1925, predicted in 1938 that the famous Eastern market was slowly disappearing while more Westerly-styled shops and buildings were to take its place. 'The Eastern market will remain a romantic and historical remnant of an economic period that has passed away', he declared in a book published that year on the economy of Eretz Israel.[24] The market, which was operated by Arabs and Jews alike, was still seen by many to have remained a nuisance—dirty, noisy, chaotic and unruly.[25]

But the Middle Eastern market was also perceived by Israeli society at large as exotic and unique: when the two weeks 'Arab market' opened (on 29 March 1967) in Tel Aviv's Migdal Shalom (with its 34 floors, the highest skyscraper in the Middle East), the papers described the 'colourful aromatic scents of an Eastern market with its exotic spices' which characterised this well-orchestrated, Jewish-imagined 'Arab market'.[26] Underlying this enterprise was an attempt to enable an economic encounter between potential

---

22 *Maariv*, 3 May 1954, p. 4.
23 *Ramla Bevinyana Uvehitpatchuta*, p. 24; *Mehanaasa Ba'ir*, p. 6; *Ramla: Seker Likrat Shikum*, p. 40.
24 Cited in Anat Helman, *Urban Culture in 1920s and 1930s Tel Aviv* (Jerusalem, 2007) [in Hebrew], p. 105.
25 Interestingly, the Arab-Israeli *suq* was sometimes even compared to the East-European market of the Jewish shtetl. When these two 'Eastern' (East European and Middle Eastern) economic institutions were juxtaposed with more modern (i.e. clean and quiet) European and American shops their Otherness and inferiority were proclaimed and made obvious. Helman, *Urban Culture*, pp. 106–109. On the discourse of modernisation, and cleanliness versus pollution see Chapter Five.
26 *Al Hamishmar*, 2 April 1967, in ISA 102//17024/9–gimel lamed.

consumers and suppliers, both on national and international scale.[27] The Israeli-Jewish representation of the Arab *suq* was therefore wrapped in layers of what Edward Said termed Orientalism: it was described as both attractive and repulsive, colourful and dirty, (re) settled and restructured, dominated and ruled over.[28]

Whether dirty, romantic, or both combined, the *suq* was here to stay: goods sold in the market were cheaper than in other places, thus posing an attraction for many.[29] The red angora fabric for Bilha Elchalal's Bat Mitzva dress, for example, was bought from 'the Arab at the *shuk*' in Ramla, since it was cheaper to purchase it there.[30] This was probably also the reason, or one of the reasons, for the survival of the Bedouin market in Beer Sheva (Beersheba in Arabic), that had been operating since its foundation by the Ottomans in 1906. Beer Sheva's market was closed down by Israeli authorities after the town's occupation, in an attempt to disconnect the association between this desert town and the Bedouin tribes living around it, but nevertheless, it was reopened in 1954 in order to cater better for the (mostly Jewish) residents' needs and demands. Safad's market, on the other hand, which existed since the sixteenth century and was a meeting point for diverse communities of Christians, Muslims, Jews, Druze and Bedouins, lost its standing after 1948 and was closed down, never to reopen; over the years it was neglected and finally destroyed.[31] If successful in traversing 'modernisation' without being destroyed in the process the marketplaces inherited by the new Jewish municipalities from their Arab predecessors have become a social space that facilitated interaction among different ethno-cultural groups.[32]

---

27 'Summary of Mr. Mordechay Meir Speech in the Opening Ceremony of "The Arab Week" in Kol-bo Shalom', 29 March 1967, SA 102//17024/9–gimel lamed.

28 Edward W. Said, *Orientalism* (London, 1985)[orig. 1978], p. 3.

29 Helman, *Urban Culture*, pp. 111–112.

30 Toren, *Sdom Vehamora*, p. 19.

31 Eitan Cohen, *Beer Sheva: The Fourth City* (Jerusalem, 2006)[in Hebrew], pp. 35–45; 165–167; *Safed: A Walk Through Time: A Walking-Tour with Yad Ben-Zvi*, Eyal Meron (ed.)(Jerusalem, 2006)[in Hebrew], pp. 92–93.

32 L.M. Pratt, 'Arts of the Contact Zone', in *Ways of Reading*, D. Bartholomae and A. Petroksky (eds.)(NY, 1999).

Another component of the modernisation of Ramla's market was linked to the change in the national and socio-economic composure of those owning and running the market's shops and stalls. In May 1955 it was published in the national press that in order to lessen the number of 'social cases'—ailing people, incapacitated folk and the elderly—in Ramla 'by offering constructive help', the municipality will be 'handing out' seventy shops in the town's new marketplace to candidates decided upon by the relevant welfare institutions.[33] This was done with the help of 'Malban'—a foundation that was part of the American Jewish Joint Distribution Committee, which helped elderly and incapacitated new immigrants.[34] In this manner the municipality, struggling to regulate and supervise the market and its everyday operation for six years, attempted to strengthen its control over it while assisting the town's welfare authorities. Unlicensed Arab (and probably also Jewish) peddlers were now replaced by disadvantaged Jews under the care of welfare organisations, who rented their stalls and shops directly from the municipality. Other renters paid Amidar, the national housing company administering national assets, including those that had been declared absentees' property. In this case 'absentees' property' included the shops in the market that were, up to 1948, part of Ramle's Muslim *Waqf,* and perhaps also shops owned privately by Muslims. The local churches in Ramla (mostly Greek and Armenian), whose property was mostly 'released' back to them by the Israeli authorities, were the owners of the remaining shops in the market.[35] Ramla's *shuk,* as real estate in town more generally, was a patchwork of diverse ownerships, representing the status of the different Arab communities in town—while Christian ecclesiastical assets were usable, Muslim *waqf* property was withheld by the Israeli state and its extensions.

By 1970, however, most shops in the market were used— rented or owned—by Jews who had immigrated to Israel from Iraq

---

33 *Davar,* 29 May 1955.
34 *Maariv,* 3 May 1954.
35 Personal correspondence with Miri Shemesh from Ramla's municipality, dated 30 December 2010; Interview with Muhammad Taji, dated 25 June 2007.

(hereafter referred to as Iraqi Jews); they have remained so to this day.[36] Did this new presence in the *shuk* consist of disadvantaged individuals, shrewd businessmen or simply men wishing to make a living? Answers to this question might be found in yet another growing economic expansion and dominance of Ramla's Iraqi Jews—around the town's cafés.

Café Appropriation

In the mid-1950s, the café owned by Hana Zakaria Hallak, a fifty-three-year-old Christian Arab and father of seven, was an emblem of neighbourly relations in Ramla. Located on 6 Jan Masaryk St. in the Old City (these days renamed Kehilat Detroit), Arabs and Jews frequented it together, while Israeli flags and posters of the Israeli President, Prime Minister and Chief of Staff hung on the counter. Yet on 6 September 1956, Jewish New Year's Eve, Hallak was stabbed to death and his son William (20) and son-in-law George Azar (29) were severely injured in a violent incident.[37]

The assailants were two Jewish residents of Ramla of Iraqi descent—Zvi Kaduri (19) and Avraham Abudi (24)—who lived

---

36 Pinchas Frank, *Proyekt Shituf Toshavim Bebinuy Upinuy: Sikum Mechkar Pe'ula* (Tel Aviv University, c. 1970–1971[?]), p. 17; personal correspondence with Miri Shemesh from Ramla's municipality, dated 30 December 2010. We find a similar economic Jewish takeover in Acre's Old City, where in a gradual process Jews bought Arabs' shops: whereas in 1951–1952 there were 131 Arab shop owners in the town's market and only 37 Jewish ones, in 1957–1958 the ratio shifted to 78 Arabs and 98 Jewish shop owners; by the early 1970s only 75 Arab shop owners remained, in comparison with 102 Jewish shop owners. Yehoshua Lurie, *Acre—The Walled City: Jews Among Arabs, Arabs Among Jews* (Tel Aviv, 2000)[in Hebrew], p. 574.

37 There is extensive documentation of this incident, in police reports, the daily press and two sessions of the Knesset Committee for Internal Affairs. I was unable to locate the relevant court documents, which had probably been burnt. See all police documents and amnesty letters in ISA, 79//2479/23–lamed; *Davar*, *Yediot Ahronot*, *Haaretz* and *Maariv*, 9 September 1956; *Maariv*, 10 September 1956; *Haaretz*, 11 September 1956; *Haolam Haze* 987 (12 September 1956); Minutes 2B and 3B (16 and 30 October 1956, respectively) of the Knesset Committee for Internal Affairs, ISA, 60//104/7–kaf.

in one of the town's Transit Camps (*Ma'abara Beth*),[38] and some of their friends. Police investigation revealed that the trigger for the attack was an incident that had occurred in Hallak's café about a fortnight prior to the killing, in which the two had felt their honour was compromised: when their food order was delayed, they demanded to be served out of line but were overlooked. Later, before avenging their insult on New Year's Eve, Kaduri and Abudi sat in the nearby Karabina Café, drinking Arak (anis-based Mediterranean liquor) in order to muster courage. When thus emboldened, they entered Hallak's café while Kaduri asked the owner, 'Do you remember what you've done to me two weeks ago?'; when answered 'so what do you want?' Kaduri began stabbing Hallak. At the same time, Abudi stabbed Hallak's son-in-law. Hallak's son was likewise stabbed by Kaduri after attempting to help his father; only after Hallak's wife, who had seen her husband collapse, started shouting for help, did the assailants escape. By the next morning the police arrested Kaduri, Abudi, and twelve other Jewish men who assisted their escape.

The police, anxious that the event might escalate into local riots, positioned large forces in the *sakne* after 'certain groups' (according to the press) tried to 'incite' the Arab population.[39] In the next days, Ramla's Arab inhabitants announced a general strike, planned to last until receiving reassurance that violent incidents against the Arab community would not recur. During the funeral procession, in which about 800 people participated, including Mayor Meir Melamed, the shops located on the route remained closed, whether owned by Arabs or by Jews.

Hallak's attackers were convicted of manslaughter and sentenced to fourteen years in prison in May 1957.[40] In May

---

38 The *ma'abara* (pl. *ma'abarot*) housed new Jewish immigrants during the 1950s; for more information on the *ma'abara* see Chapter Five.

39 This may have referred to Communist Party members who, according to a police report, tried to prevent shop owners and workers from going to work in the following days. *Davar*, 9 September 1956; ISA, 79//2479/23–lamed; Police report, 26 September 1956, ISA, 79//2479/23-lamed.

40 Undated and untitled amnesty request of Avraham Abudi, ISA, 79//2479/23–lamed.

1962—six years after Hallak's death—the town witnessed a *sulha* (traditional Arab reconciliation ceremony) between the victim's family and those responsible for the murder, in which representatives of the town's Jewish Iraqi community paid the late Hallak's family 7,900 Israeli Pounds. The practice of *sulha* in this case highlights the choice of reconciliation over revenge.[41] At the same time, it emphasises the fact that this particular Arab tradition was shared by two communities composed of different ethnic, religious and national origin: Christian-Arab and Iraqi-Jewish. Following this reconciliation, Kaduri and Abudi's sentences were commuted to ten years.[42]

The attack on Hallak's café may have been triggered by Kaduri and Abudi's injured pride, yet it was only the last incident in a string of violent incidents related to cafés in Ramla. At the end of March 1952, several violent confrontations occurred in Ramla's Old City between Arabs and Jews of Iraqi origin. Contemporary reports seem to suggest that these were orchestrated by potential Jewish buyers of Arab-owned cafés. After two cafés were bought by Iraqi Jews, the remaining cafés still in Arab hands experienced violent incidents that stopped only once they moved into Jewish ownership.[43] In one of these, three Jewish men from Iraqi descent (the brothers of Na'im Kaduri who had bought an Arab café only several months earlier) attacked a young Arab named 'Adel Amasyas while he was sitting in one of the Arab cafés in the Old City. Two drunken Iraqi Jews that were also sitting in the same café joined in and started a fight, during which Amasyas managed to escape. When five policemen arrived at the scene and arrested the people involved one of the drunken men injured a policeman with a knife. Ramla's police station reported the incident to the

---

41   Sharon Lang, '*Sulha* Peacemaking and the Politics of Persuasion', *Journal of Palestine Studies* 31:3 (2002), pp. 52–66.

42   Hallak's remaining family members immigrated to Canada, where they later opened a café named al-Kuds (Arabic for Jerusalem). Interview with Samir Dabit, 2007.

43   Minutes 3 of the Ministry of the Interior Subcommittee on Ramla Affairs, 19 August 1952, ISA, 60//89/15—kaf.

sub-district's commander in a document titled 'Iraqis and Arabs' (11 March 1952). In a return letter, the station was called 'to supervise the state of affairs between these residents [Iraqi Jews and Arabs], so that the police takes charge of the situation'.[44] The minutes and conclusions of a 1952 subcommittee of the Ministry of the Interior reveal a second violent incident in which Arabs were attacked by Iraqi Jews in another café. A third incident, on 1 July 1952, deteriorated into an assault in which stones were thrown at an Old City café owned by an Arab family named Shahin. The owner reported that before this attack, two Iraqi Jews offered him 4,000 Israeli Pounds for his café (whereas he demanded 10,000 Pounds). Three policemen protected the place, preventing further damage to property or to life and limb.[45]

As a possible key to understanding the escalating tension around Ramla's cafés and throughout the Old City in general, the subcommittee's members were informed that three cafés passed from Arab to Jewish hands in the period preceding the violent events of March and July 1952. It was not indicated which cafés exactly were involved, but if the ownership of Ramla's cafés is traced further back, it soon becomes clear that Arab cafés changed ownership as early as 1950. Around that year, a Jewish family of Iraqi descent bought an Arab-owned café and named it Karabina; this was where Abudi and Kaduri drank Arak before their assault.[46] An Armenian-owned café was likewise sold to Iraqi Jews in October 1951.[47] In addition, around that time (and before October 1951) Abu Michelle's café was bought by Na'im Kaduri. Two other cafés on the main street were likewise bought

44 '*lehishtalet 'al hamatzav*'; ISA, 79//7/2–lamed, the second letter dated 24 March 1952. See also *Divrey HaKnesset*, vol. XII, pp. 2598–2600.

45 *Divrey HaKnesset*, vol. XII, p. 2599; Minutes 2 of the Subcommittee on Ramla Affairs, 11 August 1952, ISA, 60//89/15–kaf; Minutes 3 of the Subcommittee, 19 August 1952, ISA, 60//89/15–kaf; Conclusions of the Ministry of the Interior's Committee on the Ramla Incidents, 19 August 1952, ISA, 71//1121/5–gimel lamed.

46 Interview with Samir Dabit, 11 June 2007.

47 Report dated 27 October 1951, ISA, 79//7/3–lamed; Minutes 3 of the Subcommittee, 19 August 1952, ISA, 60//89/15–kaf.

and turned into movie theatres.[48] Despite all these incidents, the subcommittee that debated these matters in 1952 could not establish a conclusive link between pressure on Arab café owners to sell their businesses to Iraqi Jews and violent incidents targeting Ramla's Arab community.[49] But why cafés?

The institution of the café has been part of the public sphere in which various types of interaction are made available, being a liminal place, in between public and private, work and leisure, male and female. While enabling interaction and acting as a meeting place for different backgrounds, the café may also enforce segregation and exclusion. In bringing together the public and the private, the eventful and the mundane, the café has been political in more than one way, enabling debates, intentional and strategic action, as well as reactive and unconscious one.[50] It is no wonder, therefore, that the cafés which operated along the Tel Aviv-Jaffa border in Mandate Palestine functioned as intersections of class, nation, gender and ethnic boundaries, or that the 1959 Wadi Salib riots in Haifa, protesting against Mizrachi discrimination, were triggered by events in local cafés.[51]

In 1950s' Ramla, as today, one could find different types of cafés—from the semi-legal gaming enclave to the familial ice-cream parlour (fig. 4). In 1951, card games played in some of Ramla's cafés were described as 'a plague', with men of all nations and ethnicities playing from morning until night. The consequences of this phenomenon concerned the police; they

48 Interview with Samir Dabit, 11 June 2007.
49 Conclusions of the Ministry of the Interior's Committee, 19 August 1952, ISA, 71//1121/5–gimel lamed.
50 Andrew Edgar, *The Philosophy of Habermas* (Chesham, Bucks., UK, 2005), p. 31; Andrew Edgar, *Habermas: The Key Concepts* (NY, 2006), p. 124; W. Scott Haine, *The World of the Paris Café: Sociability among the French Working Class, 1789–1914* (Baltimore and London, 1996), p. 237; David W. Stowe, 'The Politics of Café Society', *Journal of American History* 84:4 (1998), pp. 1384–1406 (p. 1385).
51 Deborah Bernstein, *Women on the Margins: Gender and Nationalism in Mandate Tel Aviv* (Jerusalem, 2008)[in Hebrew], p. 74; Yfaat Weiss, *A Confiscated Memory: Wadi Salib and Haifa's Lost Heritage*, trans. Avner Greenberg (NY, 2011), pp. 1–8.

Fig. 4: H. Dorfzaun, A Café in the Marketplace, c. 1962–1964 (Courtesy of www.palphot.com)

included petty theft, family ruin, and the arrival of 'negative elements' into town.[52] Despite the dominance of cafés in which cards were habitually played, other types of cafés also existed in Ramla.[53] One such example of a family-oriented establishment, in which women and children were welcome, was Arditi in the marketplace.[54] Some attracted ethnically and nationally mixed clientele, as in the case of Hallak's café or that run by Mrs. Ghattas.[55] This type of co-existence was particularly evident on the Shabbat and Jewish holidays, when the closed Jewish-owned cafés drove the town's secular Jews to seek entertainment in the Arab-owned venues.[56]

Ownership of these cafés, especially those in which semi-legal gaming took place, meant not only potential financial gain but also some social standing, and connection to the place. Through the provision of entertainment, food and beverages, the café owners came in close contact with many people and were in fact the facilitators of activity in a public sphere, whether homogenous (in terms of gender and ethnicity), or diverse. Café ownership also established and reinforced connection to the place, offering link to the actual locus where property stood (and with it to the surrounding area), in terms of ethnicity, religion or language. The status of the public-private café was even more enhanced in this period, when many of the town's people, Jews and Arabs alike, lived in poor or crowded conditions—in the *ma'abarot* or in small flats shared by several families. The café has consequently become a sort of escapade, offering both a place for conversation and a physical space in which many could assemble. Understandably, owning one was dearly coveted.

---

52 Police Report, 27 October 1951, ISA, 79//7/3–lamed.
53 By the end of 1950, thirteen cafés operated in town; a year later, in 1951, ten more business licenses were issued to cafés. *'Iryat Ramla* (1950/51), p. 10; *Ramla Bevinyana Uvehitpatchuta* (Ramla, 1952), p. 27.
54 Photograph of Arditi Café in 1965, Ramla Museum.
55 'Iraqis and Arabs', Police Report, 11 March 1952, ISA, 79//7/2–lamed.
56 *Maariv*, 9 September 1956, p. 7.

Na'im Kaduri, already mentioned above, was clearly one of the dominant figures in the Iraqi-Jewish community and in the local cafés milieu of his time. As the Iraqi Jews' *mukhtar* (Arabic for community leader)—as he was referred to in a police report of March 1952—Kaduri claimed to have 'complete control over Iraqi immigrants'.[57] As a café owner of such standing in the *sakne* (in which gambling took place and which he had bought from an Arab by 1951), he may have led a group interested in appropriating Arab cafés for semi-illegal purposes. Violence may have been one way of pressuring potential sellers. As mentioned above, three of his brothers were involved in the violent attack of 'Adel Amasyas; Kaduri and Abudi, who had been convicted numerous times for assault and public disturbance even before the incident in Hallak's café,[58] may have been his 'soldiers' too.

In order to better understand this appropriation process, we need to review the circumstances in which the key players operated—the town's original café owners as well as the new ones. Regretfully, however, as often in subaltern studies, the voices of the dispossessed are seldom heard directly; we are usually able to hear them only through the ventriloquism of the political establishment or the press.

The Original Owners' Perspective

The institute of the café existed in pre-1948 Ramle, as it did in other Arab-Muslim towns throughout the Middle East and North Africa. From the sixteenth century onwards, the coffeehouse had become a central feature of the urban Arab-Muslim society. It was the need for entertainment, time spent with one's peers, and the public experience of seeing and being seen, that attracted men to cafés in cities like Cairo, Istanbul and Jerusalem, where they

---

57 'Iraqis and Arabs', Police Report, 11 March 1952, ISA, 79//7/2–lamed.
58 Police Report (undated, but later than September 1966), ISA 79//2481/2–lamed.

could play chess or backgammon, smoke a water pipe, and enjoy live music or radio broadcasts.[59] The al-Bandour café opposite Ramle's municipality building was frequented by politicians and intellectuals; there were also the café owned by Asad, in which merchants used to sit, and the cafés of al-Zamouri, Sha'aban, Khalil al-Midawi, and others.[60] In an interview with Samir Dabit, himself the owner of a restaurant in Ramla's Old City active since 1942, he referred to six different cafés that operated in town before 1948, all of which but one (Shahin's café) were sold to Jewish owners in the early 1950s.[61]

The leisured atmosphere which characterised Ramle's cafés up to 1948 changed in the early 1950s when the town's Arab dwellers started being harassed and insecurity grew: in 1952 and again in 1956, Jews (including children) would attack members of the Arab community both verbally and physically, in cafés and on the streets of the *sakne*.[62] Ramla's Arab community saw itself as the innocent victim of religious and ethnic violence, whereas those more involved in the commercial and political affairs of the town interpreted the violent incidents as part of an organised campaign of terror designed to dispossess the town's Arabs.[63]

The local Arab leadership not only protested against what they saw as insufficient action by the municipality and local police, but also held certain Jewish individuals of Iraqi descent directly responsible for the aggression. The actual attackers were seen to be manipulated by people 'who took advantage of their influence and

59   Ralph S. Hattox, *Coffee and Coffeehouses: The Origins of a Social Beverage in the Medieval Near East* (Seattle, 1985), pp. 72–73, 90, 94.
60   Interviews with Fawzi al-Basoumi; Maliha al-Khayri; Abdel Rahman Abu Hamdeh (dated 30 August 2003). All interviewed as part of the Oral History Project of the Palestine Remembered website (http://www.palestineremembered. com/OralHistory/Interviews-Listing/Story1151.html#al-Ramla).
61   Interview with Samir Dabit, 2007.
62   *Maariv*, 28 July 1952; Minutes 1 of the Subcommittee on Ramla Affairs, 4 August 1952, ISA, 60//89/15– kaf; Minutes 2 of the Subcommittee, 11 August 1952, ISA, 60//89/15–kaf.
63   *Divrey HaKnesset*, vol. XII, p. 2599; Minutes 2 of the Subcommittee on Ramla Affairs, 11 August 1952, ISA, 60//89/15–kaf; *Haolam Haze*, 12 September 1956.

standing in these incidents'.[64] Therefore, Arab leadership saw the incidents as triggered not by blind ethnic hatred, but by avaricious individuals: 'there is no hatred between the two nations', declared the Muslim community's representative Isma'il al-Nachas in 1952, 'but certain individuals exploit certain circumstances for their private benefit'.[65]

Rostam Bastuni, one of the few Arab MPs (and a Christian),[66] used an altogether different tone when referring in the Knesset to Ramla's Arab population. He placed it in a wider context, as a triple victim suffering from the 'attacks, robbery and assassinations' of local Jewish individuals, the indifference of the police and local authorities, as well as a governmental agenda of oppression.[67] Here we see clear difference between the way in which a Palestinian politician representing broader Palestinian interests treated the subject by using a harsher terminology, and the milder attitude of the local leadership which preferred to target specific individuals.

Four years later, when another violent episode culminated in Hallak's death, Ramla's Arab community representatives who appeared before the Ministry of the Interior's committee discussing the events abandoned the appeasing tone that had characterised the Arab leadership in 1952. Instead, it was the state's 'policy of national oppression against the Arab minority' that was to blame for violence in Ramla, rather than individual perpetrators acting 'out of personal interests'.[68] The State of Israel, in other words, indirectly legitimated the assailants' behaviour. Accordingly, in 1956, the Arab representatives called for the appointment of a parliamentary inquiry committee to investigate the incidents in Ramla, as had been done in 1952. The situation in town seemed obvious to them:

---

64 Minutes 2 of the Subcommittee , 11 August 1952, ISA, 60//89/15–kaf.
65 *Ibid.*
66 Representing Mapam, the predominantly Jewish socialist party.
67 *Divrey HaKnesset*, vol. XII, p. 2599.
68 Minutes 2B of the Committee of the Ministry of the Interior, 10 October 1956, ISA, 60//104/7–kaf, p. 5.

Facts have likewise proven that there is intent to take sources of revenue from the Arabs, to make them change their livelihood. And we see that these strikes [*pgi'ot*] against Arab cafés and shops were only because their owners were Arabs. Indeed, there are many shops etc. of Jews with higher income than those of the Arabs, yet no one opposes and no one harms them.[69]

We find changing attitudes not only when we examine the events chronologically but also when we treat them through different prisms. This goes for the difference between local and national Arab leadership, but also for the difference between local leadership and individual Arabs. Thus, individual Arabs who had been attacked tried to avoid further trouble: when the police arrested eighteen of those who had stoned Shahin's café in July 1952 and summoned him to identify the attackers, Shahin 'looked at his shoes and said he recognised no one.' Others were as afraid to name known aggressors. Occasionally, matters were resolved without involving the police, and informal reconciliations were concluded between Arab and Jewish individuals and their families.[70] The town's Arab leadership, on the other hand, protested against the incidents through various means. One tactic used both in 1952 and in 1956 was declaring a general business strike.[71] Strikes of this type were not an unfamiliar occurrence in Mandate Palestine, the most obvious example being the general strike during the early stages of the Arab Revolt (1936–1939). They were, as David De Vries argues, linked closely with national conflict, 'reflecting economic processes, effecting social mobilisation, disrupting and politicising routines', and—more significantly in our case—giving a voice to those struggling to be heard and spreading further crucial public

69   *Ibid.*, p. 6.
70   Minutes 2 of the Subcommittee on Ramla Affairs, 11 August 1952, ISA, 60//89/15–kaf.
71   On the one-day strike in July 1952, see *Divrey HaKnesset*, vol. XII, p. 2599. On the three-day strike in September 1956, see *Davar, Haaretz, Yediot Ahronot*—all from 9 September and *Maariv*, 10 September 1956.

issues.[72] Another tactic used by Ramla's Arab leaders was protest rallies to which locals of all religious and ethnic backgrounds were invited, designed to draw attention to situation in town, galvanise authorities into action, and create a united front against future harassments.[73] Finally, delegations representing Arab local interests appeared before the municipality and MPs, calling for the appointment of inquiry committees and testifying before them once formed.

The New Owners' Perspective

In a 1952 session of the Subcommittee on Ramla Affairs, Bechor Shitrit, Minister of the Police and formerly Minister of Minorities Affairs, preferred to focus on the individual element responsible for the incidents—unlike the Arab MP Bastuni (mentioned above), who highlighted the oppressive state of affairs at the municipal and national levels. Acknowledging that a small group of seven or eight Jewish men of Iraqi descent attacked the town's Arabs, Shitrit claimed that the violence started 'not because of ethnic or racial hatred, but for material reasons; they [Iraqi Jews] want to take a certain place in which Arabs sit and want to dispossess them (*lenashel otam*)'.[74] Thus, the Arab claim that the violence was linked to questions of commercial ownership received indirect support from the highest level.

Again in 1956 there was at least one Jewish representative of the establishment (a Mr. Kupilevich of the Ministry of the Interior's Department of Minorities) who opined that violence

---

72 David De Vries, 'Cross-National Collective Action in Palestine's Mixed Towns: The 1946 Civil Servants Strike', in *Mixed Towns, Trapped Communities: Historical Narratives, Spatial Dynamics, Gender Relations and Cultural Encounters in Palestinian-Israeli Towns*, D. Monterescu and D. Rabinowitz (eds.)(Aldershot, 2007), pp. 85–112 (pp. 85–86).

73 On the rally in September 1956, see *Davar, Haaretz*, 9 September 1956; *Maariv*, 10 September 1956; *Haolam Haze*, 12 September 1956.

74 *Divrey HaKnesset*, vol. XII, p. 2599.

had erupted in town for commercial rather than ethnic reasons.[75] It is no coincident that such representatives were or had been active in parliamentary frameworks intended to protect Arab interests, and presumably were familiar with similar claims of Arab dispossession elsewhere.[76]

Not everyone accepted this interpretation. In the same subcommittee where Shitrit accepted this understanding of recent events, others de-legitimated it. Aryeh Altman of the right-wing Herut Party blamed the local representatives of the pro-Arab communist Maki and socialist Mapam parties for provoking unrest. Another subcommittee member, Yidov Cohen of the liberal Progressive Party, said, 'it is known that the communists tell the Arabs in Ramla that the Jews want to take over their houses'.[77] According to this line of reasoning, the assertion of dispossession was a manipulation of Ramla's Arab community by anti-Zionist political factions. Another way of belittling the issue was to legitimise the café sales by simply isolating the specific economic transaction, and ignoring prior violent incidents, the general atmosphere of fear in the Arab community, or the cafés' real financial value: 'if an Arab is given 4,500 Israeli Pounds for his café', it was claimed, 'it cannot be referred to as theft (*gezel*).'[78]

Whereas Ramla's Arab representatives presented commercial appropriation as the trigger for anti-Arab violence—with politicians accepting or rejecting this claim, as cited above—Ramla's Iraqi Jews, seen by the town's Arabs as the instigators, presented a different interpretation. As far as they were concerned, violence originated and erupted around matters of honour and pride, individual and collective alike. The attack on Hallak's café, as we have seen, was linked to a previous incident, in which the

---

75 Minutes 2B of the Ministry of the Interior's Committee, 10 October 1956, ISA, 60//104/7–kaf, p. 9.
76 See also the words of Moshe Erem, MP for Mapam, who had been representative of the Ministry of Minorities Affairs in Ramla in 1948–9. Minutes 3 of the Ministry of the Interior's Subcommittee, 19 August 1952, ISA, 60//89/15–kaf, p. 2.
77 Minutes 1 of the Subcommittee, 4 August 1952, ISA, 60//89/15–kaf.
78 *Ibid.*

attackers had felt their honour was compromised. In earlier cases, so the police reported, Iraqi Jews involved in harassing Christian Arabs claimed that these young men had been 'dating Jewish girls', and that all they intended was 'to defend the honour of the daughters of Israel (*lehagen 'al kvod bnot Israel*)'.[79] This honour also needed protection against 'impolite words' with which Arabs allegedly harassed young Jewish women.[80]

The attackers themselves did not refer directly to the social, ethnic and physical circumstances that they had experienced in Iraq or encountered later in Israel. Others, however, saw these as key causes for the Jewish-Arab tension in town. One of the underlying factors in the incidents of 1952 raised in the press was the 'miserable pairing' (*zivug umlal*) of Iraqi Jews and Arabs as neighbours:

> The immigrants from Babylon [Iraq] experienced the torment of tyranny, persecution, and exploitation and murder of their brethren. There is no wonder, therefore, that these people become instantly enraged if an Arab offends them.[81]

The same opinion was voiced by a member of the 1952 subcommittee who did not think that 'a *ma'abara* of 1,200 Iraqis should be built in a place where an Arab community exists [...] Immigrants from Arab countries should not be settled in such places'.[82] Moreover, one of the Arab subcommittee members mentioned a municipal meeting in which the 'Iraqi' delegates had brought examples of the arbitrariness with which Arabs had had treated Jews back in Iraq, in order to incite public emotions.[83]

This proximity between the two communities, and wrongs

---

79 'Iraqis and Arabs', Police Report, 11 March 1952, ISA, 79//7/2–lamed.
80 Bechor Shitrit in *Divrey HaKnesset*, vol. XII, p. 2599; *Maariv*, 28 July 1952.
81 *Maariv*, 28 July 1952.
82 Minutes 1 of the Subcommittee on Ramla Affairs, 4 August 1952, ISA, 60//89/15–kaf, p. 2.
83 Minutes 2 of the Subcommittee, 11 August 1952, ISA, 60//89/15–kaf, p. 4.

experienced in the near past were thus presented as legitimate reasons for the hostility felt by Iraqi Jews towards Arabs. These were exacerbated by the difficult financial circumstances experienced by many of the immigrants from Iraq, especially when compared with the situation of immigrants from Europe, particularly Bulgaria.

The Iraqi-Jewish immigrants settled in Ramla between May 1950 and June 1951 had had to renounce their Iraqi citizenship in order to emigrate; those who had registered to emigrate after March 1951 also had had their property confiscated before leaving the country.[84] Upon arriving in Ramla with no material assets, most of them were housed in the *ma'abarot* on the outskirts of town; few took over 'abandoned' Arab houses in which others were already living.[85] They arrived mostly from Iraqi cities, had at least high-school education, and spoke several languages (Arabic, French, and occasionally English). Among them were professionals in public administration, commerce, and banking, and also journalists and musicians.[86] Whereas a small proportion of the newcomers were of high socio-economic status, most Iraqi Jews who arrived in Israel were of medium or low financial background.[87] Their immigration to Israel was described in the Zionist narrative as a rescue operation. However, Zionist interest in Iraqi Jewry, it has been suggested, was not— or not only—attributable to an urge to protect them after the

---

84 Sylvia G. Haim, 'Aspects of Jewish Life in Baghdad under the Monarchy', *Middle Eastern Studies* 12:2 (1976), pp. 188–208 (esp. pp. 198–201); Moshe Gat, *A Jewish Community in Crisis: The Exodus from Iraq, 1948–1951* (Jerusalem, 1989)[in Hebrew], Chapters 4 and 7; Elie Kedourie, 'The Break between Muslims and Jews in Iraq', in *Jews among Arabs: Contacts and Boundaries*, M.R. Cohen and A.L. Udovitch (eds.)(NJ, 1989), pp. 21–63 (pp. 49–58). This issue is treated more fully below.

85 For example, the case of an old Arab blind woman who was attacked and then expelled from her room by a Jewish Iraqi man, who then squatted in the room; Minutes 2 of the Subcommittee on Ramla Affairs, 11 August 1952, ISA, 60//89/15—kaf.

86 Kedourie, 'The Break', p. 23.

87 Esther Meir-Glizerstein, 'The Absorption of Iraqi Jews in Israel', in *The Age of Zionism*, A. Shapira, J. Reinharz and J. Harris (eds.)(Jerusalem, 2000)[in Hebrew], pp. 271–295 (pp. 273–276).

riots of June 1941 (the *farhud*),[88] but rather to the desire to use this reservoir of Jews to improve the Jewish-Arab demographic balance in Palestine, particularly after the Holocaust in Europe.[89] Whether or not Iraq's Jews experienced Zionist longings,[90] once in Israel they did not shy away from voicing their dissatisfaction— protesting against unemployment and housing shortage, as well as lack of cooperation with the governmental policy of population distribution when sent to reside in non-urban areas.[91]

The few months' difference between the settling of Bulgarian Jewish immigrants in Ramla (the first group arriving in town in mid-November 1948), and the influx of Iraqi Jews during 1950–51 had a significant effect on these groups' status in Israel.[92] The Bulgarian Jews' early arrival (many youngsters immigrated to Israel even before 1948), as well as prior familiarity with the language, and support by Jewish-Bulgarian organisations which had been operating in the country since the 1930s,[93] provided them with a significant edge over the Iraqi Jews. Many Bulgarian immigrants who came (or were sent) to reside in Ramla were given well-built 'abandoned' Arab houses. Some of these people became quickly involved in the town's emerging municipal life: in the first city council (elected in November 1950), there were six

---

88 On these events see Haim, 'Aspects of Jewish Life', pp. 194–5; Gat, *A Jewish Community in Crisis*, pp. 17–21; and Nissim Kazzaz, *The Jews in Iraq in the Twentieth Century* (Jerusalem, 1991)[in Hebrew], Chapter 8.

89 Yehouda Shenhav, 'The Jews of Iraq: Zionist Ideology, and the Property of the Palestinian Refugees of 1948: An Anomaly of National Accounting', *International Journal of Middle East Studies* 31:4 (1999), pp. 605–630 (p. 608).

90 *Ibid.*, idem.

91 Meir-Glizerstein, 'The Absorption of Iraqi Jews in Israel'.

92 Moshe Lissak, *The Mass Immigration in the Fifties: The Failure of the Melting Pot Policy* (Jerusalem, 1999)[in Hebrew], pp. 24–25.

93 These organisations provided the recently arrived immigrants with guidance, small lawns and professional training; they also helped in finding housing solutions. Moshe Mossek, 'Kulanu Bulgarim', in *The Tribes –Evidence of Israel: Exile, Immigrations, Absorption, Contribution and Integration*, A. Mizrahi and A. Ben-David (eds.)(Netanya, 2001)[in Hebrew], pp. 238–258 (pp. 255–56); on Bulgarian Jews in Israel, see also Guy H. Haskell, *From Sofia to Jaffa: The Jews of Bulgaria in Israel* (Detroit, 1994).

Bulgarian Jews out of a total of fourteen.[94] Others slowly nurtured new careers: Moshe Eshkenzi, who came to Ramla from Bulgaria (probably at the end of 1948), was initially given a menial job by the JA—to deliver iron bed frames to new immigrant families. Over time, this turned into permanent employment with the CAP when in the early 1950s Moshe became in charge of the ongoing maintenance of the immovable assets under the CAP's administration in town—repairing houses, arranging to fix pipe leaks, shoring up walls and the like. By 1955 he was already the rising leader of the local office of the CAP.[95]

In a way, the European immigrants arriving in Ramla in 1948–49, especially the Bulgarians, quickly became the closest thing to veteran Jewish settlers, an element which did not exist in pre-1948 Ramle. They were also quick to move out of the Arab houses and into the new *shikunim* (housing projects) built in town.[96] The Iraqi Jews, who arrived later, were mostly excluded from the town's emerging socio-economical and political hierarchies.

The different living conditions were perhaps one of the most glaring manifestations of this ethnic gap, identified quite early as the backdrop for local tensions. *Maariv* journalist Dov Goldstein personally examined the living conditions experienced by Hallak's killers in the *ma'abara*. In his report he describes a 'neglected and dilapidated place' in which hundreds of decaying wooden huts and tattered tents lie scattered. He also vividly described the offensive smells, constant presence of flies, and lack of cultural and public institutions.[97] Even the miserable conditions in the *sakne* offered a more respectable existence, with a fixed roof over one's head and public meeting places such as cafés and the marketplace.

Some commentators saw a direct link between these two

---

94 The other members were a Romanian, four Poles, and two others, whose origin is not indicated, yet their surnames (Gavza and Spector) indicate Central-European descent; there was also one Arab representative. *Ramla Bevinyana Uvehitpatchuta*, p. 12.
95 Sandy Tolan, *The Lemon Tree: A Jew, An Arab, and the Heart of the Middle East* (NY, 2006), pp. 106–107, 112.
96 Chovav, *Ramla—Hair Ha'atika*, pp. 20, 58.
97 *Maariv*, 13 September 1956.

parameters—the past and present proximity of the Arab and Jewish-Iraqi communities and the latter's miserable living conditions in Ramla (especially in comparison with those of some immigrants from Europe). The first to point this connection was radical left-wing magazine *Haolam Haze*, which devoted a two-page article to the murder in 1956. Next to pictures showing Hallak's grieving widow and bereaved family as well as a bloodstained wall, *Haolam Haze* linked the unemployment and miserable living conditions in the *ma'abara*, the hatred of Arabs cultivated already in Iraq, and the resulting violent attacks on Ramla's Arab minority.[98] Herut's Altman reminded the other members of the 1952 subcommittee that

> The Iraqis are people who came to the country only a few months ago, from a place in which they were persecuted and robbed, and all of a sudden, they come and find around them Arabs who are in much better condition than they are.[99]

His conclusion, cited above, was that separation had to be maintained between Arabs and Jews from Arab countries. The Arab representatives in the subcommittee did not refer to the persecution suffered by Jews in Iraq, but the latter's current difficult situation in Ramla was referred to and interpreted as a convenient platform for incitement, and for fierce competition for the town's limited resources:

> We see that the state of Iraqi Jews in Ramla is financially difficult. People whose economic and social state is not good can be easily incited. We see that there are certain groups in town that try to take advantage of these circumstances. We feel that unemployment and difficult living conditions facilitate incitement. The inciters claim

98   *Haolam Haze*, vol. 987, 12 September 1956.
99   Minutes 1 of the Subcommittee on Ramla Affairs, 4 August 1952, ISA, 60//89/15–kaf, p. 2.

that the Arabs have taken their jobs and that they live in better houses. I mention these facts in the context of attacks on Arab shops.[100]

Circumstances of life in rundown neighbourhoods—the Arab *sakne* or the Jewish *ma'abara*—triggered feelings of degradation, discrimination and loss of personal and collective prestige among the new immigrants from Iraq.[101] Commercial appropriation of Arab businesses seems to have been one way of redeeming honour and improving socio-economic conditions. Iraqi Jews did not attempt to take over businesses owned by Jews of European descent; rather, they targeted Arab property because they identified and accepted the social hierarchy established in the young Israeli state and in Ramla in particular: Ashkenzi (or European) Jews dominated municipal and national politics and finances, whereas the Arabs were made a target for suppression and expropriation. Iraqi Jews (as those of other Middle Eastern, North African or Asian origin) were placed in between these two social and ethnic elements, and needed to secure—and with time, promote—their social, political and financial interests given that reality.

In other formerly Arab or mixed towns similar hierarchies were gradually created, but awareness to this situation resulted in more confrontational clashes between Ashkenazi and Mizrachi Jews. When discussing the 1959 Wadi Salib incidents Sami Shalom Chetrit draws attention to the fact that the setting for the two most significant Mizrachi uprisings against Ashkenazi hegemony in Israel—the Wadi Salib incidents of 1959 and the Black Panthers protest a decade later—occurred in formerly-Arab neighbourhoods in which Jewish immigrants from Arab countries had been settled, Wadi Salib in Haifa and Musrara in Jerusalem. Chetrit explains this as an ambivalence triggered by two contradicting messages: on the one hand, the state perceived and legitimated Mizrachim as heirs of the Arabs' property by

100 Minutes 2 of the Subcommittee, 11 August 1952, ISA, 60//89/15–kaf.
101 Lissak, *Mass Immigration in the Fifties*, p. 114.

providing them with 'abandoned' Arab houses to reside in; on the other hand, their growing understanding of Mizrachi low political, social and economic status in the new social hierarchy.[102]

In Ramla, the poor socio-economic conditions experienced by the newcomers from Iraq triggered the drive for commercial appropriation, facilitated by an accurate reading of the new political reality in which they found themselves. By expropriating Arab property—'abandoned' Arab houses in which Jews now resided were perhaps the most visible symbol of this dispossession—the state legitimated further appropriation. In a way, Iraqi Jews in Ramla merely extended this legitimation to the private sphere, not waiting for the state to complete the process, or perhaps giving up on the possibility that it may do so in the future.

Whereas the commercial taking over Arab businesses in Ramla was a matter of debate—some saw it as the cause for tension in town while others rejected this claim and highlighted social and national background factors instead—the symbolic component was yet another part of the conflict in early 1950s Ramla. Even if this process was in fact accomplished unwittingly, new Jewish ownership of Arab businesses extended beyond mere economic aspects. The spatial appropriation it resulted in came to symbolise the Israelisation of the Arab space in the Old City. While the *sakne*, as will be seen in Chapter Five, was habitually treated as a segregated antithesis of the new neighbourhoods which were being built in the north-western parts of town, it was also seen as requiring incorporation into the matrix of the expanding Israeli city. And whereas appropriation of the Arab space had begun with the state's expropriation of houses in the early days after July 1948, it continued into the early 1950s with the attempted commercial appropriation of Arab businesses, to which the town's Jewish municipality and Jewish individuals from Iraqi origin were directly, if not exclusively, responsible.

---

102 Sami Shalom Chetrit, *The Mizrahi Struggle in Israel Between Oppression and Liberation, Identification and Alternative 1948–2003* (Tel Aviv, 2006)[in Hebrew], p. 100.

By taking over Arab cafés in the Old City and gradually coming to dominate the market, Iraqi Jews not only served the national goal of Spatial Judaisation (*yihud hamerchav*). Perhaps more importantly, they created a place they could call their own, in which the spatial layout and architecture—familiar from their previous lives in Iraq—were retained. This area could potentially evolve into an Iraqi neighbourhood. Whereas the means of reinforcing Jewish control over the Arab parts of Ramla were debatable, at the end of the day it nevertheless served national ends of spatial expansion and Jewish ethnic dominance, even while maintaining most of the landscape's Arab characteristics.

Broader Perspectives: Beyond the City

Commercial dispossession of Arab businesses in Ramla by Iraqi Jews cannot be treated on the local level alone. As noted by a member of the 1952 subcommittee, many similar incidents occurred in Jaffa, involving dispossession of Arab-owned corrals, orchards and businesses.[103] Even if not directly, the commercial tensions in Ramla, as in other places, were also linked to more extensive discourses on population movements and international accountability in their European, Israeli-Palestinian and Jewish-Iraqi contexts.

Yehouda Shenhav has referred to this broader perspective, showing how the Israeli government linked claims for Palestinian property and Jewish assets in Iraq. This act, he argues, 'constructed a zero-sum equation between the Jews of the Arab countries and the Palestinians in Israel'.[104] The state of Iraq's Jewish community and its assets had been brought up in Knesset debates as early as 1949; later that year, the British proposed a population exchange between Israel's Palestinians and Iraq's Jews, one which

---

103 Minutes 3 of the Ministry of the Interior's Subcommittee on Ramla Affairs, 19 August 1952, ISA, 60//89/15–kaf, p. 2.
104 Shenhav, 'The Jews of Iraq', p. 621.

would include financial compensation for the newcomers from the property of those who would emigrate. This suggestion was ignored and then rejected by the Israeli government. Reluctance to accept in principle and in practice compensation of Palestinian refugees, as well as concern over a potential claim for individual compensation by Iraqi Jews, meant that this option failed to materialise.[105]

This attitude changed after the Iraqi parliament's resolution, in March 1951, on the freezing of Jewish property. This law came into effect after the parliament had passed a denaturalisation law a year earlier. The first law, of March 1950, was valid for one year and enabled Jews to renounce their Iraqi citizenship and leave the country. It did not refer to issues of property, yet it triggered such a massive Jewish response that alarmed the Iraqi government, and was therefore followed by the second law.[106] Consequently, in March 1951 the Iraqi government passed a law freezing the assets of Jews who had registered for emigration. Land transactions involving Jews were no longer processed, vehicles were confiscated, all Jewish warehouses were locked and sealed by the public custodian, and the houses of merchants and jewellers were searched.[107]

Following the March 1951 legislation, Israel was quick to establish an explicit linkage between Jewish assets in Iraq and Arab property in Israel. That same month, Foreign Minister Moshe Sharet described before the Knesset the plunder of Jewish property in Iraq, and linked this with Arab property in Israel:

> We will take into account the value of the Jewish property that has been frozen in Iraq with respect to the

105 *Ibid.*; see also Kedourie, 'The Break', pp. 45–48.
106 On the 1950 Denaturalization Law, see Haim, 'Aspects of Jewish Life', pp. 198–199; Gat, *A Jewish Community in Crisis,* Chapter 4; Kedourie, 'The Break', pp. 49–52.
107 Haim, 'Aspects of Jewish Life', pp. 200–201; Shenhav, 'The Jews of Iraq', pp. 617–618; see also Gat, *A Jewish Community*, Chapter 7; and Kedourie, 'The Break', pp. 56–58.

compensation we have undertaken to pay the Arabs who abandoned (*sic*) property in Israel.[108]

Iraqi legislation meant that private property owned by Jews was nationalised. To Israeli eyes, this served to invalidate Palestinian claims for compensation, but also put an end to the hope for any future compensation for Jewish assets left behind in Iraq.[109]

Among Iraqi Jews who arrived in their new homeland with little or none of their former assets, the hoped-for solution to the new situation was immediate individual compensation from the Arab property managed by the CAP. They were to find out, however, that by linking the two issues, the state in fact appropriated their property 'in order to use it—rhetorically, symbolically, and judicially—as state property in every respect'.[110] Once refugee property was seen as held legitimately by the Israeli government, the new arrivals from Iraq—their difficulties, needs and hopes— were overlooked, and they were left to their own devices in their new homeland, despite the state's alleged commitment for their compensation. In 1955, they still insisted on the validity of their claim for compensation from the state, and the issue of Jewish property in Arab countries remained on the agenda of the World Organisation for Jews from Arab Countries (WOJAC) from its foundation in the 1970s and until the late 1990s.[111]

When commercial appropriation in Ramla is examined from this broader perspective, the acts of Iraqi Jews, although not strictly justified, seem to make more sense. Taking over Arab businesses—whether or not through legal and/or legitimate methods—can be seen as compatible with state policies. Indeed, Zionist emissaries in Iraq reported in 1951 that they were being

108 Quoted in Shenhav, p. 619; also discussed in Kedourie, 'The Break', pp. 57–58.
109 Shenhav, 'The Jews of Iraq', p. 619.
110 *Ibid.*, p. 621.
111 *Ibid.*, p. 622; Yehouda Shenhav, 'Ethnicity and National Memory: The World Organization of Jews from Arab Countries (WOJAC) in the Context of the Palestinian National Struggle', *British Journal of Middle Eastern Studies* 29:1 (2002), pp. 27–56 (esp. pp. 41–46).

asked by Jews about to immigrate to Israel whether they would
need to present documents proving their ownership of frozen
property, and how to forward these documents.[112] Even if Ramla's
Iraqi Jews were unaware of the ongoing Knesset debates on this
matter, they nevertheless took advantage of the relative weakness
of the post-war Arab minority in Ramla and attempted to
'compensate' themselves for property left in Iraq using the latter's
assets in Israel.

This is why Police Minister Shitrit did not reject the claim that
tension in Ramla was triggered by material rather than ideological
reasons: the root cause of the violence was the local power structure
reflecting a pragmatic attitude, more than anything else.[113] As a
veteran participant in the debate on population exchange and
compensation that had been going on since 1949, Shitrit was
familiar with the claims of Iraqi Jews and even saw them as 'well
founded'.[114] He was one of few politicians who seemed able to
see the bigger picture or at least admit to it: Iraqi Jews were led to
believe they were to be compensated for their lost property from
the Arab possessions administered by the CAP; until this would
materialise, some of them took matters into their own hands.
On an even wider scale, the state legalised and legitimised the
dispossession of its Arab minority; this discriminative approach
may have been mirrored also in the acts of individuals, who
perceived Arab-owned property as available for taking.

Whereas the issues of Palestinian property in Israel and
Jewish assets in Iraq occupied centre stage, Jewish immigration
from Europe and the dispossession of Jewish property associated
with it were shadows looming in the background. In the 1952
subcommittee Jewish acceptance of the Arab claim of illegitimate
appropriation of refugee assets was devalued and made to
appear as some kind of paranoid suspicion originating in Jewish
experiences back in Europe. Any such acceptance was attributed

112 Shenhav, 'The Jews of Iraq', p. 620.
113 *Divrey HaKnesset*, vol. XII, p. 2599.
114 Shitrit quoted in Shenhav, 'The Jews of Iraq', p. 618.

to 'a psychology originating is in the Diaspora', where Jews—in Poland, for example—were pressured by 'terrorists' to 'give up their businesses' and were eventually forced to sell them to gentiles.[115] Frank Bajohr terms this 'pressure', in the case of 1933–1935 Nazi Germany, 'economic antisemitism': in a gradual process Jews were forced out of German economy, their businesses 'aryanised' through pressure from below steered from above.[116] When this argument was brought up in the 1952 subcommittee, however, it was used to *downplay* the graveness of the incidents in Ramla, instead of triggering a more in depth debate on the legitimacy of pressure put on Arab owners to sell their cafés to Jews.[117]

Four years down the line, Yisrael Shar'abi, Mapai representative and member of the 1956 subcommittee, returned to the issue of oppression and dispossession of Jews in the Diaspora. The comments of this Yemen-born MP, however, carried a different message. Firstly, he refrained from specifying the countries in which Jews had been oppressed; by this he implied not only European economic persecution of Jews, but also difficulties suffered by Jews in Arab countries.[118] In Egypt, for example, Jewish businesses were confiscated, Jewish workers fired, and payment of special taxes and 'donations' to the Egyptian government enforced, all between 1947 and 1949.[119] Secondly, and perhaps more importantly, MP Shar'abi warned against Israeli emulation of the oppression and dispossession suffered by Jews throughout the ages, now

---

115 Minutes 3 of the Ministry of the Interior's Subcommittee on Ramla Affairs, 19 August 1952, ISA, 60//89/15–kaf, p. 2.
116 Frank Bajohr, *'Aryanisation' in Hamburg: The Economic Exclusion of Jews and the Confiscation of Their Property in Nazi Germany* (NY and Oxford, 2002), p. 20; Martin Dean, *Robbing the Jews: The Confiscation of Jewish Property in the Holocaust, 1933–1945* (Cambridge, 2008), pp. 25, 28–31.
117 I do not attempt to compare here these two processes; rather, I aim to fully understand the nature of the comments raised in the subcommittee's dealings.
118 Minutes 3B of the Knesset Committee for Internal Affairs, 30 October 1956, ISA, 60//104/7–kaf, p. 4.
119 Itamar Levin, *Locked Doors: The Seizure of Jewish Property in Arab Countries*, trans. Rachel Neiman (Westport, Conn., 2001), Chapter 5.

aimed at the Palestinian minority.[120] His words—and silence—communicate clear unease with the current situation, especially since the Jewish people, having experienced its share of misery, was now treating its own Palestinian minority in similar ways.

* * *

Minor violent incidents—a drunken brawl, the stoning of a house—reflected a much broader socio-historical context. The transformation of Ramla's market and the town's shifting ownership of cafés epitomise issues linked to the contemporary process of Israelisation: need to fit into new social hierarchies, desire to advance financially, drive to take control of urban space, and search for a new identity. The ongoing ideological process of Spatial Judaisation was acted out by individuals who, whether wittingly or unwittingly, expressed and implemented national mentalities, policies, legislation and (sometimes illegitimate) acts. Despite the tension between individuals (Iraqi Jews in our case) and the establishment, as around the issue of compensation from Arab property in Israel or housing, some national agendas were achieved, even out of pragmatic rather than ideological considerations.

A vicious cycle of trauma and dispossession operated here: Iraqi Jews disowned of their property in the process of immigrating to Israel, targeted non-Jews whose assets they perceived as available. Aziza Khazzoom, viewing the dynamics of Israeli stratification as interactional, relational, and driven by an aspiration for westernisation, called this process 'The Great Chain of Orientalism': 'Israel has a three-tired orientalisation-driven hierarchy, in which Mizrachim emerge as the transformable liminal group between western Ashkenazim and unredeemably oriental Arabs.'.[121] This

---

120 Minutes 3B of the Knesset Committee for Internal Affairs, 30 October 1956, ISA, 60//104/7–kaf, p. 4.
121 A. Khazzoom, 'The Great Chain of Orientalism: Jewish Identity, Stigma Management, and Ethnic Exclusion in Israel', *American Sociological Review* 68:4 (2003), pp. 481–510.

chain of Orientalism seems to have been in work in Ramla too: the exclusion and marginalisation of one group (Iraqi Jews) by a more dominant one (European Jews) triggered further exclusion and marginalisation of a third one (Palestinian Arabs).

CHAPTER THREE

On Men and Trees:
The Town's Green Areas

Landscapes are products of human values and as such, they articulate and reproduce ideologies, power relations, and local and national identities and agendas.[1] They convey messages that need to be decoded and interpreted, read critically and deconstructed, in order to be fully understood beyond their misleadingly obvious and straightforward façades.[2] Despite attempts at presenting landscapes as predestined, they always represent an agenda, one or another human construction, and it is the double role of landscape, as W.J.T. Mitchell suggested, which is to naturalise these constructions and to represent 'an artificial world as if it were simply given and inevitable'.[3] Since they are often camouflaged, exposing the deeper meanings of landscapes requires a critical approach.

1   I. Robertson and P. Richards, 'Introduction', in *Studying Cultural Landscapes*, I. Robertson and P. Richards (eds.)(London, 2003), pp. 1–18 (pp. 2, 4); Alan R.H. Baker, 'Introduction: On Ideology and Landscape', in *Ideology and Landscape in Historical Perspective: Essays on the Meanings of Some Places in the Past*, Alan R.H. Baker and Gideon Biger (eds.)(Cambridge, 1992), pp. 1–14 (p. 5); Catherine Brace, 'Landscape and Identity', in *Studying Cultural Landscapes*, pp. 121–140 (pp. 128–9).
2   Baker, 'Introduction: On Ideology and Landscape', p. 9.
3   W.J.T. Mitchell, 'Introduction', in *Landscape and Power*, W.J.T. Mitchell (ed.) (Chicago and London, 2002) 2nd ed., pp. 1–4 (p. 2).

Palestinian Landscapes: Ideology and Practice

The fruit of a lemon tree that had stood in the garden of the Kheiri family in Ramle and was brought in 1967 to its *pater familias*, exiling in Ramallah, articulates the link between a Palestinian man and his land:

> I told you of my father and of that lemon, how I woke up from sleep in one of the lonely nights to an unfamiliar sound, turned to the source of the sound and saw my old, blind father, holding the lemon in both his hands, bringing it close to his lips and kissing it over and over again, detached from the whole world, in utter solitude, only him and the lemon. And he was hugging it with devotion, and rinsing it with tears from his extinguished eyes. [...] Yes, Rachel, for us the lemon is not merely fruit, but it is the memory of childhood concealed in every one of us. It is love; moreover, it is the homeland.[4]

In 1967, nineteen years after their displacement, the Kheiri family's only connection to the land they had once owned was a lemon, kept as a precious relic even after it dried up and shriveled. Another lemon tree which linked an uprooted Palestinian woman and her home (in Jaffa) is a literary one. In his essay 'Autocartography: The Case of Palestine, Michigan' (1995) the Palestinian writer Anton Shammas described the longing of A.'s grandmother—now living in Dearborn, Michigan—to the lemon tree she had left in 1948 in the centre of her backyard:

> Not even a room, not even the facade of a house, but just a tree in the backyard, hidden away from the bustle of main street politics; the tree under whose shadow she always imagines herself sitting, dreaming away her days.

4   Bashir El-Hairi, *Letters to a Lemon Tree*, trans. D. Brafman (Jerusalem, 1997) [in Hebrew], p. 10.

Say Palestine to her and all she sees is herself, as she is now,
not the young woman she was, sitting under that tree,
breathing in the scent of its leaves and its early flowers.[5]

For many exiling Palestinians, as both Carol Berdenstein and
Laleh Khalili show, the native landscape has become a central
component in the collective Palestinian memory. Especially native
fruit and trees, cultivated and grown in the preexilic immediate
surrounding, were made into an expression of indigenousness,
highlighting (in a nostalgic manner) rootedness on the backdrop
of actual displacement, and aiming at reinforcing national
identities intergenerationally.[6] The remembered and imagined
lands of Palestine have become, for many of the refugees living in
the Palestinian Diaspora, a paradise-like construction; a familiar
Palestinian cliché is that no fruit can taste as delicious as those
picked off local trees.[7]

This romantisation of the land and of rural life, as Manar
Hasan argues, is part of Palestinian and Zionist discourses aiming
at forgetting the Palestinian urban centres which had existed
prior to 1948; in both these discourses Palestinian society is
imagined as one whose past is mostly rural, never going through
the process of modern urbanisation. In Zionist historiography,
according to Hasan, Palestinian towns were 'forgotten' because
their existence refuted the ethos of the arrival to a desolate
country; another reason was that rural society was perceived as

5   Anton Shammas, 'Autocartography: The Case of Palestine, Michigan', *The
      Threepenny Review* 63 (1995), pp. 7–9 (p. 8); quoted and discussed also in
      C. Bardenstein, 'Threads of Memory and Discourses of Rootedness: Of Trees,
      Oranges and the Prickly-Pear Cactus in Israel/Palestine', *Edebiyat* 8 (1998),
      pp. 1–36 (pp. 29–31). Another literary work linking Palestinians and citrus
      is, of course, Ghassan Kanafani's well-known short story 'The Land of the Sad
      Oranges' from 1962, which appeared in a collection of his works *Men in the
      Sun and Other Stories*, trans. Hilary Kilpatrick (Washington, D.C., 1993);
      mentioned and discussed in Bardesntein, 'Threads of Memory', pp. 18–19.
6   Bardenstein, 'Threads of Memory', esp. pp. 18–31; Laleh Khalili, 'Grass-Roots
      Commemoration: Remembering the Land in the Camps of Lebanon', *Journal
      of Palestine Studies* 34:1 (2004), pp. 6–22, esp. pp.17–18.
7   Khalili, 'Grass-Roots Commemoration', pp. 17–18.

primitive and therefore posed less of a threat. Pre-1948 urban centres have disappeared from the Palestinian collective memory because during and following the war these were ruined and their population driven out: 'The defeat of the Palestinian town in the war of memory did not leave any alternative to the urban exiles who still carried with them urban memories, and they were forced to dress their memories in different forms of rural tradition and interweave them with history'.[8]

Mandatory Palestine's urban culture had not only existed, but was also the setting for an ongoing encounter of nature and town. The typical Middle-Eastern garden was an example of this intersection of urban setting and trees, flowers and water; it was a garden designed for both pleasure and utility, sheltering its visitors from the sun.[9] The quintessential Arab/Muslim garden, Persian in origin, was a symbol of paradise. This typically quartered garden was partitioned by water canals representing the four rivers of water, milk, wine and purified honey mentioned in the Koran, with trees and pavilions providing shade and walls that filtered external noise and intrusive eyes. The result was a place of relaxation and contemplation, epitomising a symmetrical cosmic order.[10] In the traditional Arab-Muslim city, gardens were associated with the private sphere more than the public one; and indeed, they were more common in private estates than next to the few public buildings. This served to maintain a gendered separation: the private garden, located in the innermost heart of the house, was sheltered, protective and quiet, perfectly suitable for women; the public garden, on the other hand, represented the exclusively male public sphere in which civil errands could

---

8   Manar Hasan, 'The Destruction of the City and the War on the Collective Memory: The Victorious and the Defeated', *Theory and Criticism* 27 (2005), pp. 197–207 [in Hebrew] (p. 203).

9   Kenneth Helphand, *Dreaming Gardens: Landscape Architecture and the Making of Modern Israel* (Santa Fe, NM, 2002), pp. 49–50.

10 John Brooks, *Gardens of Paradise: The History and Design of the Great Islamic Gardens* (London, 1987), pp. 17–23; Emma Clark, *The Art of the Islamic Garden* (Marlborough, Wiltshire, 2004), pp. 25–26, 39–40; D. Fairchild Ruggles, *Islamic Gardens and Landscapes* (Philadelphia, 2008), esp. Chapter 4.

mix with political discourse. Female presence in such public places, as in the marketplace, was rigidly regulated through attire and women were marginalised 'to the point of making them "invisible"'.[11]

These two types of gardens featured also in British Mandate Palestine: the traditionally private *bustan* and the public garden.[12] The *bustan* was a private family garden, which suited the enclosed lifestyle of the extended Arab family of the time. It included mainly fruit-trees, scented bushes, vegetables and herbs which served the needs of its owners and were not aimed at creating sellable surplus. The *bustan* was in essence a modest vernacular Arab garden that suited the local climate, landscape and culture, and could have been found in both rural and urban areas.[13] One such *bustan* to have survived (even if standing in ruins) is that of the Chiat family in Wadi Siach in Haifa. Built and planted in 1936 by 'Aziz Chiat, one of Haifa's distinguished and rich residents, it provided his family with a special place outside the hustle and bustle of the city, a place to relax and enjoy. In the six and a half dunum terraced *bustan* were fruit trees (pomegranate, strawberry and fig), several pools, water fountains and water canals.[14]

The Palestinian public garden, situated next to public buildings, was rarer than the *bustan*. In general, the traditional view in terms of city planning tended to see allocation of urban plots for public gardens as a waste of potential building space. The British Town

11 Anton Escher, 'Construction of the Public Sphere in the Middle Eastern Medina During the First Half of the 20ᵗʰ Century', in *Middle Eastern Cities 1900–1950: Public Places and Public Spheres in Transformation,* Hans Chr. Korsholm Nielsen and Jacob Skovgaard-Petersen (eds.)(Aarhus, 2001), pp. 164–175 (p. 165).

12 Ruth Enis, 'Historical Gardens in Eretz-Israel and their Pioneer Designers', in *Point of View: Four Approaches to Landscape Architecture in Israel,* Lipa Yahalom et al. (eds.)(Tel Aviv, 1996)[in Hebrew], pp. 7–18 (p. 7).

13 Alisa Braudo, 'The Bustan: A Garden of the Past in Today's Landscape' (MA Thesis, University of Oregon, 1983), pp. 16–17.

14 Gili Sofer, 'Siach Brook in Haifa: The Bustan', *Masa Acher* 180 (September 2006), pp. 104–106 [in Hebrew]. For the last thirty years the *bustan* has been in the hands of the municipality of Haifa, which included it in its list of places for conservation. Nevertheless, it stands dilapidated and neglected.

Planning Ordinance (Hebrew *pkudat binyan 'arim*) from 1921 changed matters slightly: its implementation in Palestine's towns triggered the foundation of several public gardens.[15] One such garden was that located on the premises of the Dajani hospital in Jaffa during the 1930s. It circulated the hospital's main building and included several trees, some rose bushes, a small lawn and a symbolic grapefruit orchard.[16] These public gardens were not inherent to the Middle Eastern and Muslim tradition, in which private gardens dominated; rather, they evolved out of British influence which considered public gardens to be an integral element of the modern city.

Utopian and Real Zionist Landscapes

The imagined garden Theodor Herzl described in *Altneuland* (An Old-New Land) from 1902, was the symbolic epitome of his envisioned Zionist dream coming to life in Palestine: in this garden, set in the house of the artist Isaacs, palm trees prospered and marble statues were scattered around. It was not a big garden, yet it felt so because of its bushes' design. In its centre stood a water fountain, and comfortable couches were positioned in the garden's corners, encouraging conversation.[17] This was a garden that combined both Arab and European elements, representing in microcosm Herzl's wish to combine Palestine's local traits with European ideas, technologies and designs.[18]

Outside the territory of books newcomers and visitors to Eretz-Israel encountered only few gardens adjacent to public buildings; to the private *bustan* they probably did not have easy

---

15 Gideon Biger, 'Unit 3: Regulative Planning in Towns in Palestine During the Period of British Mandatory Rule', *in Settlement Geography of Israel: Spatial Experiments* (Tel Aviv, 1996)[in Hebrew], pp. 208–211.

16 For a 1933 sketch of this garden see Helphand, *Dreaming Gardens*, p. 51.

17 Theodor Herzl, *Altneuland* (Tel Aviv, 2004)[in Hebrew], p. 198.

18 Tal Alon-Mozes and Shaul Amir, 'Landscape and Ideology: The Emergence of of Vernacular Gardening in Pre-state Israel', *Landscape Journal* 21:2 (2002), pp. 37–50 (p. 41).

access.[19] Only gradually did Zionist gardens—in *kibbutzim* and in urban areas—develop as vernacular expression of cultural life, their roots being, as in Herzl's book, both indigenous Palestinian gardening and European-modelled gardens; another inspiration in the creation of the vernacular Hebrew gardening style were Middle Eastern gardens, such as in Lebanon and Syria. The result of this dialectic between 'inside' and 'outside' influences, between European and therefore 'cosmopolitan' and Middle Eastern and therefore 'provincial' sensibilities 'was an eclectic mix'.[20]

Zionism, as Dan Yahav commented, 'developed the rhetoric of the garden culture as an efficient instrument for its ideology'.[21] Although Zionist ideology saw the urban project as inferior in comparison to the rural one pre-1948,[22] new Zionist gardens could symbolise the idea of *kibush hakarka*—the physical and emotional conquest and appropriation of the land through its cultivation. The forests planted between 1850 and 1950 by the Jewish National Foundation (JNF) (and, until 1948, also the British authorities), likewise reflected Zionist goals and national policies and was 'vital for materialising the Zionist plan'.[23] First and foremost, afforestation had a legal purpose, with desirable political and national side-effects: claiming ownership, especially in the face of continuous Arab dwelling on lands acquired by the JNF.[24] Other Zionist goals were providing employment for new Jewish immigrants, strengthening the bond with world Jewry through afforestation donations, and even—as on Mount Carmel—attracting potential homeowners and protecting existing

---

19 *Ibid.*, p. 38.
20 Alon-Mozes and Amir, 'Landscape and Ideology', p. 39; Helphand, *Dreaming Gardens*, pp. 89–90.
21 Dan Yahav, *Gardens and Gardening in Tel Aviv-Jaffa* (Azur, 2006)[in Hebrew], p. 26.
22 Erik Cohen, 'The City in Zionist Ideology', in *Towns in Israel: A Reader*, A.Sachar, D. Weintraub, E.Cohen and L. Shelach (eds.)(Jerusalem, 1973)[in Hebrew], pp. 5–10 (p. 5).
23 Nili Liphschitz and Gideon Biger, *Green Dress for a Country: The Afforestation in Eretz-Israel, The First Hundred Years 1850–1950* (Jerusalem, 2000)[in Hebrew], p. 50.
24 *Ibid.*, p. 57.

flora and fauna.[25] As in other settler societies—in Australia, South Africa, or the United States—physical takeover was a means of marking land ownership and creating a new local identity for the recently arrived settlers.[26] This also meant that any other (i.e. Arab) potential claim was contested and invalidated. Another Zionist battle was that for the conquering of wilderness (*kibush hashmama*) or the making of desert bloom (*hafrachat hashmama*). This ethos was influenced by a Calvinist approach, according to which whoever 'tames' nature for their own needs is entitled to claim it their own.[27] Through these discourses Zionism's right to what was perceived as an empty, desolate and uncultivated country was established.[28]

Another way of appropriating the country and its landscape was through knowledge, as part of a comprehensive project which set as its goal getting to know the country (*yedi'at haaretz*). This programme of indoctrination was implemented since the 1920s in Eretz Israel's (and later the State of Israel's) institutions of education, and at its centre was acquaintance with the flora and fauna of the country, as with its historical, geographical and geological traits. The project was perceived as imperative because its addressees were immigrants from other countries (and their offspring) who came to Eretz Israel and lacked familiarity with its landscape; another reason for its intensified implementation was ambition to bridge the gap between, on the one hand, the idea of

25 *Ibid.*, pp. 50, 59; Nurit Kliot, 'Ideology and Afforestation in Israel: Man-Made Forest of the Jewish National Fund', *Studies in the Geography of Israel* 13 (1992), pp. 87–106 [in Hebrew]; Yossi Ben-Artzi, *The Creation of the Carmel as a Segregated Jewish Residential Space in Haifa, 1918–1948* (Jerusalem, 2004)[in Hebrew], p. 262 and Chapter 9.

26 Oz Almog, *The Sabra—A Profile* (Tel Aviv, 1997)[in Hebrew], p. 252. See also Gershon Shapir, 'Land, Work and Population in the Zionist Colonization: General and Unique Perspectives', in *Israeli Society: Critical Perspectives*, Uri Ram (ed.)(Tel Aviv, 1993)[in Hebrew], pp. 104–119; Oren Yiftachel and Batya Roded, 'To be Your Prisoner of Love: Judaizing Space in Israel/Palestine', *Motar* 11 (2003), pp. 35–44.

27 Almog, *The Sabra*, p. 440, n. 146.

28 Later writers, however, doubted this ethos and invalidated it as propaganda. See, for example, Alan George, 'Making the Desert Bloom: A Myth Examined', *Journal of Palestine Studies* 8:2 (1979), pp. 88–100.

a 'return' of the Jewish people to its homeland and, on the other hand, the fact that this 'homeland' was, in practice, unfamiliar and foreign.[29] The term *Yedi'at haaretz*, as Oz Almog suggested, highlights sensual and erotic aspects since the expression brings to mind the carnality of 'knowing of a woman' (*lada'at isha*); this, in turn, emphasises the joining of knowledge with emotion, science with ideology.[30]

Zionist landscape in general, and gardens in particular, had also practical and mundane purposes, like in contemporary Palestinian culture. Aharon Halewi, planner of Tel Aviv's first municipal garden, claimed in 1933 that gardens benefit the population as they provide relaxation for the tired citizen, offer a spiritual and aesthetic experience in nature and a public meeting place, and present school teachers with an opportunity to educate children on nature.[31] Landscape architect Shlomo Weinberg believed that the local public garden should 'search for a synthesis between the westernised garden and the special needs of our country's climate': trees for shade, spotted with some grass, bushes and flowers.[32] An Eretz-Israeli gardening style was gradually taking shape, combining English-styled landscape design (of a more 'natural', wild-looking garden) with the symmetry and straight lines of the French style. British presence in Palestine over previous decades certainly inspired this development. Not surprisingly, the Persian/Arab garden was overall not adopted in the Israeli garden-culture because of its rigid lines and meticulous design and aesthetics, but presumably also because of its association with the culture of the Arab 'Other'.

29 Bardenstein, 'Threads of Memory', pp. 3–4.
30 Almog, *The Sabra*, p. 256.
31 Aharon Halewi, 'The City Garden "Gan Meir" at Tel Aviv', *Hatteva' Vehaaretz* (Nature and Country) 2 (1933), pp. 105–110.
32 Quoted in Joseph Ben Arav, *Gardens and Landscape in Israel* (Tel Aviv, 1981) [in Hebrew], p. 69.

The Olive Tree

Seeing them as a medium of thought Douglas Davies suggested that 'trees are not simply good to climb, they are good to think'.[33] Palestinian and Israeli trees, as elsewhere, can hardly be described as merely an indigenous natural entity or a plant imported from a foreign country; rather, they are a cultural construction through which Israeli-Palestinian relations can be discussed and further understood. Among the trees that have grown to become (sometimes contested) national emblems are citrus trees, especially orange, olive, eucalyptus, and pine. Despite the fact that it is not a tree, the prickly pear cactus (*sabra* in Arabic, *tsabar* or *sabres* in Hebrew) may be added to this list.[34]

In her book *Planted Flags: Trees, Land, and Law in Israel/ Palestine* Irus Braverman juxtaposes and contrasts two trees— olive and pine—as representing each 'the quintessential symbol of Palestinian and Israeli national discourses':

> The pine is synonymous with the Zionist project of afforesting the 'desolate' land of Israel, and the olive has become emblematic of the Palestinian struggle against Israel's occupation and for national independence.[35]

This bifurcated reading of the landscape has been criticised, since it ignores the inherent asymmetric nature of the power relations between the two discussed national entities.[36] Moreover, as Braverman herself acknowledges in the book's epilogue, 'these

---

33   Douglas Davies, 'The Evocative Symbolism of Trees', in *The Iconography of Landscape: Essays on the Symbolic Representation, Design and Use of Past Environments*, D. Cosgrove and S. Daniels (eds.)(Cambridge, 1988), pp. 32–42 (p. 34).

34   Bardenstein, 'Threads of Memory'; Nasser Abufarha, 'Land of Symbols: Cactus, Poppies, Orange and Olive Trees in Palestine', *Identities* 15 (2008), pp. 343–368.

35   Irus Braverman, *Planted Flags: Trees, Land, and Law in Israel/ Palestine* (Cambridge, 2009), p. 10.

36   *Ibid.*, p. 13.

natural and national bifurcations could be and are in fact contested, subverted, and perhaps even transcended'.[37] The olive tree is a fascinating example of this type of contestation, subversion, and appropriation of tree symbolism and hermeneutics, especially when analyzed in the framework of an overall discussion on the town of Ramle/Ramla.

In Palestine's traditional agriculture and economy the olive tree had a special place, particularly due to its two central end products of oil and soap. In the aftermath of the First World War demand exceeded local supply, and Palestine's *fellahin* (villagers) started replanting olive trees. The biennial cycle of the fruit, however, and the influence of climatic factors, affected the shifting crop prices, and enhanced the difficulties experienced by small-scale cultivators. During Palestine's Mandatory rule British authorities attempted to strengthen the position of these small-scale villagers through regulation and education, for example by founding the Olive Oil Committee or by selling trees to cultivators at a subsidised price. Towards the end of the 1930s there were in Palestine almost 600,000 dunams on which olives were grown; olive was Palestine's crop of preference.[38]

This long tradition of Palestinian olive cultivation has embedded the olive with symbolic characteristics. Palestine's olive trees were not merely an economic industry; they also held special meaning in Palestinian culture, featuring in popular harvest songs, and given a sacrosanct aura when associated with tombs of saints. After 1948 these trees gradually became a representation of Palestinian nationhood, symbolising particularly the ideas of *sumud* (steadfastness) and rootedness. It was especially the longevity of the olive tree that made it into a 'proxy Palestinian witness' to the shifts and turns in the history of this nation, expressed in poetry

37 *Ibid.*, p. 201.
38 Shaul Ephraim Cohen, *The Politics of Planting: Israeli-Palestinian Competition for Control of Land in the Jerusalem Periphery* (Chicago, 1993), pp. 51–52.

and visual imagery alike.[39] The sense of communality that has been traditionally part of the olive's cultivation, especially during harvest time, has transformed to represent intergenerational reciprocity and willingness to sacrifice.[40]

Israeli culture, on the other hand, has highlighted the olive as a universal symbol of peace, based on the biblical story of the dove bringing an olive branch to Noah's ark as a proof that the flood had receded (Genesis 8:11). Two olive branches carry this meaning on the emblem of the State of Israel (presented in February 1949), alongside a representation of the Menorah that had stood in the Temple and the word 'Israel' in Hebrew. The olive branches in this heraldic national symbol were meant to express, according to artist Gavriel Shamir who created the emblem, 'the love of peace within the people of Israel'; at the same time, they were also 'a very decorative element'.[41] However, this interpretation of the olive as an Israeli peace symbol has been ironically subverted by its vernacular use: olive is also the official colour of Israeli military uniform, whereas some officers' ranks in the IDF are represented by olive branches.

The olive tree, therefore, has become a polisemic symbol, carrying on its imagined and real branches conflicting and contesting ideas and representations: while standing for Palestinian nationality, rootedness and communality, it has also been claimed as a symbol of the universal lingering hope for peace, and, even more poignantly, of Israeli statehood and militarism. By using the olive as a national symbol, Israeli-Jewish culture appropriated it to the ends of expressing and articulating its statehood. While doing so, it also challenged the olive's role as a Palestinian national emblem.[42] As a consequence, these contesting semiotic

---

39   Bardenstein, 'Threads of Memory'; Carol B. Bardenstein, 'Trees, Forests, and the Shaping of Palestinian and Israeli Collective Memory', in *Acts of Memory: Cultural Recall in the Present*, M. Bal, J. Crewe and L. Spitzer (eds.)(Hanover, NH, 1999), pp. 148–168; also Braverman, *Planted Flags*, pp. 121–129.

40   Abufarha, 'Land of Symbols', p. 358.

41   Alec Mishori, *Lo and Behold: Zionist Icons and Visual Symbols in Israeli Culture* (Tel Aviv, 2000)[in Hebrew], Chapter 6 (quote on p. 152).

42   Braverman, *Plated Flags*, pp. 206–207.

uses highlight not only Israeli statehood, but also Palestinian lack thereof.

Green Areas in Pre-1948 Ramle

Ramle's green area up to 1948 was quite typical of a contemporary Palestinian town, consisting of suburban orchards and groves, an unknown number of private *basatin* (plural of *bustan*) and one municipal garden.[43] Located in inner courtyards, Ramle's private gardens were enjoyed by their residents only. One such garden was that in the Kheiri house, which stood on the town's eastern outskirts. In this garden had grown not only the lemon tree mentioned above, but also scented rose bushes, a jacaranda tree and a fragrant plumeria.[44] The only public green area in Ramle up to Jewish occupation was the municipal garden to be discussed extensively below.

In pre-1948 Ramle, one could find not only flourishing gardens but also groups of trees, scattered throughout town and on its periphery. Within residential quarters, trees were found mainly in courtyards; some scattered trees can be seen in Mandatory maps near schools and in cemeteries—most of them outside the town's municipal boundary—offering shade to schoolchildren and mourners alike. One line of trees stretched along the road which marked the town's south-eastern boundary, perhaps designed to mark a visible and symbolic border between the town's El Mufti Quarter and the cemetery located to its east; the boulevard of trees also decorated and shaded the path for those entering this quarter from the direction of Jerusalem.

43 For the description of Ramle's layout during the 1930s and 1940s I have used the following maps: AA45 1930 ('Lydda and Er-Ramle', 1:10,000); BD 900A-[1] 13/14 1930 ('Er Ramle', 1:20,000); AA Er Ramle [1] 135–145.7 1931 (1: 1,250); AA45 1937 ('Ramle', 1:5,000); AD900A-[1]13/14 1941 ('Er Ramle', 1:20,000); AD 900A-[1] 13/14 1942 ('Er Ramle', 1:20,000); KC 900A [2] 13/14 1943 ('Er Ramle', 1:25,000); AA45 1947 ('Ramle', 1:2,500).

44 Tolan, *The Lemon Tree*, p. 5.

Some orchards and groves were planted within the town's boundaries around its north-eastern (olives and orchards), western (citrus), and southern (olives, orchards and citrus) outskirts. Beyond the town's boundaries, Ramle's residents cultivated mainly olives, a common practice since the Middle Ages, when olive trees provided the town with raw materials for two of its famous industries of olive oil and soap.[45] Whereas some of the local groves and orchards were *waqf* property, most were privately owned.[46]

Whereas privately owned green areas existed in Palestinian Ramle in abundance, there are several explanations for the relative scarcity of public greenery in town. One was the inherent traditional predominance of private spaces over public ones in Arab-Muslim culture more generally. The municipal garden thus suited the minimal needs of local community. In several other public spaces—schools, cemeteries and on one particular road—trees provided shade and/or marked symbolic borders. Another possible explanation is historical water scarcity in Ramle, whose sandy terrain made water irrigation particularly challenging, though various solutions for this problem were suggested throughout the ages—as building an aqueduct, accumulating water in large underground cisterns, or digging deep wells, for instance.[47] In the first report of the Israeli Municipality of Ramla (referring to the period between July 1949 and September 1950), serious water shortage is mentioned as threatening plans for vegetable patches and industrial development. The town's water system was described as dilapidated.[48] Whereas in a private garden

45 Shimon Gat, 'A Flourishing Arab City: The Economy of Medieval Ramla', *Cathedra* 123 (2007), pp. 33–66.
46 See AA Er Ramle [1] 135–145.7 1931 (1: 1,250), plan III; also letter from the lawyer of the Fanus family, complaining to the Minister of the Interior that olive trees located on the family's private land were uprooted to enable construction. Letter dated 9 November 1952, ISA, 1966/80–gimel.
47 On water supply in Ramle see S. Gat, 'The City of Ramla in the Middle Ages', pp. 102–125.
48 *Iryat Ramla: Sikum Pe'ulot Ha'irya* (for the period 1 July 1949 to 30 September 1950) (Ramla, 1951), pp. 14–15.

vegetation could be cultivated with relatively simple means of irrigation, and the owners of citrus orchards and olive groves had a financial interest in somehow watering their trees, public gardens would have been a much more complicated and unprofitable project. Thus, cultural inclinations and geographic parameters operated jointly throughout Ramle's history to shape the town's green environment.

Green Areas in post-1948 Ramla

A local essay competition celebrating a decade of Israeli independence in Ramla produced essays later published in a special municipal leaflet, including a piece by a seventh-grade student named Menachem:

> Once Ramle was a small Arab town
> In which the Jews did not dare pass through
> Nowadays Ramla is big, clean and pretty
> The trees grow, the flowers bloom
> Ramla is a town like all towns [...][49]

For Menachem, the sign of normality and of matching up to national standards was Ramla's appearance: the trees' presence and beauty of flowers symbolised for him, as for many others, modernity and transformation. Indeed, in Zionist worldview gardens were seen as symbols of progress and modernity. They became an important component of the modern Jewish town, especially when contrasted with its Arab contemporary, conceived by the Jewish settlers as dirty, crowded, and devoid of greenery. Tel Aviv's founding fathers, for instance, envisioned a 'garden city' reminiscent of modern Western capitals, the very opposite of neighbouring Jaffa.[50]

49 *Yediot Ramla* (Ramla, 1958), last page.
50 Yahav, *Gardens and Gardening*, pp. 83–84.

Ramle's occupation in July 1948 and its gradual process of Israelisation over the next decades changed not only the town's demographics and dominant nationality, religion and culture, but also its urban landscape and sense of place. Ramla's post-1948 planners were no doubt inspired by the goals and experience of the pre-state Zionist gardening and afforestation efforts.

In the immediate aftermath of the war, an attempt was made in Ramla to preserve and continue cultivating the local orchards and especially olive groves, mainly out of economic needs and for financial gains.[51] Symbolically, Ramle's Arab olive trees were culturally appropriated and given an Israeli-Jewish character when juxtaposed with the Star of David on Ramla's new municipal emblem.[52] Over time the preservation and continued cultivation of Ramla's once-Arab groves and orchards clashed with the national and local goal of housing the growing flow of new immigrants. Once the 'abandoned' Arab houses were occupied, new housing projects were initiated. As discussed in Chapter Five below, these stretched to the town's north-west, at the expense of former orchards and groves. A letter from 1952, written by the lawyer of an Arab family who remained in Ramla to the Minister of the Interior protested against the uprooting of the family's olive trees on the lands that had been in their possession until 1948 in preparation for construction.[53]

In the Israeli-Palestinian cultural context, uprooting trees has had much deeper meanings and broader resonances. Since both national ideologies hold trees as symbols of rootedness and connection to the land, the act of uprooting them represents an attempt to erase memory and facilitate collective oblivion. In Palestinian post-war poetry, fiction and memoirs, trees that remain standing represent a nostalgic yearning for the lost

---

51 Meeting dated 7 October 1948, IDF Archive, 1860/50/31; 'Ramla', report dated 2 January 1949, signed by Shlomo Asherov, ISA, 49//297/5–gimel; 'Report on the Activities of the Military Administration in Ramle and Lydda for January 1949', IDF Archive 1860/50/31.
52 See Introduction for a discussion on Ramla's municipal emblem.
53 Letter dated 9 November 1952, ISA, 1966/80–gimel.

homeland. An example is Abu Salma's poem *I Love You* (1978): '... The little orchards weep for us, gardens grow desolate,/ the vines are forever saddened'.[54] Whether rooted out, planted over or left to be, Ramle's trees—and its Palestinian past more generally— kept shadowing the town's old and new neighbourhoods in one way or another, creating configurations 'which in part develop quite independently of each other, and in part overlap, converge and interact with each other', generating a combined discourse on past and present.[55]

Public Gardens

Gardens were seen in both Palestinian and Zionist worldview as spaces for leisure: be it relaxed contemplation, leisure, or spiritual reconnection with the land, they offered those visiting them a real and metaphorical breeze of fresh air. Current discourse of leisure tends to understand it as a more complex field—contextualised in the historical, political, economic and social aspects. If critically analysed, leisure can be seen as instrumental and coordinated from above (despite the feeling of choice an individual may have when selecting a preferred form of leisure), a source of social discipline, identification or cohesion, or a means for moral transformation.[56] Much like law and landscape, leisure can also use as an ideological tool, masking 'the artifice and ideological nature of its form and content' by 'becoming part of the everyday, the taken-for-granted, the objective, and the natural'.[57]

---

54 Bardenstein, 'Threads of Memory', p. 28.
55 *Ibid.*, p. 1.
56 John R. Kelly, *Leisure Identities and Interactions* (London, 1983), pp. 18, 30, 32; 'Contemporary Trends: Introduction', in *Sociology of Leisure: A Reader*, C. Critcher, P. Braham and A. Tomlinson (eds.)(London and NY, 1995), pp. 3–4; John Clarke and Chas Critcher, 'Leisure and Inequality', in *Sociology of Leisure*, pp. 247–255 (p. 247).
57 James S. Duncan, *The City as Text: The Politics of Landscape Interpretation in the Kandyan Kingdom* (Cambridge, 1990), p. 19.

One of the first advocates of the modern public park was British writer and designer John Claudius Loudon, writing in the 1820s. He considered the public garden to be not only a place to walk around and enjoy fresh air, but also an instrument of social reform.[58] A renaissance of the public garden ensued in the early twentieth century and was particularly linked to nascent ideas of urban planning. One of the first partakers in this reborn trend were Germany's city planners, architects and landscape designers who created several new public parks in the first two decades of the century, mainly in Berlin and Hamburg.[59]

It was this combination, of German and English ideas and practices concerning public gardens and parks, which inspired Zionist landscape architecture in this period; whereas many of the local landscape designers were trained in Europe, especially in Germany, British Mandate's influence was a given presence in the country. With the foundation of the State of Israel, gardening in towns experienced a surge, affected by Western urban planning of open green areas. In Tel Aviv, for instance, the territory of its public gardens more than doubled in the period between 1948 and 1953: from 66 dunum of public gardens Tel Aviv grew to have 150 dunums of them.[60]

While new neighbourhoods were planted at the expense of uprooted Arab trees, the new Ramla needed public gardens too, in which children could play and their parents and grandparents relax, in keeping with new ecological and social ideologies. Indeed, '[t]he municipality devotes particular attention to laying out gardens and parks to be used as shaded spaces of relaxation and rest for the town's inhabitants', Ramla Municipality formally announced in a 1952 leaflet.[61] During the 1950s, several public gardens were planted in developing areas of town. The first, in

---

58   Michael Lancaster, 'Public Parks', in *The Oxford Companion to Gardens* (Oxford, 1991), pp. 456–461 (p. 457).
59   *Ibid.*, p. 461.
60   Ruth Enis, *Documentation of Three Gardens in Israel (1935–1950)*(Haifa, 1988) [in Hebrew], p. 23.
61   *Ramla Bevinyana Uvehitpatchuta* (Ramla, 1952), p. 21.

1953, was a garden on Kikar Hamedina (National Square); in 1954, another was planted in one of the new residential quarters, Neve David. 'A nice little garden' was inaugurated above St Helena's Cisterns on 14 November 1956, celebrating the eighth anniversary of the arrival of the first Jewish new immigrants to Ramla. A large municipal park was planned around the White Tower area, never to have been materialised,[62] and three other gardens will be discussed below. In addition, tree lines were planted along Ramla's main street (now Herzl Blvd.)(fig. 5), and in smaller streets, all of them located between the Old City (but not in it) and the new neighbourhoods.[63]

On the whole, this trend privileged the new neighbourhoods and emerging stronger socio-economic groups—new Jewish residents who could afford the new houses—over former and new Arab inhabitants, as well as some Jewish families residing in the *sakne*. This discrimination was expressed through removal of the once-Arab orchards and groves in favour of housing projects, as through the geographical location of the new gardens; in other words, no public gardens were planted in the *sakne* and no young trees were to line its streets.

This observation raises questions related to the real and symbolic appropriation of space, exclusion and inclusion, and cultural, ethnic and national identification. It is obvious, for example, that the inauguration of the small garden above St Helena's Cisterns manifested the Zionist linkage of planting with immigration. Moreover, by endowing this historical landmark with a Zionist identity, Ramla's municipality not only symbolically appropriated

---

62 For the garden on Kikar Hamedina see Ramla's Municipal Archive, Town Council resolutions, resolution no. 77 from 22 November 1953; for the garden in Neve David see Ramla's Municipal Archive, Town Council resolutions from 9 September 1954; for the garden above St Helena see *Mehana'asa ba'ir: Igeret le'ezrachey Ramla* 4 (Ramla, April 1957), p. 6; for the planned big park see Ramla's Municipal Archive, Town Council resolutions, decision from 9 December 1951, also *Ramla Bevbinyana Uvehotpatchuta*, p. 21 and *Mehana'asa Ba'ir: Igeret le'ezrachey Ramla* 4 (April 1957), p. 6.

63 These streets were Dani Mas, Bar Kochva, Hagdud Ha'ivri and Bialik. Ramla's Municipal Archive, Town Council Resolutions from 12 May 1954.

the ancient site, but also excluded anyone who was not part of the
Zionist project of Jewish immigration. These issues, apparent in
many of Ramla's gardens, will now be discussed and elaborated
on through three case studies: those of Gan Hanasi (President's
Garden), Gan Hahaganah (Haganah Garden) and the British War
Memorial Cemetery.

Fig. 5: Y. Dorfzaun, Trees on Ramla's High Street, c. 1962 - 1964 (Courtesy of www.palphot.com)

The Municipal Garden / Gan Hanasi

The garden on Ramla's main street, known since the mid-1950s as Gan Hanasi, used to be Arab Ramle's municipal garden—'the big garden', as it was locally referred to.[64] Israelised and made into the municipal garden of Israeli Ramla, it is nevertheless the only public garden to have survived the 1948 watershed. Ever since the garden changed hands, and throughout the years since its Israelisation, it has been standing also as a reminder of the town's Arab 'past', as its original layout was not altered in the process. This garden caters for multiple memories, representing two temporal narratives—that of the Palestinian 'past' as well as that of the Israeli-Jewish 'present'.[65] Concurrently, it also embodies two parallel constructions of time and space, one mythical, the other mundane. Whereas the first manifests through time and space the two grand narratives at the same time (both Zionist and Palestinian, both in the past and in the present), it also hosts the more worldly routine activities that characterise daily life in the garden.[66]

In the years that followed the town's conquest, this garden's land was appropriated by the state, which rented it out to the Ramla Municipality on an annual basis.[67] Before 1948, it had been the property of Ramle's Arab municipality. Yet it was probably

64 Interview with Maliha al-Khayri (dated 18 March 2005). Interviewed as part of the Oral History Project of the Palestine Remembered website (http://www.palestineremembered.com/OralHistory/Interviews-Listing/Story1151.html#al-Ramla).

65 Bardenstein, 'Threads of Memory', p. 2.

66 On these two constructions, and their implementation in relation to Gan Hakovshim, on the border between Tel Aviv and Jaffa, see Tali Chatuka, 'Parallel Realities: Gan Hakovshim and its Surroundings, Tel Aviv 2003', in *Birshut Harabim: Mechva leganan ha'ir Tel Aviv, Avraham Karavan*, Ya'el Moriya and Sigal Bar Nir (eds.)(Tel Aviv, 2003), pp. 68–77.

67 See, for example, lease for renting the garden in the years 1952/53 (Lease no. 114), Ramla's Municipal Archive; Minutes of Town Council Meeting, 1955/56: decision to approve the contract dated 30 April 1956—renewal of the rent of block no. 1 parcel 4441 for the purpose of municipal garden, for a period of two years (1.4.56–31.3.58), Ramla's Municipal Archive, Minutes of Town Council Meeting 1955/56.

not an original local construction: the traditional Arab-Muslim city, up to the first half of the twentieth century, usually lacked large open spaces; rather, it was the colonial powers that usually initiated their planning.[68] Indeed, Arab Ramle's municipal garden was constructed under British influence during Mandate years.

The earliest marking of the garden in maps is from the early 1930s, where it is referred to as 'Municipal Garden'. Maps clearly show a quadrangular space with a round clearing at its centre (representing a round stone stage), where stood a café frequented by the town's notables.[69] Two water fountains and four paths divided the garden, while trees were scattered throughout, some along the garden's peripheral walls, others along its four paths and around the small stage; symmetrical rows of palm trees (in place today) added stateliness to the garden's overall appearance.[70] This was a local variation on the Persian garden theme, discussed above. Since according to the date engraved in stone above the entrance to the town's municipality and/or post office building it was erected in 1922, we may assume that the adjacent 'Municipal Garden' was created around this date or later.

The first report of the Israeli Ramla Municipality (for the period between July 1949 and September 1950) states that the one municipal garden in town 'used to look like a junkyard'. Over the report period, the garden 'was organised and is used these days as a relaxation place for the residents and as playground for toddlers'.[71] No reason is given for the garden's dismal state prior to its re-organisation by the new municipality, but it could definitely have been the result of air and ground strikes the town

---

68 Escher, 'Construction of the Public Sphere' p. 164; also Nikita Ellisséeff, 'Physical Lay-Out', in *The Islamic City*, R.B. Serjeant (ed.)(Paris, 1980), pp. 90–103 (pp. 99–100).
69 Hila Keren-Steinmetz, 'The Location and Place of Ramle's Old Market' (work submitted to Geography Department, Bar Ilan University, 2010)[in Hebrew], p.21.
70 AA45 1930 ('Lydda and Er-Ramle', 1:10,000); AA Er Ramle [1] 135–145.7 1931 (1: 1,250), plan II.
71 *Iryat Ramla: Sikum Pe'ulot Ha'irya* (for the period 1 July 1949 to 30 September 1950) (Ramla, 1951), p. 18.

experienced in July 1948, as well as the result of an influx of thousands of Arab refugees from Jaffa and other places.[72]

The initial re-organisation of the garden was apparently not satisfactory; therefore, in the beginning of December 1951 the town council decided to approve Zvi Miller's new plan for the garden's redesign.[73] Miller immigrated in 1935, bringing from his native Germany knowledge, skills and professional terminology of gardening and landscape design. Having graduated from Mikve Israel (the first Jewish agricultural school in Palestine), he entered London's School of Planning and Regional Reconstruction in 1945; in 1951 he was appointed to head Haifa's gardening department.[74]

During the work on the garden, planned to be inaugurated in the summer of 1953, Israel's first President Dr. Chaim Weizmann, passed away (9 November 1952).[75] The practice of renaming public institutions and gardens after recently deceased political and national leaders has obviously countless examples throughout the world; in this case too, Weizmann's demise, and the wish to honour his memory, provided the town with a new and suitable name for this hitherto 'nameless' garden. Naming, however, 'rather than mimicking reality, in effect constitutes it',[76] and the garden's renaming as 'Gan Hanasi'—President's Garden—contributed through this toponymic act to the ongoing appropriation of the once-Arab landscape. By this act, Ramla joined a more general post-1948 tendency, accomplished throughout the country by cartographers and settlers alike, of replacing Arab place names with biblical ones. Meron Benvenisti has interpreted this toponymy

72 B. Morris, *The Birth of the Palestinian Refugee Problem Revisited* (Cambridge, 2004), pp. 424–5.
73 Ramla's Municipal Archive, Town Council resolutions, resolution no. 83 from 9 December 1951.
74 Kenneth Helphand, *Dreaming Gardens*, pp. 105–108.
75 Ramla's Municipal Archive, Town Council resolutions, resolution no. 19 from 12 March 1953.
76 *Re-Naming the Landscape*, Jurgen Kleist and Bruce A. Butterfield (eds.)(NY, 1994), p. x.

not as a representation of contempt to Arab heritage, but rather as a declaration of war on it.[77]

The decision to name the garden after Israel's first president had commemorative and Zionist symbolic aspects: Weizmann was not only a widely accepted icon of the diplomatic struggle towards Jewish State, but also the personification of its presidency following these efforts.[78] The garden's inauguration thus made it into an Israeli garden, replacing both physically and in title the 'nameless' Arab garden which had been there before.[79]

Activities carried out in Gan Hanasi were also different from those that had taken place there before 1948; various photographs from the 1950s and 1960s archived in Ramla's city museum testify to its becoming a popular spot, with families, mothers with their children, the elderly, all enjoying the garden and playing the roles designated by local landscape planners. The garden also hosted two national and religious collective rituals: public dancing on Independence Day,[80] and the circuits of Simchat Torah, celebrating the completion of the annual Torah readings.[81] After 1948, Independence Day was celebrated by dancing circles, one of the markers of national identity.[82] The religious Simchat Torah

---

77 Meron Benvenisti, *Sacred Landscape: The Buried History of the Holy Land since 1948*, trans. M. Kaufman-Lacusta (Berkeley, [2000]), Chapter 1, esp. p. 47.

78 Dr. Chaim Weizmann was seen to have been the person responsible for the Balfour Declaration of 1917. In 1929 he was elected as President of the Jewish Agency. When he was elected as the first president of the nascent Israeli state, Ben-Gurion hailed him as one who has done more than anyone else for the creation of the Jewish State. Norman A. Rose, *Chaim Weizmann: A Biography* (Jerusalem, 1986), trans. Karmit Guy [in Hebrew], p. 289.

79 The surname 'Weizmann' sounded foreign, and that was presumably one of the reasons for preferring the title to his name, as was the case with the settlement Eshel Hanasi (The President's Tamarisk). See Benvenisti, *Sacred Landscape*, pp. 35–36. However, the name had another aspect, that of linking past and present and personifying the Jewish people's return to the homeland: the head of the Sanhedrin, who was the Jewish religious and political leader in the period of the Second Temple, was also referred to as 'Hanasi'.

80 See, for example, *Mehana'asa Ba'ir* 5 (Ramla, May 1957), reporting the plan for Independence Day celebration; also interview with Yonatan Tubali, 30 March 2008; interview with Shmulik Partush, 31 March 2008.

81 Interview with Shmulik Partush, 31 March 2008.

82 Almog, *The Sabar*, p. 362.

holiday also involved merry-making and elated collective dances, which likewise enhanced communal Israeli-Jewish identification and stressed collective mores and beliefs.

It is interesting to note that despite the location of Ramla's Israeli municipality halfway between the Old City and new neighbourhoods to its west, celebrations were held in Ramla's old civic centre, next to the *sakne*. The inherited municipal character of Ramla's first public garden may have contributed to this, as did the round stone stage in the middle of the garden (about one meter in height and 10–15 meters in diameter) which acted as the platform on which the Torah scrolls were placed during Simchat Torah celebrations. The garden may have retained its original Arab layout and role as a public space, but, at the same time, it also changed its national, religious and cultural orientation.

Gan Hanasi was also a place for political rallies. Mapai's Eliezer Livne, for example, was very impressed by a political gathering there in 1954. Speaking to the Knesset, he lauded the well-kept garden in the new town of Ramla as 'a model for the older cities' (i.e. those with Jewish majority prior to 1948). The civilised manner in which the meeting took place and its dispersal 'in an atmosphere of camaraderie and self-assurance', as well as the garden's cultivation, left Livne struggling to believe that the Jewish presence in Ramla was only six years old.[83]

Public events in the garden selected, concentrated and interrelated themes of existence (lived and imagined) that in the everyday tended to be more diffused, dissipated and obscured.[84] By using it for Independence Day celebrations, Simchat Torah festivities and political rallies the garden was made into a place where individual and collective, national and religious, civic and political identities were formatted, moulded and enhanced in their local Zionist and Jewish context.

Ramla's Arab inhabitants, living only a few blocks away, were

83 *Divrey HaKnesset*, vol. XVI, p. 2349.
84 Don Handelman, *Models and Mirrors: Towards an Anthropology of Public Events* (Cambridge, 1990), pp. 15–16.

usually excluded from these activities. On the whole, the local Arab community refrained from visiting Gan Hanasi.[85] Arguably, Ramla's Arab residents were never explicitly denied entrance to the garden, and could have avoided it because of different views on public spaces in general and garden culture in particular. It is more likely, however, that they preferred the relative safety of the 'ghetto', particularly in times of heightened national and religious awareness, as those discussed in Chapter Two.

Gan HaHaganah

In a series of postcards describing Ramla's tourist attractions in the early 1960s, the garden chosen as one of Ramla's symbols was not Gan Hanasi, but Gan HaHaganah. The postcard shows green lawns and trees, a few paths crossing them; no one is at sight, and in the background, on the garden's margins, are a couple of buildings and the red rooftops of several two-storey houses.[86] Inaugurated in 1960, this garden, located near the new municipality building, became the town's new face in the following decade.

Mandatory maps show that orchards had once stood on the land, from as early as 1918. In 1947, they were still there, included within the town's municipal boundaries.[87] At some point between July 1949 and September 1950, Churshat HaHahagna—the Haganah Thicket—was planted in what was then Kaf-Gimel St. and

---

85 Interview with Samir Dabit, 1 April 2008; Interview with Shmulik Partush, 31 March 2008. One exception was the May Day parade discussed in Chapter Four.

86 'Ramla, The Haganah Garden', Palphot postcard no. 6508, c. 1962–1964.

87 JB900 A-[1] 68 1918 ('Ramle', 1:50,000); BD 900A –[1] 13/14 1927 ('Er Ramle', 1:20,000); BD 900A—[1] 13/14 1930 ('Er Ramle', 1:20,000); AA45 1930 ('Lydda and Er-Ramle', 1:10,000); BD 900A-[1] 13/14 1930 ('Er Ramle', 1:20,000); AA Er Ramle [1] 135–145.7 1931 (1: 1,250); AA45 1937 ('Ramle', 1:5,000); AD900A-[1]13/14 1941 ('Er Ramle', 1:20,000); AD 900A-[1] 13/14 1942 ('Er Ramle', 1:20,000); KC 900A [2] 13/14 1943 ('Er Ramle', 1:25,000); AA45 1947 ('Ramle', 1:2,500)

later renamed Haganah St.[88] In 1955 the town council decided to turn this thicket into a municipal garden to be planned by Miller;[89] it was finally inaugurated in 1960.[90] Commemorating the soldiers killed during the battle for Ramle, the garden was named after Eliyahu Golomb, Haganah's unofficial commander (1893–1945).[91] His widow Ada honoured the inauguration with her presence.

Also present was Zusman Jawitz, Ramla's Military Governor in 1948–9. Why was he still part of life in Ramla? How was he linked to the garden? Answers to these questions associate its foundation to the Zionist ideology of reviving the land in the most interesting ways. They are revealed in a press report on the party that celebrated the end of military administration in Ramla. In this farewell event, Jawitz's request from the town was for a thicket to be planted by school children. He wished it to be named Churshat HaHaganah, and to be planted gradually, with new trees added once a year, on Tu Bishvat.[92] In its Zionist metamorphosis Tu Bishvat included the planting of new trees as a symbol of the Zionist renewal of Jewish return to the biblical motherland, with this holiday becoming a national ritual of putting down roots.[93] Jawitz's request was fulfilled to the letter and the original thicket eventually became a municipal garden with an abundance of trees. In this request, Jawitz achieved two goals. The first was to honour the Haganah, of which he was a member from 1921 until its integration in the IDF in 1948, as the fifth Haganah commander

---

88 *Iryat Ramla: Sikum Pe'ulot Ha'irya* (for 1 July 1949 to 30 September 1950) (Ramla, 1951), p. 18.

89 Ramla's Municipal Archive, Town Council Resolutions, Resolution no. 114 from 22 July 1955.

90 *Mehana'asa Ba'ir: Igeret le'ezrachey Ramla* 4 (Ramla, April 1957), p. 6.

91 For a biography of Golomb, see Ahuvia Malkin, *Ha'activist: Sipur Chayav shel Eliyahu Golomb* (Tel Aviv, 2007).

92 'Ezrachey Ramla ve Lod Nifradim Me'anshey Hamimshal Hatzva'i', undated and unidentified newspaper article from the Jawitz family private archive. I wish to thank Zusman's wife, Esther, and their children Ruti and Shay for their kind help and hospitality.

93 Eliezer Smoli, 'Letoldot Chag Haneti'ot', *Teva Va'aretz* 9 (1966), pp. 70–72; Kliot, 'Ideology and Afforestation in Israel', p. 90; Bardenstein, 'Threads of Memory', pp. 7–8.

in Tel Aviv, in charge of the city's *slikim* (weapon caches).[94] Jawitz's second goal was to commemorate the fallen soldiers in a way that implied not violence and bloodshed, but growth and vitality. In this manner, through the link with Tu Bishvat, Jawitz was fulfilling the Zionist agenda of cultivating the land while facilitating its appropriation on the practical as well symbolic levels.

This early link between the garden and the Haganah is felt to this day. The association of war, death and sacrifice on the one hand, and memory and vitality on the other, is also articulated in a memorial erected in 1958 near one of the entrances to the garden. Like other memorials in Israel, it manifests in the most refined way Israeli and Jewish existence, linking past and present together.[95] The memorial is dedicated to 'the protectors of the homeland' (*meginey hamoledet*), and more specifically, to the soldiers of Regiment 42 of the Kiryati brigade, who perished in the battles over Ramle. Made of cement, iron and marble, the monument is shaped like a tree struck by lightning, whose branches nevertheless bloom,[96] while its inscription 'And through their death/ They bade a life be ours' (*'uvemotam tzivu lanu et hachaiym*'), — the concluding line of the poem *If You Would Know* (1898) by national poet Chaim N. Bialik[97]—highlights the ethos of sacrifice in which the loss of soldiers was constructed as the 'price' for Israel's survival, a 'debt' to the bereaved families repaid by immortalising the fallen.[98]

---

94   Mussa Brener, *Asara Mi Yode'a? (Aseret Mefakdey HaHaganah Shel Ha'ir Tel Aviv)*(Tel Aviv, 1988), pp. 52–53; Gershon and Aliza Rivlin, *The Stranger Cannot Understand: Code-Names in the Jewish Underground in Palestine* (Tel Aviv, 1988)[in Hebrew], p. 83.

95   Avner Ben-Amos, 'Theatres of Death and Memory: Monuments and Rituals in Israel', in D. Dominey and F. Lebée-Nadav, *Everywhere: Landscape and Memory in Israel*, M. Vigoder (ed.)(Tel Aviv, 2002)[in Hebrew], pp. 18–20.

96   D. Dominey and F. Lebée-Nadav, *Everywhere: Landscape and Memory in Israel*, ed. M. Wigoder (Tel Aviv, 2002)[in Hebrew], pp. 109–110.

97   Chaim Nachman Bialik, *Poems from the Hebrew*, L.V. Snowman (ed.)(London, 1924), pp. 49–51.

98   M. Weiss, 'Bereavement, Commemoration and Collective Identity in Contemporary Israeli Society', *Anthropological Quarterly* 70:2 (1997), pp. 91–101 (p. 92).

The whole nation was indebted to the falling soldier.[99] By stressing this relationship between the dead and the living, between sacrifice and renewal, this garden and monument forged a bond between the town and its conquerors, whose death gave life to the town's newcomers. In this socialisation process, producing and reproducing national and local identities, Ramla's inhabitants were taught that their life in an Israeli Ramla was made possible only by the sacrifice of others who did not survive, that they were now obliged to commemorate the dead, and make their own sacrifices by contributing to the state and town. In other towns similar memorial gardens were likewise constructed; a hilly area in Safad, planted in 1924 by Arab and Jews alike, was redeveloped into a garden after 1948 by the architect Shlomo Weinberg, who designed it into a big park, called The Fortress Garden. It included, at its highest point, a large monument commemorating the Jewish soldiers who had perished while occupying (or releasing, according to viewpoint) Palestinian Safad.[100]

As part of this process of linking past and present, the Haganah garden in Ramla became during the 1960s a public space associated with Memorial Day: garlands were laid and memorial ceremonies held there.[101] This obviously further stressed the garden's meaningful role in the town's life as a reminder of past sacrifices, and endowed this local manifestation of Israeli commemoration culture with a 'language of commitment', cutting across ethnic divisions and historical periodisations within the Jewish population. Don Hendelman characterised Israeli Memorial Day and Independence Day, which occur on consecutive days, as 'a semiotic set'—at the same time separated from and related to each other.[102] These two occasions were manifested spatially

99 Yael Zerubavel, 'Patriotic Sacrifice and the Burden of Memory in Israeli Secular National Hebrew Culture', in *Memory and Violence in the Middle East and North Africa*, Ussama Makdisi and Paul A. Silverstein (eds.)(Bloomington, 2006), pp. 73–100 (p. 73).
100 Enis, *Documentation of Three Gardens*, p. 24.
101 See, for example, *Ramla: Bita'on Iryat Ramla* 1 (Ramla, 1966), p. 2.
102 Handelman, *Models and Mirrors*, Chapter 9.

in Ramla, creating an imaginable route stretching between Gan HaHaganah, where Memorial Day was marked, and Gan Hanasi, where Independence Day was celebrated. This symbolic layout endowed the gardens and main street between them (Ramla's 'Herzl Blvd.', aptly named after the prophet of Zionism) with complementary notions of willing sacrifice and national victory.

Although, as mentioned above, Arab orchards had existed on its location, Gan HaHaganah was not built on the grounds of an earlier garden as was Gan Hanasi; in this sense, it was a new creation, laden with no undesired memories. It could be moulded at will, the memories associated with it freely chosen rather than remodelled. The trees planted in this garden—mostly cypress and pine—also communicate newness. Unlike olive and palm trees, associated with Jewish biblical past or with the oriental Arab landscape, cypress and pine were 'Zionist' trees commonly planted by the JNF in its large-scale afforestation projects. In a way, the JNF's decision to prefer fruitless trees (taken before the First World War and still implemented today)[103] created a symbolic connection between Zionism and its adopted landscape.

The garden's location near the new municipality building and Ramla's new neighbourhoods also identified it with the Hebrew Ramla and new beginnings. It was located away from the *sakne*, detached from the town's previous existence. This was, of course, only an illusion, since the land on which the garden was planted was part of pre-1948 Ramle; it also belonged, before that year, to one or more of Ramle's Arab residents. Moreover, the town's Arab past was implicit in the memorial's commemoration of soldiers fallen while conquering the Arab town. Whether knowingly or unwittingly, the past was engraved in the garden's landscape through deliberate acts of remembering as through quiet forgetting.

The Haganah garden was designed to invite the visitor in: cypress and pine trees shaded the perimeter, green lawns added beauty and colour, and the garden was accessible from several

---

103 Nili Liphschitz and Gideon Biger, 'Afforestation Policy of the Zionist Movement in Palestine 1895–1948', *Cathedra* 80 (1996), pp. 88–108 [in Hebrew].

directions. Like other public gardens in the period, it was designed for young families and the elderly. Yet, its distance from the old centre of town, with its Arab and lower-income Jewish families, made it practically inaccessible to some of this target audience. The garden's blatant nationalist and military orientation further excluded the Arab community on the symbolic level as well.

The British War Memorial Cemetery

One 'garden' which was distinctly *not* part of the Zionist project was the British War Memorial Cemetery on the north-eastern outskirts of town. This is the biggest memorial war cemetery of six built in Palestine after the First World War: 3,769 soldiers who died during and in-between the two world wars are buried there.[104]

Like its equivalents in Palestine and worldwide, this is a sprawling garden surrounded by high stone walls. Evergreen and cypress trees decorate its perimeters and a green lawn stretches inside, where lines of uniform gravestones commemorating the fallen are located next to flower beds; a big stone cross—the Cross of Sacrifice—stands nearby, representing the Empire's Christian identity, despite a variety of creeds among its soldiers.[105] The land for this cemetery was allocated in 1920 by 'the people of Eretz Israel', and to this day graves are being maintained, as in all British memorial war cemeteries around the world, by the Commonwealth War Graves Commission (CWGC), with the help of local gardeners and administrators (fig. 6).[106]

---

104 Ron Fuchs, 'The Planning of the British War Cemeteries in Mandatory Palestine', *Cathedra* 79 (1996), pp. 114–139 [in Hebrew].
105 *Ibid.*
106 Fuchs, 'The Planning'; Eli Shiler, 'The British Cemeteries in Eretz Israel', *Ariel* 171–172 (2005), pp. 196–223 [in Hebrew]. For a description of the cemetery in Ramla, and on the annual memorial ceremony there, see Shay Rozen, 'A Tour around the British Cemetery in Ramla', *Ariel* 175 (2006), pp. 90–107 [in Hebrew].

Fig. 6: Moshe Milner, The Anglican Bishop, Greek Orthodox Clregyman and Jewish Army Chaplain Conducting the Armistice Day Memorial Service at the British War Cemetery in Ramla, 14 November 1976 (Courtesy of the GPO).

The cemetery was also used for more intimate purposes. In her autobiographical memoir, Bilha Toren, who grew up in Ramla, explains: 'The place was perfectly peaceful and calm, away from curious eyes—a place with no worries.'[107] She goes on to praise the soft European lawns, which added to its allure and sense of escapism. No doubt, the garden's main attractions were its beauty, peacefulness and geographical distance, but it was not only that. The British War Memorial Cemetery was an alternative space, liminal and different, away from 'civilisation' in which usual norms and hierarchies applied. This was where young men and women could spend leisurely afternoons and make love, away from their parents' homes and the spying eyes of neighbours. Toren narrates how the old Arab guard, who was also the gardener, offered couples

107 Bilha Toren, *Sdom Vehamora: Sipurim—Lo Liyladim!* (Tel Aviv, 2004), p. 97.

who visited there 'places for conquest'.[108] The military language was used here with an ironic wink, replacing military occupation with sexual conquest, only to emphasise the Arab guard's acceptance of the intimate activity carried out in the perimeter under his responsibility. This garden was, therefore, an exterritorial space, neither Jewish nor Arab, where national politics were irrelevant and love and youth prevailed.

The garden was open to Jews, Muslims and Christians, locals and foreigners alike; yet it seems that the only ones to have shown interest in it, except for dignitaries and visitors during formal ceremonies, were young Jewish men and women from Ramla and nearby Lydda. Older Jewish folk may have found this 'garden' too far to walk to; naturally, this was also not a place suitable for children, despite the luscious lawns. For Ramla's Arab population the distance and sobriety of the place were probably a deterrent factor, and with the imposed and/or chosen segregation in the *sakne*, it seems there was no reason for them to go there.

* * *

This analysis of three of Ramla's gardens contributes to a much needed research on Palestine's gardens and their transformation in the years that followed Israeli occupation. Some Palestinian gardens survived—if not very gracefully—the vicissitudes of time; *bustan* Chiat in Haifa is a case in point. Other gardens, similarly to Ramle's municipal garden remade into Ramla's Gan Hanasi, went through a process of Israelisation. One such garden is Gan Allenby (after General Edmund Allenby, the British military commander who occupied Palestine in 1917, d. 1936) in Beer Sheva's Old City. It was initially designed in 1901 as a public garden, adjacent to the Saraya House (Ottoman governance building). Its name— Jamal Pasha Garden (after the Ottoman governor of Syria, d.

108 *Ibid.*, idem.

1922)—was given to it on the eve of the First World War.[109] This
is a Palestinian garden turned into an Israeli one, but there were
also Palestinian gardens which were razed to the ground, leaving
no visible evidence of their existence but in fading memories
and written recollections. Acre's municipal garden, which was
inaugurated during the 1920s, was located near the Muslim
cemetery, a well-kept public space with trees, benches and a water
fountain at its centre. Despite the best intentions to nurture and
even expand it, the garden was destroyed during the 1950s in
order to make place for the new residence of Acre's Navy Officers
School.[110] In this case, the Palestinian garden—which served also
Jewish visitors in Acre's mixed city of the early 1950s—gave way
to the town's rising symbol of young ambition and future national
success on the sea.

The landscapes discussed in this chapter served various interests
and agendas. In Ramla, as elsewhere, some of these were political
and national, such as the celebrating of Independence Day or the
bond between deceased soldiers and the town's new immigrants.
Others were more mundane, as spaces for recreation and leisure
aimed at different age groups. Access was restricted to none of
Ramla's public gardens discussed above. Even the British cemetery
and Gan Hanasi, which were surrounded by walled gates and
locked at certain times, were open to the public during most of
the day. Yet, these gardens' special features and characters, as well
as the typical activities carried out in them, made them in effect
more attractive for certain audiences, and less so for others. Their
symbolic appropriation was made visible through their design and
use in the post-1948 period; overall, this appropriation served to
exclude the town's Arab community.

109 Nimrod Luz, 'The Re-making of Beersheba: Winds of Modernization in Late
    Ottoman Sultanate', in *Ottoman Reforms and Muslim Regeneration: Studies in
    Honor of Prof. Butrus Abu Manneh*, I. Weissman , F. Zachs (eds.)(London and
    NY, 2005), pp. 187–210 (p. 196).
110 Mustafa Abbasi, 'Families of Arab Notables in Acre at the End of Ottoman
    Rule and During the Mandate Period: Continuation or Change?', *Cathedra*
    130 (2009), pp. 51–74 (p. 66) [in Hebrew]; Yehoshua Lurie, *Acre—The Walled
    City: Jews Among Arabs, Arabs Among Jews* (Tel Aviv, 2000), p. 539.

CHAPTER FOUR

Walking the City:
Communal Processions as
Spatial Performance

Urban spaces have always been linked to parades and processions that use the symbolic temporary appropriation of streets as a means to propagate ideas and agendas—political, religious, and national, frequently all these intertwined. Neil Jarman sees parades not only as 'expressions of culture, displays of faith and acts of domination', but also as 'intimately linked to the wider political domain'.[1] Processions are often a manifestation of the political culture and of real or desired power, whether asserted by minority groups or by the majority. Be it triumphal imperial entries in Roman times, confessional processions in the Middle Ages, progresses of foreign rulers in Renaissance Italy, or the commemoration of leaders in the young American Republic, parades reiterate a message of power.[2] They constitute performances of presence: the

---

1 N. Jarman, *Material Conflicts: Parades and Visual Displays in Northern Ireland* (Oxford and NY, 1997), p. 124.
2 For studies of particular processions and parades see, for example, M. McCormick, *Eternal Victory: Triumphal Rulership in Late Antiquity: Byzantium, and the Early Medieval West* (Cambridge, 1986), Chapter 3; M. Rubin, *Corpus Christi: The Eucharist in Late Medieval Culture* (Cambridge, 1991), pp. 243–271; Andrew Brown, *Civic Ceremony and Religion in Medieval Bruges c. 1300–1520* (Cambridge, 2011); M. Bonner, *The Majesty of the State: Triumphal Progresses of Foreign Sovereigns in Renaissance Italy 1494–1600* (Florence, 1986); Susan G. Davis, *Parades and Power: Street Theatre in Nineteenth-Century Philadelphia* (Berkeley and London, 1986); Simon P. Newman, *Parades and the Politics of the Street: Festive Culture in the Early American Republic* (Philadelphia, 1997).

banners, costumes and flags, as well as the crowd's hierarchical or organised progression through town, may be compared to those of a marching army, dominating the locality, if only for the day. Seen from the outside, the procession is meant to represent a visible *tour de force*, in which the streets stand for conquered or re-conquered ground.

Processions can be seen as an articulation of existing power relations, but also as a means of negotiating this power. The marching of parades—much like other acts conducted in the public sphere—highlight the fact that power, at least the way Michel Foucault perceived it, is dynamic and (re)produced from one moment to the next;[3] inherent to processions, therefore, is a *moment* of power and with it of appropriation, whether symbolic or concrete. One of the sources for the power highlighted through processions is what Émile Durkheim termed (in his 1912 *The Elementary Forms of Religious Life*) 'collective effervescence'—the sacredness of the communal gathering, and the dynamic moments reproduced in the process; through these, a heightened sense of collective identity is generated and society celebrates itself.[4] As a spatial ritual, the parade also takes hold of the landscape and changes the normal order of things—stopping traffic, altering daily behaviour—and thus often needs to be pre-licensed by the authorities. It represents a transitory moment of liminality and anti-structure,[5] in which power is temporarily deposited in the hands of the marchers.

---

3   Joseph Rouse, 'Power/Knowledge', in *The Cambridge Companion to Foucault*, G. Gutting (ed.)(Cambridge, 1994), pp. 92–114 (p. 105).
4   Émile Durkheim, *The Elementary Forms of Religious Life*, trans. Carol Cosman (Oxford, 2001), see, for example, on p. 158.
5   Victor Turner, *The Ritual Process: Structure and Anti-Structure* (London, 1969), pp. 95–96.

Processions and Parades in Palestine/Eretz Israel

Parades and processions formed part of Palestinian life, especially in the urban context. Religious processions regularly took place among Christian and Muslim Arabs alike, such as the traditional Palm Day procession during Easter week. Occasionally, these events intermingled with political undercurrents, as happened during the Nabi Mussa festivities of 1920. Nabi Mussa, believed by Muslims to be buried five miles south of Jericho, is the focus of annual week-long celebrations in his honour (began in the Friday preceding Easter), which used to be the largest and most important festivity of its kind. They included a procession from Jerusalem to Nabi Mussa's burial site, culminating in ensuing merriment.[6] In April 1920, impassioned speeches carried out by religious leaders triggered the attack of Jews in Jerusalem's Old City by Arab aggressors. Funerals posed another opportunity for processions, especially when of eminent public figures. The funeral procession of the national leader (and Jerusalem's mayor between 1918 and 1920) Musa Kazim al-Husseini in March 1934 attracted great crowds to the streets of Jerusalem, wishing to pay respects.[7] Political rallies and parades also figured in the Palestinian political culture of the early twentieth century. One such protestation took place in Jerusalem on 16 August 1929, when about 2,000 Muslims marched along a marked route from the Temple Mount to the Wailing Wall, in order to voice their stand on the issue of Jewish access to this revered place; it escalated within days to attacks on Jews throughout the country.[8]

6   For the site and the historical and modern celebrations of Nabi Mussa, see Sharon Talmor, 'Back to Nabi Mussa', *Eretz ve'Teva* 99 (2005), 60–66 [in Hebrew]; Arnon Dancho, 'Nabi Musa Rituals', *National Geographic* 34 (2001)(no page number)[in Hebrew]; Ifrah Zilberman, 'The Renewal of the Pilgrimage to Nabi Musa', in *Sacred Space in Israel and Palestine: Religion and Politics*, Marshall J. Breger, Yitzhak Reiterad and Leonard Hammer (eds.) (London and NY, 2012), pp. 103–115.

7   Walid Khalidi, *Before Their Diaspora: A Photographic History of the Palestinians, 1876–1948* (Washington D.C., 1991), p. 111.

8   Tom Segev, *Palestine under the British* (Jerusalem, 1999)[in Hebrew], Chapter 13 (esp. p. 255).

In the Jewish Yishuv and later in the State of Israel, parades have also been used as a key discursive element in political and national life. Processions marched the streets of the Yishuv from the early 1900s, combining Zionist elements, traditional characteristics, as well as features adopted from foreign countries. Holidays such as Hanukkah and Purim were celebrated during the 1920s and 1930s in the main streets of the first Hebrew town, Tel Aviv; whereas the *Adloyada* procession in Purim was a carnivalesque affair, Hanukkah was a celebration of light and included a parade of children holding small candles and adults carrying torches.[9] May Day was originally celebrated by the young socialists who were part of the second Jewish immigration wave (1904–1914) using symbols adopted from the Soviet Union.[10] May Day's processions were not always a peaceful affair—on the first week of May 1921, the collision of two alternative May Day processions triggered violent riots in Jaffa that ended with the death of 95 people.[11] With the foundation of the Israeli state, it was the military parade that began to march annually, every year in a different location, celebrating unity, military power and loyalty.[12] This new tradition was accepted enthusiastically. In general, these outdoor processions of various types and characteristics often incorporated Zionist symbols representing an antithesis to the indoor culture of the Diaspora.[13]

9   Nili Arieh-Sapir, 'Carnival in Tel Aviv: The Purim Festival in the "First" Hebrew City', *Jerusalem Studies in Jewish Folklore* 22 (2002), pp. 99–121; Hizky Shoham, *Mordecai is Riding a Horse: Purim Celebrations in Tel Aviv (1908–1936) and the Building of a New Nation* (Jerusalem, 2013)[in Hebrew]; Nili Arieh-Sapir, 'The Procession of Lights: Hanukkah as a National Festival in Tel Aviv, 1909–1936', *Cathedra* 103 (2002)[in Hebrew], pp. 131–150.

10   Rachel Sharaby, 'May Day Ceremonies in the State of Israel's First Decade: From a Sectorial to a National Holiday', *Megamot* 44 (2005)[in Hebrew], pp. 106–136 (p. 108).

11   Segev, *Palestine under the British*, pp. 148-153.

12   Eliezer Don-Yehiya, 'Festivals and Political Culture: The Celebrations of Independence Day in the Early Years of Statehood', in *State, Government and International Relations* 23 (1984), pp. 5–28; Maoz Azaryahu, *State Cults: Celebrating Independence and Commemorating the Fallen in Israel 1948-1956* (Beer Sheva, 1995)[in Hebrew], Chapter 3.

13   Arieh-Sapir, 'Carnival in Tel Aviv'; Arieh-Sapir, 'The Procession of Lights'.

The act of collective procession—framed by constantly overlapping and merging ideas on class, nationality and religion—thus enables an examination of questions related to the real and symbolic appropriation of Ramla throughout the 1950s, on the backdrop of three types of processions which marched the streets of town around that period.

Israel's Sixth Military Parade (1954)

The military parade has become a conventional political ritual in the modern state, a cultural production that combines various patriotic goals. Its characteristic integration into the ceremonial construction of national holidays enhances the message it propagates, that of foundation and dominance of a certain political order.[14] France's Bastille Day, for example, is commemorated every 14 July with a military parade which marches from l'Arc de Triomphe, down the Champs Élysées, to the Place de la Concorde, celebrating the foundation of the French Republic.

In its relatively short time span of existence the Israeli military parade, as Maoz Azaryahu shows, went through various phases. The two first parades (in 1948 and 1949) were prominent demonstrations of Jewish nationhood and military prowess that by 1950 were given a fixed date: Independence Day, celebrated on the fifth day of the Hebrew month of Iyar. Over the 1950s and 1960s Independence Day military parade became routinised and was gradually shaped into a new custom. In 1968, Azaryahu argues, this construed tradition reached its zenith when the twentieth anniversary of Israeli victory in 1948 collided with the euphoria experienced in the aftermath of the military triumph a year before, in the Six Day War. In the years that followed, Israel's military parade marched only on special occasions or jubilees,

---

14 Maoz Azaryahu, 'The Independence Day Military Parade: A Political History of A Patriotic Ritual', in *The Military and Militarism in Israeli Society*, Edna Lomsky-Feder and Eyal Ben-Ari (eds.)(NY, 1999), pp. 89–116 (pp. 90–92).

such as Israel's twenty-fifth Independence Day in 1973. By 1978 there were growing voices that called for the abolishment of this recently-invented tradition, which created an overly-militaristic image of Israel abroad; the military parade, however, was to resurface in the early 1990s.[15]

The decision to choose the mixed town of Ramla as the backdrop to Israel's sixth military parade excited and surprised many while disappointing others. During the parade's heydays in the mid 1950s Ramla was hardly the most obvious candidate to host this important, nationwide event. 'Ramla, the year-round sleepy and dusty town, today resembles Cinderella of the fairy tale', exclaimed *Yediot Ahronot* on 4 May 1954, two days before the set date:

> [...] for twenty-four hours it will become the country's capital [...] The President, Prime Minister, senior diplomats, and tens of thousands of spectators from all over Israel will come in its gates, and the IDF will have its great Independence Day Parade right there.[16]

Despite the town's alleged greyness, the narrowness of its main street which was to force certain restrictions on the parade's organisers, and potentially dangerous houses and rooftops that might collapse under the weight of too many people, Ramla was chosen to host the 1954 military parade.[17] Why Ramla, rather than one of the more obvious candidates such as Tel Aviv (as in 1949), Jerusalem (1950 and 1951) or Haifa (1953)? According to governmental sources, Ramla was selected because of its central location enabling easy access by 'many of the people of Tel Aviv, Jerusalem and the vicinity'.[18] Nonetheless, Ramla was given the honour also because

---

15   *Ibid.*
16   *Yediot Ahronot*, 4 May 1954.
17   *Yediot Ahronot*, 4 May 1954; *Davar*, 6 May 1954; 'Instructions for Ramla's Residents', ISA, 46//391/14– gimel.
18   Minutes of the Meeting of the Independence Day Committee 1954, 9 February 1954, Archive of the City of Tel Aviv-Jaffa, alef/3/33/4.

it was a heterogeneous and mixed town that presented an ideal test case in the socialisation process of the Israeli public. The goal of Independence Day—and of the military parade that was its central feature—was for the individual to identify with the country,[19] and Ramla posed a spectacular challenge, precisely because of the various communities that came to see it as their home.

One important target audience was that of new immigrants. In the government meeting that debated the matter, the cities proposed for the honour were Jerusalem, Tel Aviv, Beer Sheva, Tiberias and the Ramla-Lydda area. Ramla-Lydda seemed to offer the ideal location: central and therefore enabling easy access for civilians, diplomats and tourists; cheap and convenient for transportation of army units and vehicles (due to its centrality and the proximity of a nearby army base); and, most importantly, because 'it is a place near masses of new immigrants'.[20]

The parade was expected to reinforce the new immigrants' identification with the state and its army. Ramla's new citizens— be they of Polish, Bulgarian, Turkish or Moroccan origin—were expected to respond with excitement and patriotic pride. Indeed, as *Haaretz* reported in the aftermath of the parade, tears were seen in the eyes of one of Ramla's residents, a new immigrant from Iraq, when he saw the army marching through town: '"The government did well when it chose our town to host the parade"', he was quoted as saying, and the reporter concluded: 'indeed, the IDF parade was a great experience for new immigrants'.[21] The disappointment voiced by Pesach Lev, the Mayor of nearby Lydda, testifies to the same link between the presence of new immigrants in town and the need for an enhanced sense of patriotism created by the procession. In a letter to the Ministry of the Interior he protested against the decision to hold the military parade in Ramla. He claimed that Lydda was likewise populated by new immigrants who needed the atmosphere triggered by the parade,

19 Don-Yehiya, 'Festivals and Political Culture', pp. 17–18, 23.
20 Minutes of the Fourth Government 18ᵗʰ Meeting, 20 December 1953, pp. 11–16, ISA, Minutes of Fourth Government Meetings, vol. XVI.
21 *Haaretz*, 7 May 1954.

which created a bond between them, the nation and the state. The mayor ignored all formal conventions by using an emotional and expressive language to describe the significance of military parade for the new immigrants in his town:

> Independence Day celebrations and especially military parades are like a remedy to the souls of these people, lifting their failing spirit from everyday troubles and nurturing in them national pride and love of the motherland. Only one who had seen the tears flowing from these people's eyes, tears of joy and of pride, when the IDF parade passes before them, could understand the full value of this event.[22]

The parade's inclusive motivation was not restricted to Jewish new immigrants. One of the army units that attracted much attention in the 1954 parade was the minorities unit, consisted of Druze, Bedouin and Circassian soldiers. As the parade's rearguard, the camel-riders who were part of this formation were the big highlight, attracting much attention and photo opportunities, and giving the parade 'a somewhat exotic appearance'.[23] Rising to the occasion, claimed the press, the unit's Druze soldiers refused to wear their traditional *kaffiyas*, insisting on wearing IDF khaki berets instead; it was therefore difficult to distinguish between them and the Jewish soldiers also serving in this unit.[24] Whether this was actually the soldiers' wish to assimilate or an order from above, it is clear that there was an interest to incorporate the non-Jewish soldiers in the army, and, moreover, inform the public about it. The parade thus posed the option of integration for those who wished to serve their country, whether by enlisting or, more

22 Letter from Lydda's Mayor Pesach Lev to the Minister of the Interior, 3 February 1954. IDF Archive, 642/56//244.
23 Appendix listing the marching and driven units. IDF Archive, 642/56//244; *Haaretz*, and *Davar*, 7 May 1954. For pictures see, for example, *Haaretz* and *Davar*, 7 May 1954; *Haolam Haze*, no. 864 (13 May 1954), p. 11.
24 *Haolam Haze*, no. 864 (13 May 1954), p. 11.

generally, by accepting Jewish hegemony and refraining from subversion. This message of inclusion and possible assimilation, however, highlighted the problematic situation in which only certain non-Jewish communities were accepted into Israeli-Jewish society through military service, whereas others (like Muslim and Christian Arabs) were excluded.

Military parades seem to have two objectives: unifying the nation and dissuading the enemy, by presenting the army's potential strength.[25] I propose that choosing Ramla for the sixth IDF parade promoted both these objectives, in more than one way. The first was already discussed: be it new Jewish immigrants or loyal non-Jewish individuals, all were invited to partake in the parade (as marchers or spectators) and in the building of the nation. The second objective was also attempted in 1954. This was a particularly important element of the military parade of that year, following escalating incidents on the borders with Egypt, Syria and Jordan:[26] the participating units and their equipment testified to the IDF's constantly developing abilities (fig. 7).[27]

Yet, whereas enemy countries were the stated target audience of this *tour de force*, there was another public at which the parade was aimed, albeit less explicitly, that of Israel's Arab citizens. There was no official policy as to participation of Arabs in Independence Day celebrations, which was inherently ambivalent: a minority of different nationality living in a country that celebrates the hegemonic national identity of its majority. On the one hand, the Arab public was encouraged to mark the occasion as an expression of loyalty; on the other, sensitivity was also shown, avoiding from forcing it to take part in or initiate extravagant celebrations.[28]

---

25 Don-Yehiya, 'Festivals and Political Culture', p. 13; also Azaryahu, 'The Independence Day', p. 98.
26 Azaryahu, *State Cults*, p. 83.
27 Appendix listing the marching and driven units. IDF Archive, 642/56//244.
28 Azaryahu, *State Cults*, pp. 67–68.

Fig. 7: Teddy Brauner, Independence Day Military Parade in Ramla, 6 May 1954 (Courtesy of the GPO).

The 1954 military parade targeted Israeli Arabs, especially Muslims, who were symbolically represented in the event by Ramla's Arabs. Implicitly, it warned Israel's Arab residents against any latent disloyalty: the army's role as protector, stressed in the 1954 parade by balloons that formed the words 'IDF protects' in the sky,[29] was a subtle reminder to the Arab minority that the army sleeps with one eye open. On the ground, the route of the 1954 military parade was uncomplicated yet minutely planned. A sketch in the IDF archive clearly marks the straight path through which the units were to march, beginning in the eastern entrance to town (the direction of Jerusalem), and ending five miles away, outside Ramla, in the Tzriffin (Sarafand) military base. It also indicates the location of the spectator platforms, and the exact places where

29   *Yediot Ahronot*, 7 May 1954.

salutation should commence and conclude.[30] The Israeli army—
with its soldiers, vehicles and even camels—was to march through
Ramla's main street, basically crossing the town from east to west.
A flyover demonstrated the IDF's aerial capabilities, also drawing
attention to the open skies above Ramla.[31]

It has been suggested that military parades represent the ideal
military activity—short, predictable and victimless.[32] In that
sense it can be argued that almost six years after Arab Ramle was
occupied, the Israeli army returned to town for a second, this
time well-rehearsed and carefully planned, performance. 'In the
same street where in those days passed the jeeps and armoured
vehicles stormed through town', exclaimed *Davar*'s reporter in
the aftermath of the parade, '...now marches a great army, to the
sounds of an orchestra, in front of tens of thousands...'[33] Ramla
was also re-conquered from the air, by airplanes forming the
Hebrew letters Chet-Aleph, acronym for Air Force. The balloons
mentioned above also served to re-establish aerial hold over
town.[34] The parade was indeed a bloodless battle in which Ramla's
streets were reoccupied and symbolically appropriated, linking
not only past and present, but also the future.[35] Whereas in 1948
the Israeli army advanced through Ramle towards Jerusalem, the
parade's route six years later advanced in the opposite direction.[36]
This was a reversed, bloodless and predicted reconstruction of
past events, but also a declaration of the present state of affairs,
as of an anticipated future. The parade represented—and, in a
way, made possible—the aspiration for a strong, secure, densely
populated and united Israel, in which the Arab population is a

30   IDF Archive, 642//56/80; also *Haolam Haze*, no. 864 (13 May 1954), p. 16.
31   *Yediot Ahronot* and *Maariv*, 7 May 1954; *Haolam Haze*, no. 864 (13 May
     1954), pp. 9–11.
32   Azaryahu, *State Cults*, p. 77.
33   *Davar*, 7 May 1954.
34   *Yediot Ahronot* and *Maariv*, 7 May 1954; *Haolam Haze*, no. 864 (13 May
     1954), pp. 9–11.
35   Jarman, *Material Conflicts*, p. 107.
36   Map showing platforms for tourists, officers and the salutation stage. IDF
     Archive, 642/56//80; *Haolam Haze*, no. 864 (13 May 1954), p. 16.

cooperative and loyal minority. The parade enabled a momentary rest on collective laurels, while propagating messages designed for different publics. State and army leaders could feel proud: new immigrants, who did not know 'how poor was the power of the army in those days, six years ago, when it had to stand up to well-trained and equipped invaders',[37] felt privileged to have arrived in an already established and safe homeland. Tourists and foreign diplomats were expected to report back to their countries on the power of the Israeli army. Finally, Israeli Arabs, for whom this reversal of the town's conquest was a reminder of traumatic experiences, as well as present realities, could muse on their becoming a minority, marginalised in their town and country, and decide whether they prefer to remain loyal to the Israeli regime or risk undermining it. The parade was meant to convey unity, yet it managed to create only an illusion of collectiveness.

Being a one-way type of parade, according to the typology proposed by Louis Marin, this symbolic march from 'Jerusalem' to 'Tel Aviv-Jaffa' along Ramla's main street implied irreversible movement, and a schematic reproduction of narrative, with its end-point representing victory.[38] The fact that the parade began in 'Jerusalem' and ended in 'Tel Aviv' created a symbolic reversal of past victory: when Ramla had been conquered in 1948 Jerusalem had not yet been in Israeli hands; in 1954, on the other hand, the fact that the (imaginary) starting point was in Israeli hands, made it a victory parade. The arches bearing the slogan 'rejoice Ramla and be merry with the IDF entering your gates' positioned just before the platform destined for the army's senior officers, were linked to the triumphal arches in Republican Rome, and aimed to symbolise the honour due to a victorious army returning from the battlefield.[39]

---

37   *Haaretz*, 7 May 1954.

38   L. Marin, 'Notes on a Semiotic Approach to *Parade, Cortege,* and *Procession*', in *Time Out of Time: Essays on the Festival*, Alessandro Falassi (ed.)(Albuquerque, 1987), pp. 220–228 (p. 224).

39   The slogan was mentioned in *Davar*, 5 May 1954; it repeated that used in the military parade of the year before in Haifa. Map showing platforms for tourists, officers and the salutation stage. IDF Archive, 642/56//80; Batya Donner, 'Shkifut Hakoach Hanir'e', in *Hod Vehadar: Tiksey Haribonut Hayisraelit, 1948–1958* (Tel Aviv, 2001), pp. 8–61 (pp. 13–15).

The highlight of the ritualistic military parade is arguably the moment when the army passes in front of the state's leaders while saluting them; this is usually done on the backdrop of a holy site.[40] The hand-drawn map depicting part of the 1954 parade route clearly indicates where the marching soldiers should begin saluting, and where they should end; altogether, it comes to about a hundred yards.[41] In this particular case, no holy site was situated next to the platform. There was nevertheless great significance to its chosen location near a crossroads leading to the four corners of the country (Lydda, Tel Aviv, Jerusalem, and Rehovot), symbolically controlling the whole area, further emphasising the results of Ramla's (and the country's) conquest six years earlier. Thus, as the IDF soldiers marched on, saluting the state's leaders, they spatially commemorated and reaffirmed struggle, victory and occupation.

This analysis of the sixth military parade of 1954 could have ended here: soldiers marching according to a planned route at a set pace, saluting at the right moment in front of anticipating leaders, who represent the epitome of structure and premeditated symbolic and propagandistic national pride and power, a perfect display of citizenship and solidarity. However, things are seldom executed according to preconceived plans. When comparing the Brazilian carnival with the military parade, Roberto Da Matta suggested reading the latter not only as a structured formal celebration, but also as one encompassing moments of *communitas* and anti-structure. In order to fully analyse the military parade, claimed Da Matta, one needs to study it throughout the entire process: from the preparations, through the marching, to the crowd's dispersal.[42] Indeed, the 1954 military parade and its 100,000 spectators left chaos and destruction behind them. The disorder

40   Roberto Da Matta, 'Constraint and License: A Preliminary Study of Two Brazilian National Rituals', in *Secular Ritual*, S.F. Moore and B.G. Myerhoff (eds.)(Amsterdam, 1977), pp. 244–264 (p. 247).
41   Sketch showing platforms for tourists, officers and the salutation stage. IDF Archive, 642/56//80
42   Da Matta, 'Constraint and License', p. 251.

was apparent already while the parade was in progress, with several hundreds of spectators taking over the seats reserved for foreign dignitaries, streaming through fences and creating confusion. Disarray also marked the end of the parade, with apparently no specific planning for dispersal; this resulted in heavy traffic (it was reported that it took three hours to get from Ramla to Tel Aviv, normally half an hour's drive), three deadly car accidents, delayed trains (because of passengers climbing on train rooftops), and much diplomatic embarrassment.[43] The parade left Ramla's streets filthy, with gardens and recently planted trees trampled, tanks left deep potholes in the main street's hot asphalt, a roof collapsed under the weight of spectators, and many were injured of the barbed wire that restricted access to the parade route.[44]

It is interesting to note that whereas some of the newspapers reporting preferred to ignore these negative and chaotic aspects of the parade, others were more willing to describe the event over-all picture, referring to elements representing both structure and anti-structure.[45] *Haolam Haze*, for one, published a satirical and subversive account of the event as it was seen 'from within', stressing the inherent confusion and lack of enthusiasm among the marching soldiers, the unbearable heat, boredom and long waiting, and the relief when it was all over.[46]

No doubt, there was a gap between the pre-planned, structured parade and its disorderly conclusion. One of the papers exclaimed that 'the independence of Israel came to Ramla, mounted on tanks', stressing the parade's intended goal of demonstrating the IDF's power and contribution to independence. In the process, Ramla was re-occupied as a commemorative display of its occupation six years earlier. A non-euphoric reporter concluded: 'In the evening we returned to Ramla. It was a pitiful sight, as if

---

43 *Haaretz* and *Maariv*, 7 May 1954.
44 *Haaretz* and *Maariv*, 7 May 1954.
45 For example, *Davar* and *Yediot Ahronot*, as opposed to *Haaretz* and *Maariv*, all reporting on 7 May 1954.
46 *Haolam Haze*, no. 864 (13 May 1954), pp. 9–11, 16.

the town were occupied by a foreign army.'[47] The town was left to lick its wounds and recover.

The May Day parade, to be discussed next, marched along a very similar route, delivering, however, an almost antithetical message.

May Day Processions (1949–1959)

Established in the Paris Congress of the Second International (1889), the first of May was made a day of universal work stoppage, meant to unite the working class worldwide in demand for a fixed working day of eight hours. It also commemorates the Haymarket Affair in Chicago (1886), where a rally in support of striking workers ended in civilian deaths. In the Jewish Yishuv, the occasion was first marked in 1906 by members of the Po'aley Zion party.[48] Only in 1920 did May Day become a major public event, celebrated by both Arab and Jewish workers.[49] From the early 1920s it became a bank holiday, displaying the growing power of labour Zionism, while after 1948 and in the first decade of statehood May Day was gradually embedded with nationalist messages.[50]

Nevertheless, the greatest challenge of Marxism in the emerging State of Israel remained that of internationalism versus nationalism. Were workers to identify themselves with the international class struggle and disregard nationalist agendas, or were they to adhere to national aspirations and fight exploitation as long as it went hand in hand with the Zionist, Palestinian or Arab agenda? This issue has preoccupied many of the scholars of Communism in Palestine/Eretz Israel; a debate prevails as to whether the Jewish or

47   *Haaretz*, 7 May 1954.
48   Sharaby, 'May Day Ceremonies', p. 108.
49   Avner Ben-Zaken, *Communism as Cultural Imperialism: The Affinities between Eretz-Israeli Communism and Arab Communism 1919–1948* (Tel Aviv, 2006) [in Hebrew], p. 50.
50   Sharaby, 'May Day Ceremonies'.

Arab communists held 'true' internationalist views, and which of the two groups was national deviationist.[51]

Incidentally, one of the first answers to this conundrum was given in Ramle in 1906, when Po'aley Zion's *Ramle Platform* emphasised the equal importance of class *and* national struggle.[52] During the 1920s, the Histadrut labour federation debated the question of an Arab labour organisation. If an Arab section would be formed within the Histadrut, it was agreed, it should be non-national, or even anti-national in nature, allied to the Zionist movement rather than Arab nationalism.[53] This, it seems, was *not* an ideological position, but rather a practical one: whereas acknowledging Arab nationalism was clearly out of the question, Zionism was seen as perfectly compatible with the Histadrut's proletarian agenda. After 1948 the Israeli government and the Histadrut ensured that Arab workers be excluded from the economy, ignoring Mapam's and Maki's demands to incorporate Arab workers into the Histadrut. The Palestine Labour League (PLL) was re-established as the Arab branch of the Histadrut, enabling the latter to keep a close eye on it.[54]

In the mid 1940s, Ramle's Arab workers were organised in an association which acted—together with those of other communities—to unify the Arab proletariat. The changes that occurred as a result of the war and which contributed to increasing levels of working class consciousness and activism, were therefore not without precedent.[55] A new Marxist element in post-war Ramla (although excluded from voting in the local elections) were about eight hundred workers from Nazareth brought to work in town,

51 Joel Beinin, *Was the Red Flag Flying There? Marxist Politics and the Arab-Israeli Conflict in Egypt and Israel, 1948–1965* (Berkeley, 1990), p. 260.
52 Zeev Sternhell, *The Founding Myths of Israel: Nationalism, Socialism, and the Making of the Jewish State* (Princeton, 1998), p. 84.
53 Zachary Lockman, *Comrades and Enemies: Arab and Jewish Workers in Palestine, 1906–1948* (Berkeley, 1996), p. 84.
54 Lockman, *Comrades and Enemies*, p. 358.
55 *Yediot Po'alim*, 16 December 1945, in Lavon Institute for Labour Research, IV-219–70; on this topic see also in Aharon Cohen, *The Arab Worker's Movement (in Egypt, Palestine, Lebanon, Syria, Iraq): History, Summaries, Problems* (Haifa, 1947)[in Hebrew], pp. 53–60.

many of whom were members of the communist Arab Workers' Congress (AWC).[56] In the early months of military administration in town, the presence of these workers was undesirable. The Military Governor did not think 'entry licence to Ramla should be given to Arab communists from other places', due to the hitherto virtual non-existence of communists in town.[57] The next step was to send back to Nazareth all non-licensed workers; this, however, proved not particularly helpful in the fight against spreading communism among Ramla's Arabs, since the AWC members from Nazareth simply passed the torch to younger local men.[58] Moreover, the military administration's freedom of action was limited by the presence of Jewish communists in Ramla.

Many of the new Jewish immigrants from Europe held socialist and communist views. Micko and Loti, who had arrived in Ramla from Bulgaria in December 1948, were members of the communist party. When they discovered the town's 'ghetto' their initial reaction was to express their camaraderie by asking those enclosed on the other side of the fence whether there were any communists among them; the Arab couple they had met on that occasion—Suhil and Amin—became their friends.[59] The agenda, leadership and organisation skills of Ramla's communist and socialist crowd were promptly put to the test in a combined operation: on the morning of 25 April 1949, about three hundred unemployed workers from Ramla arrived to the Knesset where they were stopped by police; they then proceeded to the Ministry of Labour, demanding to speak to the minister. At the same time, back in Ramla, shopkeepers closed their businesses in a show

56 *Kol Haam*, 13 August 1950; Letter from Nazareth workers in Ramla to District Officer, 25 June 1950, ISA, 85//2277/26–gimel; Letter from the AWC Congress to Ramla's District Commander, 20 July 1949, ISA, 85//2277/26–gimel; Police 'Bi-Weekly Survey—Issues Relating to Arabs', 9 November 1950, ISA, 79//7/7–lamed.

57 IDF Archive, 1860/1950//33 [sheet 3].

58 Police 'Bi-Weekly Survey—Issues Relating to Arabs', 9 November 1950, ISA, 79//7/7—lamed.

59 R. Bidas, A. Moshe, R. al-Nablusi and Y. Tamari, *Zochrot et al-Ramle* ([?], 2004), p. 8.

of solidarity. When, after negotiation, the demonstrators in Tel Aviv were offered 5,000 Israeli Pounds, they refused, insisting on securing permanent employment for the unemployed, and declared they will continue demonstrating until employment was found.[60]

Ramla's municipality was also of left-wing orientation: members of the first town council elected in November 1950 included more votes for socialist Mapam and communist Maki than the two parties had received in the first countrywide elections of January 1949.[61] Indeed, the May Day parades in Ramla were a spectacular affair, attracting a crowd of hundreds each year. During the 1950's the procession would usually start in the town's proletarian stronghold—the Histadrut's Workers' Council House—and then turn into Ramla's main street (Herzl Blvd.). Marching along the town's most central route, which used not only as the main municipal road but also as the thoroughfare connecting Jerusalem and Tel Aviv-Jaffa, the marchers would be highly visible with their banners, festive clothes and orchestrated shouting of slogans. The procession would pass the entrance to the market and Gan Hanasi, finally turning back at the central bus station at the eastern edge of town. Back through the main street, they would parade to the municipality building; on some years the procession arrived as far as the road to Lydda, only then turning back to its point of departure.[62]

---

60 *Kol Hhaam*, *Haaretz* and *Davar*, all reporting on 26 April 1949; *Maariv*, 25 April 1949.

61 Other parties in Ramla's first elected city council were from Herut (two representatives); Hadatiyim (one); Hazionim haKlaliyim (one) and Haichud Vehakidma (one Arab representative), altogether thirteen city council members. *Ramla Bevinyana Uvehitpatchuta* (Ramla, 1952), pp. 12–13. Although Mapai was slightly weaker in Ramla than nationally (30.7% and 35.7%, respectively), Mapam and Maki were much stronger locally (23% vs. 14.7%, and 7.7%, vs. 3.5%, respectively). For the elections to the first Knesset, see http://www.knesset.gov.il/faction/heb/FactionListAll.asp?view=1 (accessed 16 July 2013); in Ramla: *Ramla Bevinyana Uvehitpatchuta*, p. 12.

62 Letter to Ramla's police HQ from the local May Day committee, 28 April 1958; Letter from Mr. Stein, secretary of Ramla's Workers' Council to District Officer, 24 April 1959; Handwritten letter from Ramla Police to the Commander of the Ramla/Rehovot District, 2 May 1959, all in ISA, 79//161/14–lamed.

On May Day of 1949—the first celebrated in the mixed town, then still under military administration—more than three hundred Arab demonstrators left the enclosed Arab neighbourhood to join the parade on Ramla's main street.[63] This unique gathering of a unified Arab-Jewish proletarian front in Ramla was described by one enthused reporter as 'an uncommon experience'.[64]

This event was photographed by Zoltan Kluger, a Hungarian-born photographer who had arrived in Mandatory Palestine in the early 1930s.[65] One of his photographs shows people marching along the town's main street, carrying signs in Arabic and Hebrew and dressed in their Sunday best (fig. 8). The various languages on the signs in Kluger's photographs of that day seem to articulate a message of unity and camaraderie: Arabic, Hebrew for the Jewish immigrants from Arab countries and native Israelis, Bulgarian and Yiddish for immigrants from Europe.[66]

As a photographer employed by Zionist national institutions, Kluger documented events, people and landscapes, occasionally directing his subjects as he saw fit. He has been recently described as *the* photographer of the Zionist propaganda machine, creating a utopian reality that served Zionist terminology and goals.[67] Like most of his other pictures, his photographs of Ramla's May Day of 1949 had to be sold, ideally to an institution such as the Jewish National Fund. Therefore, they needed to show what the intended audience expected to see: solidarity of nations, with the mixed town of Ramla acting as a display window for Israel that had allowed Arabs to celebrate May Day 'freely for the first time, and with much enthusiasm', as reported by *Davar*.[68]

Kluger, however, whether deliberately or unwittingly, depicted in his photographs also the tension inherent in this situation.

---

63 *Kol Haam*, 2 May 1949.
64 *Al Hamishmar*, 5 May 1949.
65 Kluger studied photography in Hungary and worked, during the 1920s, in a Berlin newspaper. Rona Sela, *Photography in Palestine in the 1930s—1940s* ([Tel Aviv], 2001)[in Hebrew], p. 163.
66 Ben Zakan, *Communism as Cultural Imperialism*, p. 105.
67 Sela, *Photography in Palestine*, p. 165.
68 *Davar*, 2 May 1949.

The ideological challenge of internationalism in opposition to nationalism, the innate hostility between victor and vanquished are all there in his May Day pictures. The various languages on the banners stress national and ethnic differences, and the Arab houses visible on the farther side of the street stand for the changes the town had gone through when 'abandoned' Arab houses became homes for new Jewish immigrants.

Fig. 8: Zoltan Kluger, Jewish and Arab workers marching in the May Day Parade, 1 May 1949 (Courtesy of the GPO).

In May Day of 1949, all these intertwined: class unity and calls for equality on the one hand and manifest national differences on the other. Mapam's *Al Hamishmar* lauded the 'spectacular parade', which united all local workers; other newspapers also referred to the fact that workers of both nationalities celebrated

May Day together for the first time.[69] The coming out of about three hundred Arab members of the AWC and PLL to join their Jewish counterparts on Ramla's main street indeed conveyed a powerful message of equality, yet it also highlighted the physical segregation of the town's Arab population. Speaking for the AWC in the 'festive assembly' organised that day by the Histadrut, Amin Kudkha demanded that military administration be revoked and 'the racist discrimination' against Arabs abolished.[70] Such voices were unheard in most newspapers; even the communist *Kol Haam* preferred to emphasise class unity, and its 'huge impression on the townspeople', rather than blatant inequality.[71]

Despite the note of hope expressed by the Histadrut's speaker in the assembly, where he wished that the next May Day would be celebrated in a unified Jewish-Arab Histadrut, due to Mapai's reluctance Arabs would not be able to become full members before 1959; they were allowed to vote in Histadrut elections only from 1965.[72] Mapai also gradually nationalised May Day events during the first decade of statehood, leading to growing national and political tensions in the parades of the following years.[73]

Already in May Day of 1950, a fight broke out and cut the celebrations short, after an Arab man was blamed for taking down and 'desecrating' the Israeli flag during a speech by a Mapai representative. In retaliation, a group of Jews from mainly Turkish origin attacked the Jewish-Arab communist club, wounding several members.[74] Even if the original aggression was an ideological act against nationalism (which is uncertain), the violent retaliation was clearly nationalistic.

May Day of 1959 was as tense, with several incidents that could have easily erupted into violence. During the march, a 'gang' of

69 For example, *Al Hamishmar*, 5 May 1949; *Kol Haam*, 2 May 1949; *Davar*, 2 May 1949.
70 *Kol Haam* and *Davar*, 2 May 1949.
71 *Kol Haam*, 2 May 1949.
72 *Kol Haam* and *Davar*, 2 May 1949; Lockman, *Comrades and Enemies*, p. 359.
73 Sharaby, 'May Day Ceremonies'.
74 Letter from Chayun, Ramla-Lydda District Officer to the Head of Tel Aviv District Police, 30 May 1950, ISA, 85//2277/26–gimel.

about ten men walked along the parade, booing and shouting derogatory remarks at the marchers from Banki (Maki's youth movement). Another incident occurred towards the end of the parade, when Mapai members tore one of Banki's signs, allegedly saying 'down with the State of Israel' in Arabic. At the end of the day, with the parade over, rumours started circulating: one such claim, according to which Mapai's secretary had been beaten up at the Maki club, resulted in a great crowd encircling the place, only to be stopped by the police; according to another rumour, Maki members tore the Israeli flag.[75] It seems obvious that all these incidents, particularly those involving the national flag, expressed and exacerbated existing tensions. Some elements in Ramla were apparently agitated by the May Day activist presence of Arab elements on the town's main street, and their refusal to remain confined to the alleys of Ramla's designated Arab neighbourhood.

May Day parade created a discourse around issues of class and nationalism, perceived differently by participants and spectators, whether communist, socialist or capitalist, Jewish or Arab. At times, it was articulated in a civilised and polite manner; at other times, it became verbally abusive and even physically violent. Towards the late 1950s, May Days in Ramla gradually turned into excuses for clashes: ideological differences may have been the context or subtext, yet nationalism was the real driving force. National differences, or rather the fear of their potential power, stand at the backdrop of the marginalisation of yet another procession, that to the Nabi Salah Tomb.

---

75   Handwritten letter from Ramla's Police to the Ramla/Rehovot District Officer, 2 May 1959, ISA, 79//161/14–lamed.

Procession to the Nabi Salah Tomb

On the first Friday after the Greek-Orthodox Easter, the Muslim celebration of Nabi Salah was traditionally celebrated in Ramle since the Middle Ages. Townspeople and peasants from all the area took part in this celebration, making pilgrimage to the assumed resting place of the prophet who, according to the Koran, preceded Mohamed in advocating belief in one God (7:71–77).[76] The procession would advance westward from Ramle's Great Mosque (Al-Jami al-Kabir or Jami al-Umari) through the White Mosque (Al-Jami al-Abyad) and Tower, and to the outskirts of town, where Salah the Prophet was believed to be buried.[77] The processors left the Great Mosque, walking through the market area, meandering through little alleys and wider streets and progressing towards the Muslim cemetery, which is part of the White Mosque compound (fig. 9). Unlike the parades discussed above, these processors did not march along the town's main road, but preferred to walk through the most crowded residential quarters of what had come to be known as the Old City.[78] Upon arrival, a prayer would be heard, after which verses lauding Nabi Salah would be recited, ending with a reading of the Koran's first *sura*. Then the crowd would temporarily disperse, with groups of pilgrims entering the small edifice around the tomb, kissing the green cloth that covered Nabi Salah's burial place and wiping their face with it to receive God's blessing. After completing this liturgy, some would pay a visit to deceased relatives in the nearby cemeteries. With nightfall, the various groups would reassemble

76 'Feasts, Celebrations and Pilgrimage to Saints' Tombs', in *Religion and Ritual and Tombs of Muslim Saints in Eretz Yisrael*, Eli Shiller (ed.)(also referred to as *Ariel* 117–118 (1996), pp. 190–191 [in Hebrew]; Yosef Drori, 'Nabi Salah', *Moreshet Derech* 10 (1985), pp. 18–19.

77 E.W.G. Masterman and R.A.S. Macalister, *Occasional Papers on the Modern Inhabitants of Palestine: Tales of Welys and Dervishes* (1915), pp. 170–176, as cited in 'Feasts, Celebrations and Pilgrimage to Saints' Tombs', pp. 190–191 [in Hebrew].

78 I would like to thank Dr. Shimon Gat, an expert on medieval Ramle, for his advice on this matter; interview with Muhammad Taji, former Head of the Ramla Waqf, 3 March 2008.

and make their way back in unison, with much excitement and loud voices. The procession's return to the Great Mosque would mark the end of celebrations, after a silent prayer.[79]

The procession celebrating Nabi Salah could be seen as a round trip. In this type of procession the 'turning point', here Nabi Salah's resting place near the White Tower, is pregnant with meaning, since it is the procession's symbolic origin and end.[80] The 'real' point of both departure and return, in our case the Great Mosque—originally a Crusader church converted into a mosque— is not 'identical spatially' when it is left and when it is returned to. In returning to it after the procession, this point too is endowed with legitimacy, gained through movement in space and its special semiotic.[81] The Great Mosque's historical origin as a church further stresses the need to reaffirm this site's Muslim identity and importance.[82] The procession thus marked an extra layer on the town's cognitive map; it was a sacred layer, which identified the route and therefore space between the two most important Muslim symbols of Ramle, turning in the process into two borderlines: the Great Mosque to the east and the White Mosque to the west. Nabi Salah procession hallowed the space between the two mosques, marking it as a sacred Muslim territory, at least for the day. Through this procession and in this imagined space the Muslim community was reunited, and participants'

---

79 'Feasts, Celebrations and Pilgrimage to Saints' Tombs', pp. 190–191.
80 Marin, 'Notes on a Semiotic Approach', p. 124. After excavations carried out by the Department of Antiquities in 1949, the compound of the White Mosque was claimed to be an Islamic relic from the late seventh century; alternatively, it was argued later that the mosque and its nearby buildings were built in the twelve century. J. Kaplan, 'Excavations at the White Mosque in Ramla', *Atiqot* 2 (1959), pp. 106–115; A.D. Peterson, 'Preliminary Report on an Archaeological Survey of Historic Buildings in Ramla', *Levant* 27 (1995), pp. 75–100 (p. 79); Shimon Gat, 'The City of Ramla in the Middle Ages' (PhD Thesis, Bar Ilan University, 2003)[in Hebrew], pp. 93–94.
81 Marin, 'Notes on a Semiotic Approach', p. 124.
82 On the Great Mosque see Peterson, 'Preliminary Report', p. 79.

Fig. 9: Matson Photo Service, Nabi Salah Procession Walking the Streets of Ramle, 30 April 1943 (Courtesy of the G. Eric and Edith Matson Photography Collection, Library of Congress, LC-M33-12797).

identity inscribed into the town's physical geography, symbolically appropriating it in the process.[83]

The vicissitudes characterising the Nabi Salah celebration throughout the ages mirror changing socio-political and religious circumstances more generally. Originating possibly during the Mamluk Period (1260–1517 A.D.), two main interpretations have been suggested for its development and character. Some scholars see this procession as originating in an environment of religious cooperation and good neighbourly relations between Muslims and Christians. This view also helps in explaining its timing, based on the Christian calendar. A symbolic relic of this tradition of coexistence may be seen in the more modern processions, some of which were led by a band of Greek-Orthodox scouts.[84] Others, on the other hand, claim that the Nabi Salah celebration (as those of Nabi Mussa and Nabi Rubin) originated in religious tension, and was meant rather to highlight the Muslim presence in Palestine during and after the Crusaders' arrival, while conveying a visible message to European pilgrims that the country was no longer under Christian control.[85]

From the early 1920s, the Nabi Salah celebrations became more agitated, at times verging on violence. In 1921, an attack of celebrants on the neighbouring Jewish settlements of Rehovot, Rishon LeZion and Ekron was thwarted.[86] It seems that as in the Nabi Mussa celebrations of that time, celebrants were incited to attack Jews.[87] During the early 1930s, the Nabi Salah festival was becoming, like the other two celebrations, more politically intense, peaking in the Arab Revolt of 1936–39.[88] Ramle's former

---

83 Neil Jarman discusses this symbolic (Protestant) unity which is created through the Twelfth of July Parade in Belfast, as well as its inscription of identity into the physical geography. Jarman, *Material Conflicts*, pp. 89, 98.

84 Drori, 'Nabi Salah', pp. 18–19.

85 Talmor, 'Back to Nabi Mussa', p. 63; Sasson, 'The Ziyara', p. 211; Drori, 'Nabi Salah', p. 18.

86 Uri M. Kupferschmidt, *The Supreme Muslim Council: Islam Under the British Mandate for Palestine* (Leiden, 1987), p. 234.

87 Dancho, 'Nabi Mussa Rituals'.

88 Kupferschmidt, *The Supreme Muslim Council*, p. 234; Zilberman, 'Renewal of Pilgrimage', p. 106.

inhabitant Maliha al-Khayri (born 1924) records the participation of the Palestinian Muslim leader and Mufti of Jerusalem, Haj Amin al-Husseini, in the Nabi Salah festivities, probably around this time:

> Haj Amin al-Husseini would arrive from Jerusalem on a train, and alight at the new market station. We used to prepare flags for him, with every town or village carrying its local flag. Everyone would celebrate his arrival in the train station with [national] songs.

Upon his arrival in town, Al-Husseini used to ride a horse to the White Tower compound; when he finally reached his destination he changed his outfit into a ritual dress of green and gold before entering the compound.[89]

In the early 1930s, Jewish fears of the Nabi Rubin festivities led to pressure by Zionist leaders on the British authorities to arrange for a temporary police station to operate during the month-long celebrations in the nearby Jewish Beyt Chanan.[90] In Nabi Mussa, the authorities' reaction to presumably similar anxieties, as well as its own concern, was to forbid mass assemblies: around 1938–39, only representatives of some of the most distinguished Muslim families were allowed to pray at the site.[91] The Nabi Salah celebrations came to be seen as threatening to Jews due to the high number of participants and Arab leaders' tendency to take advantage of the event to voice their national agendas. This procession was viewed by outsiders (Jews and British alike) as an alarming assertion of Muslim power. By pressuring the already concerned British authorities, the Yishuv managed to downscale these celebrations during the 1930s.

Following 1948 the Nabi Salah celebrations changed their

89   Interview with Maliha al-Khayri (dated 18 March 2005), as part of the Oral History Project of the Palestine Remembered website (http://www.palestineremembered.com/OralHistory/Interviews-Listing/Story1151.html#al-Ramla).
90   Sasson, 'The Ziyara', p. 217.
91   Dancho, 'Nabi Mussa Rituals'; Zilberman, 'Renewal of Pilgrimage', p. 106.

nature. Military administration tried to protect and enable religious practice in Ramla between July 1948 and July 1949, with Zusman Jawitz, Military Governor of Ramla and Lydda, attempting to clarify this matter in a report from October: 'every citizen was given a chance to run his life according to his religious practice, subject to the framework of security requirements only'.[92] Another concern of the military administration of Ramla was the physical maintenance of the town's holy places. 'One of the first worries', reported Jawitz, 'was the securing and guarding of all the holy places of all religious denominations with no exception [...]. This was done successfully [...]. All holy sites of all denominations have been preserved and are intact and fit for use'.[93] A survey from December found Ramla's mosques in good condition; the only exception was Nabi Salah's tomb, found to desecrated.[94] In the next few months, access to the White Mosque compound was denied, with the excuse of preserving the place and protecting it against further sacrilege. Between March and June 1949 (and in ensuing years as well), archaeological digs and repair works were pursued on site.[95] In order to protect the compound archaeologically and against desecration the Military Governor was asked to declare the area 'off limits for all ranks'; soon afterwards a Jewish guard was appointed by the Muslim Department in the Ministry of Religious Affairs.[96]

92 'Monthly Report on the Activities of the Military Governor of Ramle-Lydda from 1 September to 10 October 1948', IDF Archive 1860/1950//31.
93 *Ibid.*
94 'Report on a visit to Sidna Ali, Jalil, Lydda and Ramle', 5 December 1948, IDF Archive 1860/1950//31 [sheet 168].
95 Letter titled 'Transfer of Budget', 28 March 1949, IDF Archive 1860/1950//31 [sheet 248]; letter titled 'Transfer of a Water Pipe in the Territory of the White Mosque in Ramla', 1 June 1949, IDF Archive 1860/1950//31 [sheet 146]; letter titled 'Placing Water Pipes in the Territory of the White Mosque', 25 May 1949, IDF Archive 1860/1950//31 [sheet 147].
96 Letter titled 'Guarding the Square Tower and Excavations', 3 May 1949, IDF Archive 1860/1950//32 [sheet 168]; Report titled 'The Holy Places for Muslims in er-Ramle', July 1949, in Natali Mesika, 'Archaeology in Ramla: Findings Report and Bibliography' (1996)[unpublished, in Hebrew], p. 33. In this report Governor Jawitz and his deputy Hagler were lauded for protecting these sites.

What may have been a sincere wish to protect non-Jewish holy places in town and enable worship in them was perhaps beset by ulterior motives. Jawitz's accommodating policies had to yield to overriding security requirements, resulting in a heavy regulation of worship. In practice, this meant that a group of worshippers that wished to take part in certain prayers was escorted by an armed guard to and from their mosque.[97] Freedom of worship was limited to begin with: during this period, entry was 'strictly forbidden' to some of the Ramla's mosques; others were closed, and license had to be obtained to visit the one operating mosque in town, in which the governor appointed the *muezzin* (who calls for prayer).[98]

Travel was supervised not only in religious contexts. Israeli authorities wished to minimise movement between Arab communities. The 'unnecessary great traffic of Arabs' between Jaffa, Lydda and Ramla needed to be reduced, urged a secret police letter in August 1949, and it was also possibly the constant fear of 'infiltration' (*histanenut*, as entry of Palestinian refugees from across the border was called) that made Israeli authorities reluctant to have Arabs travelling and congregating *en masse*.[99]

It seems as if a double message was conveyed to non-Jewish, especially Muslim, worshipers in Ramla in the immediate aftermath of the war. On the one hand, military administration tried to facilitate religious practice and protect the holy sites; on the other, access was denied to these very places. It could be that encouraging worship was only a means to keep the Arab population and those struggling to protect its interests (such as Ministry of

---

97 'Monthly Report on the Activities of the Military Governor of Ramle-Lydda from 1 September to 10 October 1948', IDF Archive 1860/1950//31.

98 'Report from the Visit to Ramla and Lydda', 10 September 1948, IDF Archive, 1860/1950//31. Around September 1952 the 'recently restored' Great Mosque was (still?) padlocked. 'Note about Ancient Monuments Ramle, Ascalon', ISA, 48//7304/11–gimel lamed.

99 Letter titled 'Jaffa-Lydda-Ramla', 30 August 1949, ISA, 79//7/13—lamed; Letter titled 'A Note for the Inhabitants' from Ramla-Lydda Military Governor to the committees in Ramle, Lydda, and the Train-Station [Neighbourhood] in Lydda, 27 March 1949, IDF Archive 1860/1950//32 [sheet 45].

Religious Affairs) satisfied. It is more probable, however, that there were indeed good intentions of providing freedom of worship as far as it were considered safe to do so. These intentions may have been overlooked in the first few months and years after the war, when Israeli-Jewish dominance had to be asserted. In any case, in the first years of statehood the Nabi Salah procession, with its visible message of Muslim unity and strength, was no longer able to march and reaffirm symbolic ownership of the town's streets. By enforcing this prohibition, Israeli authorities asserted their own domination of Ramla's streets.

In the following years Nabi Salah celebrations became a more subdued, local affair, discreet enough not to require the Israeli authorities' permit, or to enable them to overlook its lack thereof.[100] Yet, in 1961, the Secretary of Ramla's Muslim Committee claimed that Nabi Salah's *maqam* (holy place) has been and still is a pilgrimage site for the people of the area.[101] Presumably, he meant that Nabi Salah's tomb still functioned as a place of worship, albeit without mass celebrations, but by 1964 the event drew enough attention to be reported in *Davar*. In a short article were described the flag-carrying procession that walked Ramla's streets on Friday morning, and the midday prayer at the mosque from which celebrants continued to Nabi Salah's tomb, where they stayed until the afternoon.[102] Were these festivities carried out in defiance of Israeli authorization, or were they legitimated by the authorities? It seems that there has been a gradual process through which authorization, legitimation, prohibition, and the mechanisms that enabled or withheld Nabi Salah celebrations were constructed.

100 I could find no documents to show that either the military administration (July 1948 to July 1949) or the police were requested to authorise such a gathering in the years after the war and until the early 1960s. This was also confirmed by Muhammad Taji, former Head of the Ramla Waqf, in an interview from 3 March 2008.

101 For example, the following files in the ISA, dealing with demonstrations, rallies and gatherings and their relevant requests and permits: 79//2284/30—lamed (1949–50); 79//6/33—lamed (1954–55); 79//189/9–lamed (1958–59); 79//161/11—lamed (1960–61). 'Tour of Ramla and Lydda', 22 December 1961, ISA, 98//6370/8–gimel-lamed.

102 *Davar*, 10 May 1964.

Nabi Salah's full-scale processions were resumed gradually after 1967. Following the Israeli victory Chief of Staff Moshe Dayan revoked all travelling restrictions on the Arab population, which had been in force since 1948.[103] During the late 1970s and early 1980s, Nabi Salah celebrations enjoyed a renaissance.[104] A vivid account from 1985 describes pilgrims arriving from all over Israel: not only Ramla and its environs, but also from Ramallah, Gaza, Jerusalem, Nablus, Hebron, Nazareth, and Haifa. The atmosphere was deliberately non-radical, neither in the religious nor in the political sense. A conscious attempt was made by the organisers to leave out any unwanted nationalistic elements or zealous potential troublemakers; perhaps the large tent, occupied by Israeli police, encouraged this anti-extremist attitude.[105]

These renewed, large-scale, celebrations, however, did not last long. When the first *Intifada* broke in late 1987, Muhammad Taji, Head of the Waqf and organiser of the Nabi Salah procession, was asked by police to see to the crowd's safety and security (by arranging for ambulances, ushers etc.). In those years celebrations attracted about 40,000 people.[106] It may have been also concern for Ramla's Jewish residents, which led the police to apply these new restrictions. Reluctant to be held exclusively responsible for so many people in such a volatile period, the Head of the Waqf appealed to all potential celebrants not to arrive to Ramla. Nowadays no official processions and celebrations are held, although Nabi Salah's resting place is still visited by pilgrims year round.[107]

Nabi Salah procession thus underwent several incarnations over the years, according to the powers which were in control and their agendas. For Muslim celebrants the procession and ensuing

103 Moshe Dayan, *Moshe Dayan: Story of My Life* (NY, 1976), p. 397.
104 Interview with Muhammad Taji, former Head of the Ramla Waqf, 3 March 2008.
105 Drori, 'Nabi Salah', pp. 18–19.
106 Interview with Muhammad Taji, former Head of Waqf in Ramla, 13 January 2008.
107 Interview with Muhammad Taji, former Head of Waqf in Ramla, 13 January 2008; 3 March 2008.

celebrations were meant to revere a prophet; in doing so, they also marked and symbolically appropriated the town's streets, and asserted Muslim identity. In some periods, and at least for some celebrants, the procession and festivities were also designed to propagate political messages. For British authorities and later for the Israeli-Jewish military and civil establishment the same event posed a threat both real and symbolic; consequently, they sought to restrict and marginalise it in various ways, unless they felt secure enough—as after 1967—to allow it.

* * *

The three processions discussed in this chapter converge to highlight Ramla as the unique and complex town it has become after 1948. In this 'mixed' town of various ethnic affiliations, ideological agendas and religious denominations, ever-present notions linked to nationality, class and religion allowed for co-existence but also engendered conflict. Space and identity in Ramla were not always clearly marked and correlated; rather, at least during certain public events, the town could become a relational field in which such notions were simultaneously challenged and ratified.[108]

The processions discussed above took agendas of unison and inclusion to their extreme. They stressed, encouraged and invited an individual assimilation in a collective identity. In the military parade, spectators were encouraged to become as Israeli as the soldiers marching on. In the May Day procession, on the other hand, Jews and Arabs alike were called upon to become part of the unified body of workers. Finally, in the Nabi Salah procession the marchers asserted their belonging to a Muslim collective, as well as their national awareness as Palestinians. The three processions were occasions on which Ramla was pulled out of its usual

---

108 For the theoretical framework of 'relational field' see Daniel Monterescu, 'Estranged Natives and Indigenized Immigrants: A Relational Anthropology of Ethnically Mixed Towns in Israel', *World Development* 39:2 (2011), pp. 270–281.

peripheral marginality to become the temporary centre reported on in newspapers, as they touched on issues that had nationwide resonance.

The three processions also brought to the fore, at times subtly or even unwittingly, issues linked to divergence and exclusion. In that, they demonstrated the ways in which power can be negotiated through space and its symbolic, temporary appropriation. The military parade crossed Ramla from one side to the other demonstrating its threatening capabilities to potential enemies, but also leaving a mess for the locals to clean up. May Day processions, which brought conflictual issues linked to class and nationality to the town's main street, triggered tension between Jews and Arabs. Finally, Nabi Salah procession along its traditional route was perceived as a threat by the Israeli authorities and was consequently marginalised. Processions were thus used and misused in the ongoing Israelisation process of Ramla during the 1950s. They also highlighted its general layout and planning, to which we now turn.

CHAPTER FIVE

The Old and the New City: Segregation, Incorporation and Expansion

In a leaflet published by the municipality in 1952, Ramla's role as a melting pot is stressed throughout. The municipality's aim, announced Mayor Meir Melamed is

> [T]o turn new immigrants from diasporas with different past, tradition, education, cultural levels, [and] Jewish-Zionist background, into permanent residents of status and self-recognition, who carry a shared burden, [and] to make them into citizens of equal rights and obligations towards their city.[1]

Who exactly was an Israeli citizen and who had the right to become one, was decided in the 1952 Nationality Law, which granted Israeli citizenship by right of return (for Jews), residence (non-Jewish denizens), birth, or naturalisation; immediate nationality was given only to 40% of the Arab population, creating in the

---

1 *Ramla Bevinyana Uvehitpatchuta* (Ramla, 1952), p. 7.

[167]

process various legal complications to arise in the years to come, especially in the context of Israel's Arab minority.[2]

Citizenship, however, is determined not only at nation-state level; cities, too, 'are places where the very meaning, content and extent of citizenship are being made and remade', where the sociological (or informal) spheres of citizenship evolve next to its legal (or formal) rights and obligations.[3] Moreover, citizenship is the continually changing product of struggles and power relations—Engin F. Isin's 'genealogy of citizenship'—rather than an easily defined universal institution.[4] Ramla's Arab community resented the concealed message of inequality and discrimination in the 1952 law, and was preoccupied from as early as April of that year with organising gatherings and collecting donations in order to encourage people to act against it.[5] They were not alone: days before the law's enactment leaflets were distributed also in Nazareth, calling to act against it by sending protesting telegrams and letters to the Knesset; another mode of action was a one-day business strike.[6]

Despite their lack of 'Jewish-Zionist background', Ramla's Arab residents were part of the town's human matrix, even if this was not touted in the municipal leaflet cited above. The city's physical layout included the Old City area (also known as *sakne* or the 'ghetto'), where Ramla's Arabs were concentrated, together with impoverished Jewish families, themselves mostly of Arab

2   Much was written on the Nationality Law since its enactment in April 1952. See, for example, Haim Margalit, 'Enactment of a Nationality Law in Israel', *The American Journal of Comparative Law* 2:1 (1953), pp. 63–66; Sabri Jiryis, 'Domination by Law', *Journal of Palestine Studies* 11:1 (1981), pp. 67–92 (esp. pp. 78–83).

3   Engin F. Isin and Myer Siemiatycki, 'Fate and Faith: Claiming Urban Citizenship in Immigrant Toronto', CERIS Working Paper Series, Working Paper no. 8 (June 1999), pp. 1–30 (pp. 5–7).

4   Engin Isin, 'Who is the New Citizen? Towards a Genealogy', *Citizenship Studies* 1:1 (1997), pp. 115–131.

5   Yair Boymal, 'Ekronot Mediniyut Ha'aflaya klapey Ha'aravim BeIsrael', in *Iyunim Bitkumat Israel: Studies in Zionism, the Yishuv and the State of Israel* 16 (2006), pp. 391–410 (pp. 396–397); 'Arab Response to the Law of Nationality' (letter from Ramla's police station), 24 May 1952, ISA, 79//7/2—lamed.

6   *Davar*, 13 and 15 July 1952.

descent. In a brief note, Melamed assured the leaflet's readers that 'obviously' (*muvan me'elav*), all Ramla's Arab citizens enjoy equal rights and obligations.[7] Was this ideal achieved and manifested in the city's overall planning or were residential pockets part of the urban landscape, hinting at some level of segregation? Alternatively, can we typify Ramla as a site of spatial heteronomy, in which the national-ethnic territorial logic is dynamic rather than exclusory?[8]

Pollution vs. Cleanliness

David Sibley draws our attention to the centrality of dirt in the discourse of exclusion, 'as a signifier of imperfection and inferiority'.[9] The theoretical-structuralist approach of anthropologist Mary Douglas in her now classic work *Purity and Danger* (1966) saw impurity as the result of anomalous deviation from accepted order and structure. This out-of-boundaries irregularity was seen to embody danger, and therefore needed to be separated, demarcated and cleansed. Sibley further stresses the validity of these ideas in a society feeling that its identity is threatened,[10] as was Israeli society in the 1950s.

Tour guides from the 1920s and 1930s described the difference between the new Jewish neighbourhoods of Haifa and its older Arab quarters, stressing the dichotomy between the neglected Arab town and its beatified Jewish counterpart.[11] Juxtaposition of Jaffa and Tel Aviv around this period (as after 1948) manifested similar perceptions of an existing dichotomy between Jaffa's filth, ugliness and lack of aesthetic beauty, and the cleanliness and healthiness

7   *Ramla Bevinyana*, p. 8.
8   Daniel Monterescu, 'Estranged Natives and Indigenized Immigrants: A Relational Anthropology of Ethnically Mixed Towns in Israel', *World Development* 39:2 (2011), pp. 270–281.
9   David Sibley, *Geographies of Exclusion* (London, 1995), p. 14.
10 *Ibid.*, p. 38.
11 Yfaat Weiss, *A Confiscated Memory: Wadi Salib and Haifa's Lost Heritage*, trans. Avner Greenberg (NY, 2011), p. 64.

of beautiful Tel Aviv.[12] In the town of Lydda, on the other hand, the dichotomy of clean/dirty was articulated not exclusively in geographical terms, but also chronologically: in a municipal leaflet from 1952 the town was described as changing from an underdeveloped, neglected town into a clean and organised one.[13]

In Ramla too, the Old Ramle and the New Ramla became a recurring theme in the sources describing the town after 1948. The town's occupation was seen as a chronological watershed that helped pinpoint ideas on pollution and cleanliness, linked also to issues of backwardness and modernity. Whereas the discourse of dirty/clean and old/new had a chronological aspect, it also had a spatial dimension, contrasting the Old City area with Ramla's high street and with some of the new neighbourhoods built in the north-west of town.

The chronological dichotomy between a pre-1948 dirty and primitive Arab Ramle and a post-1948 clean and modern Israeli Ramla was expressed already in a municipality report which hailed the first new immigrants in town for coming 'to inhabit and revive the dilapidated town of Ramle' and described the first Israeli municipality as forced 'to purify the town of filth'.[14] Two years later, the municipality's goal was to plan 'a modern organised and clean town', presumably in contrast to the old and backward Arab town.[15] We find this differentiation also in essays and poems written by Ramla's schoolchildren in 1958, where they refer to the small dusty town that Ramle had used to be, as opposed to the sprawling beautiful new city they knew.[16] By 1967, this view

---

12 Mark Levine, 'Planning to Conquer: Modernity and Its Antinomies in the "New-Old Jaffa"', in *Constructing A Sense of Place: Architecture and the Zionist Discourse*, Haim Yacobi (ed.)(Aldershot, 2004), pp. 192–224 (pp. 194, 202).

13 Haim Yacobi, 'Planning, Control and Spatial Protest: The Case of the Jewish-Arab Town of Lydd/Lod', in *Mixed Towns, Trapped Communities: Historical Narratives, Spatial Dynamics, Gender Relations and Cultural Encounters in Palestinian-Israeli Towns*, D. Monterescu and D. Rabinowitz (eds.)(Aldershot, 2007), pp. 135–155 (p. 142).

14 '*Iryat Ramla: Sikum Pe'ulot Ha'irya* (for the period between July 1949 and September 1950), p. 4.

15 *Ramla Bevinyana*, p. 21.

16 *Yediot Ramla* (Ramla, 1958), last page.

had already become Ramla's foundation myth, a sort of common knowledge: 'From a pitiful Arab town [Ramla] has become a beautiful city'.[17]

With Ramla's gradual growth and development, the chronological perspective slowly gave way to a spatial emphasis on the fundamental difference between the two 'Ramlas'. It may have also taken an outsider to notice this: Emmanuel Porat wrote in *Maariv* (18 August 1959) on a Ramla made of alleys, ruins and dust that existed beyond the beauty and cleanliness of the high street. Another journalist, writing in *Herut* (20 January 1960) similarly commented on the disparity between the fancy buildings on the tree-lined high street and the litter, derelict houses and dangerous empty wells of the Old City.[18] The sharp contrast between the old and new town was also stressed in a social survey conducted in town around 1968:

> Whoever crosses Ramla on their way from Jerusalem to Tel Aviv wonders as to the city's dilapidated appearance— derelict houses about to collapse, neglect, stench, scattered hawkers' stands and unpaved roads. However, this is not the true image of Ramla. In the city's outskirts, new housing projects were built and well-kept clean areas appeared.[19]

Derelict Ramla depicted here was only a mirage. 'The true image of Ramla', communicated in order to fight the city's stereotype as dirty, was rather that of the recently built modern neighbourhoods, magically 'popping' out of nowhere. Nevertheless, the dilapidated houses of the Old City were harsh reality for some.[20]

17   *Ramla: Bita'on Iryat Ramla* 3 (Ramla, April 1967), p. 5.
18   *Herut*, 20 January 1960.
19   Chagit Chovav, *Ramla—Ha'ir Ha'atika—Seker Chevrati* (1968), p. 1.
20   *Ramla—Seker Likrat Shikum* (part I)(April 1970).

Residential Patterns

Despite the fact that the right for housing has not been formally recognised in the Israeli law system, the government nevertheless has traditionally seen itself responsible for housing, particularly of Jewish new immigrants but also of more veteran Jewish population.[21] The principle at the core of this welfare policy was defending weaker elements within society from exposure to the 'real' (i.e. private) housing market. By providing subsidised accommodation, the state facilitated rent or even purchase of flats and houses by those who otherwise would not have been able to do so.[22]

Israel's housing policy from the 1950s (and, in a way, until today) carried also political overtones. The state's dual goal—absorption of new immigrants and geographical dispersion of the population– contributed in creating a new reality, in which Jews were directed to settle areas of thin Jewish presence or Arab majority. The state's housing policy was therefore also a means to display and achieve Israel's sovereignty and territorial control. At the same time, the state's socio-democratic housing vision was implemented in a differential manner, bolstering some while excluding others. Whereas the veteran Jewish population (mostly Ashkenazi, of European origin) had had various funding solutions and housing options in the centre of the country and in the cities, Mizrachi new immigrants (from Middle Eastern, Asian and North-African countries) were directed, following the goal of population dispersion, to more peripheral areas. Israel's Arab population was almost totally excluded from the state's scheme of affordable housing.[23]

Ironically, the first to be allocated a new residential area in Ramla were the Arab residents left in town in the aftermath

---

21 Lu-Yon and Kalush, *Diyur BeIsrael: Mediniyut Ve'i- shivyon* (Tel Aviv, 1994), p. 1.

22 Zeev Rosenhek, *The Housing Policy Toward the Arabs in Israel in the 1950s-1970s* (Jerusalem, 1996)[in Hebrew], pp. 7–8.

23 Rosenhek, *The Housing Policy*, pp. 9–16; Lu-Yon and Kalush, *Diyur BeIsrael*, pp. 2–6, 32.

of Ramle's occupation. Before 1948 Ramle's original Arab community was concentrated mainly to the south-east of the Jaffa-Jerusalem road which cut through town, forming its high street. Several residential pockets existed also to the north of this road; others stretched westwards.[24] The town's occupation and ensuing military regime restricted this community into a small area confined between four streets in the centre of town (today known as Herzl Blvd., and Bialik, Jabotinsky and Hama'apilim Sts.); this area came to be known as the *sakne*, or 'ghetto'. Residential segregation enforced in Jaffa after the war has been explained by Arnon Golan as aiming not only to separate Arabs from Jews, but also to ensure potential accommodation for newly arriving Jews.[25] This may have been the purpose of residential restriction in Ramla as well.

Outside this fenced-off Arab residential area 'abandoned' Arab houses were promptly appropriated by the state. As seen in Chapter One, the houses in this area, which became known to the Jews as the Old City, were subsequently occupied by the first wave of (mainly Ashkenazi) Jewish immigrants, as well as by Israelis employed in town (as teachers or police officers). Whereas few of these were practically palaces, at times producing what the geographer Amiram Gonen referred to as 'mismatch' between house and tenant,[26] others were much simpler buildings, with facilities such as bathroom or kitchen often located outdoors; under these conditions, women resorted to creative solutions such as cooking on the wide stone window-seals, for lack of a proper kitchen space.[27] Crowded living conditions were prevalent among Jewish immigrants settled in Arab houses—in Jerusalem, for instance, despite the Absorption Department's recommendation

---

24 AA Er Ramle [1] 135–145.7 1931 (plan I, II, III, IV)(1:1250); AA 45 1947 (1:2,500) sheets 1 and 2.

25 Arnon Golan, *Wartime Spatial Changes: Former Arab Territories Within the State of Israel, 1948–1950* (Beer Sheva, 2001)[in Hebrew], pp. 94–95

26 Amiram Gonen, *Between City and Suburb: Urban Residential Patterns and Processes in Israel* (Aldershot, Hants., 1995), p. 51.

27 Serene Husseini Shahid, *Jerusalem Memories*, trans. Mali Baruch (Tel Aviv, 2006)[in Hebrew][orig. 1999], p. 149.

to settle two or three people in a single room, in the spring of 1949 rooms were shared by four to five family members; there were also cases of six or seven people inhabiting a single room.[28]

With the arrival of new immigration waves, which now included also Jews from Arab countries, the town's housing reserves were exhausted. Temporary accommodation was provided by the municipality and by Amidar (the national affordable housing agency founded in 1949), in the form of wooden huts in empty lots within the Old City. These included two rooms with outdoor kitchens and toilets that were either bought or rented from Amidar.[29] *Ma'abarot* (pl. of *ma'abara*, or transition camps) on the outskirts of town provided the cheapest solution—tents and huts made of wood, textile and tin. Ramla's *Ma'abara Bet* ("B") existed since late 1951 and absorbed 500 immigrant families from Iraq, North Africa, Iran, Turkey and the Balkans; *Ma'abara Gimel* ("C") was founded in late 1952, with the dismantling of tents in *Ma'abara Alef* ("A"). It was home to 210 immigrant families from Yemen, Iraq, Turkey, and North Africa.[30]

This temporary solution sometimes became more permanent than anticipated; some of the tenants spent more than seven years in the *ma'abara*, suffering from unsanitary environment, lack of roads, pests, and dangerous pits.[31] In fact, as sociologist Moshe Lissak commented, an entire generation 'got stuck' in these 'temporary' dwellings.[32] In 1950 Tiberias, for instance, a *ma'abara* was established where thousands of new immigrants resided; five years down the line, 798 families still inhabited the *ma'abara's* tin shacks.[33] There were worse examples still: the

28 Arnon Golan, *Wartime Spatial Changes*, p. 56.
29 Pinchas Frank, *Proyekt Shituf Toshavim Bebinuy Upinuy: Sikum Mechkar Pe'ula* (Tel Aviv University, c. 1970–1971[?]), p. 18.
30 *Yediot Ramla* (Ramla, 1958), p. 14.
31 Minutes of Town Council Meeting, 31 May 1957, ISA, 50//2024/26–gimel; Minutes of Town Council Meeting, 29 June 1960, ISA, 50//1909/12–gimel.
32 Moshe Lissak, *The Mass Immigration in the Fiftees: The Failure of the Melting Pot Policy* (Jerusalem, 1999)[in Hebrew], pp. 26–33.
33 *Mituv Tverya: Dapim Lecheker Tverya*, Rephael Yankelevitch (ed.)(Jerusalem, 1988), pp. 63–64.

three *ma'abraot* which had been built in Ashkelon (formerly Arab Majdal) in 1950 and 1951 were dismantled finally only during the 1960s.[34] In Ramla, *ma'abarot* were also used to house people vacated from 'dangerous houses' in the Old City (see below);[35] at the same time, people who left the *ma'abarot* came to reside in old Arab houses within the Old City, creating a vicious circle, with people moving between bad and worse living conditions.[36]

In order to provide permanent and adequate housing solutions, three public housing projects were built on the edge of Ramla's Old City during the late 1950s and early 1960s: Agaf Hashikun (1957–8), Bilu (1960–61) and *Taf-Zain* (1963–4). These were designated for 'social cases' and *ma'abarot* evacuees.[37] During the 1950s and 1960s public accommodation was built not only in Ramla but throughout the country—these were Israel's heydays of construction for public purposes. Carried out either by the Labour Ministry's Housing Department or by public housing companies (such as Amidar, Shikun or Rasko) that operated under governmental supervision and funding and were therefore state subcontractors, public building was in full swing.[38]

The construction of Ramla's new housing projects did not require demolition of any earlier buildings—they were built on a wide plot referred to in pre-1948 maps as 'El Bustan' ('the garden').[39] New neighbourhoods built in other areas, such as Neve David or Sprinzak (both founded in the later 1950s), hinted at the direction in which municipal planning progressed: the north-western parts of town (fig. 10). Whereas Neve David was built

34 N. Gal (Gale), 'From Rural to Urban Center: Ashkelon as a Case Study of Israeli Socio-Regional Changes from the Establishment of the State of Israel to the Mid-Ninetees' in *Ashkelon Bride of the South: Studies in the History of Ashkelon from the Middle Ages to the End of the Twentieth Century*, Z. Safrai and N. Sagiv (eds.)(Ashkelon, 2002), pp. 213–232 (p. 222).
35 See, for example, Minutes from Town Council Meeting, 30 March 1959, ISA, 50//2028/13–gimel.
36 Shabtay Tevet, 'Ir Olim La'ad', *Haaretz*, 19 October 1956.
37 Chovav, *Ramla—Ha'ir Ha'atika*, pp. 9–10.
38 Rosenhek, *The Housing Policy*, p. 11.
39 AA Er Ramle [1] 135–145.7 1931 (plans III and IV); AA 45 1947 (1:2500), sheet 2.

on land on which olive trees had been cultivated up to 1947, Sprinzak was erected on a pre-1948 residential foundation already in place.[40] Both new neighbourhoods included different types of public housing—for new immigrants, for veterans, for state employees and so on—and expanded local residential options by enabling the renting or purchase of a flat, with relatively flexible funding terms.

Fig. 10: Fritz Cohen, Appartment Houses in Ramla's New Neighbourhoods, with Cows Grazing in the Foreground, 1 January 1962 (Courtesy of the GPO).

The new neighbourhoods triggered further change in Ramla's residential patterns, which had not only spatial, but also ethnic consequences: whereas the new neighbourhoods became identified with the higher socio-economic status of upwardly mobile Ashkenazi Jews, the Old City area became, and has remained to

40   AA 45 1947 (1:2500), sheet 1.

this day, the residential area of lower-income families of Mizrachi or Oriental Jews and Arabs.[41] In the classical Oriental tradition, Ramla's Old City in the east came to represent backwardness and uncleanness, whereas the new neighbourhoods in the west were made into the epitome of European modernity.

In one of his articles on Ramla, journalist Shabtay Tevet summed up the situation neatly by claiming that there were two classes in Ramla, living in different types of accommodation and in separate parts of town. Whereas the first group, which no longer needed social support and lived in better houses, consisted of immigrants from European countries, the other one, relying on welfare and living in poorer conditions, consisted of immigrants from Asian and African countries.[42] Despite writing only a month and a half after the murder of Arab café owner Hallak by two young Iraqi Jews (see Chapter Two), Tevet failed to mention the third important element in Ramla's society—the Arab community.

Following Aziza Khazzoom's analysis of segregation in Israeli development towns in the 1950s, we find two models of behaviour associated with ethnicity, capital and period of residence in the country and region: one is of 'movers', who change their housing conditions and location, another is of 'stayers', who remain where housing had been allocated for them. [43] In this sense, many of the Ashkenazi Jews in Ramla were 'movers', leaving the original Old City housing which they had been given to the new neighbourhoods or even to other towns. On the other hand, all the Arabs and many of the Oriental Jews were 'stayers' who continued to suffer from substandard living conditions in the Old City.[44] This difference between Ashkenazi 'movers' and Mizrachi 'stayers' was in effect a national phenomenon typical of other formerly Arab or mixed cities. Jewish households who had been originally settled in

41 Chovav, *Ramla—Ha'ir Ha'atika*, pp. 19–20.
42 Shabtay Tevet, 'Hachaiym Vehametim BeRamla', *Haaretz*, 22 Ocotber 1956.
43 Aziza Khazzoom, 'Did the Israeli State Engineer Segregation? On the Placement of Jewish Immigrants in Development Towns in the 1950s', *Social Forces* 84:1 (2005), pp. 115–134 (p. 121).
44 Chovav, *Ramla—Ha'ir Ha'atika*, pp. 18–20.

Haifa's Lower City left the area and moved instead to other parts of town which offered improved housing conditions and higher social standing. Similarly, Jewish residents of Jaffa's older quarters, who had been given the opportunity, preferred to move out of the area and into the suburbs of neighbouring Bat-Yam or Holon, or even farther away, to the northern neighbourhoods of Tel Aviv.[45]

Even at the end of the 1960s, Jewish population in Ramla's Old City area was still characterised as suffering from a process of negative selection, in which the more successful elements were leaving, whereas the weakened stayed.[46] Was it equally possible for an Ashkenazi Jew, a Mizrachi Jew, a Muslim or a Christian Arab to leave the Old City for one of the new neighbourhoods? Was this spatial segregation a result of municipal planning, capitalist market demands, or personal preferences?

'The geographic division also inheres social division', emphasised Maki's representative in one of Ramla's municipality council meetings in 1959: 'we have given better service to those who are in better condition and neglected those who are less well-off.'[47] No doubt, municipal planning and resource distribution had a huge impact on the city's layout. After 1948, neighbourhoods were built in hitherto thinly populated areas. In Neve David, for instance, at the northwest part of town, Rachel Ben Zvi Yana'it (wife of President Ben Zvi), found white houses with gardens, and flowers that 'make one forget the busy street'.[48] The civic centre that provided municipal services for both new and old neighbourhoods was located centrally, on the main street, west of the old Arab centre. Shopping and leisure options, and especially gardens, as discussed in Chapter Three, tended to crawl towards the north-west in order to cater for the new neighbourhoods. While remaining fairly central in terms of the town's overall planning, they were nevertheless growing distant for Old City residents.

45 Gonen, *Between City and Suburb*, p. 95, 196–197.
46 *Seker Likrat Shikum* (part II).
47 Minutes of Town Council Meeting, 5 February 1959, ISA, 50//2028/13–gimel.
48 Rachel Ben-Zvi Yana'it, 'Ramla', *Davar*, 9 April 1954.

From a different perspective, the Old City was significant in that it offered a social space that facilitated interactions among different ethno-cultural groups.[49] In the market Jews and Arabs transacted commercially, providing at least a theoretical opportunity for social interaction. A contact zone of a different type was created through the thriving local music scene during the late 1960s. Young Jewish men and women, mostly of Mizrachi origin or proletarian background, flocked to listen to Rock n' Roll bands in Ramla's Old City.[50] For those who could not become part of the cultural hegemony of the period, Ramla's Old City and this particular music genre provided not only a refuge, but also a means to express defiance.[51] The liminal character of the area attracted those who did not feel part of the establishment, and the unique location created a space that was betwixt and between.[52]

The following description of the Calypso Club in town sheds light on its attractiveness for those wishing to redefine their social identity through 'hip' music:

The place is located between a mosque, an Arab café with scattered stools and a church with a tall bell tower. Narrow and unpaved alleys meander from here within the crumbling walls of the Old City; in the near corner, Shalom Konstantino's butcher shop is open till late in the evening...; the hair salon opposite the club is also open, and a last-minute shave is given to young dandies rushing to the dance floor. The Arab café owner turns up the radio to full volume, but the Oriental tune is knocked out by the wild shake beat already on the first round.[53]

49 L.M. Pratt, 'Arts of the Contact Zone', in *Ways of Reading*, D. Bartholomae and A. Petroksky (eds.)(NY, 1999).

50 Nissan Shor, *Dancing with Tears in Our Eyes: History of Club and Discotheque Culture in Israel* (Tel Aviv, 2008)[in Hebrew], pp. 74–75.

51 *Ibid.*, p. 81.

52 Victor Turner, *The Forest of Symbols: Aspects of Ndembu Ritual* (NY, 1967), Chapter 4.

53 *Haaretz Supplement*, 17 March 1967.

This was an open-ended place of somewhat exotic surrounding and indefinite hours, and clubs such as the Calypso, Pe'er or HaKarish were located in this formerly Arab architectural and socio-cultural environment.

Despite this location, power relations remained rigidly asymmetrical: not only was the club music louder than the 'Oriental tune', but Arab youngsters were not welcome in Old City clubs. They could only sit in the nearby Arab café, and stare with envy.[54] As a contact zone, Ramla's Old City thus facilitated only a limited degree of interaction without challenging current power structure. It was a very different contact zone than the one Deborah Bernstein identifies in Mandate Tel Aviv during the 1930s. Tel Aviv's beach front, she notes, was 'a multifaceted space', frequented by thousands of people—locals (Jews and Arabs) and foreigners (British and of other nationalities) alike—especially during the summer. Cafés around the border between Tel Aviv and Jaffa were another contact zone. In them various borders were crossed—those of gender, nationality, ethnicity and class. In Tel Aviv-Jaffa's contact zones barriers elaborately erected in other arenas were subverted and dismantled.[55] In Ramla's Old City, on the other hand, power relations were merely reproduced.

Although important urban locales such as the marketplace (and its cafés, as described in Chapter Two) and central bus station remained in the town's pre-1948 centre, it was clear that the modern, Israeli Ramla was heading north-westwards, leaving its Old City behind. We might even suggest that these locales, together with growing industrial areas, were located around the south-eastern end of town exactly because they created a focus for dirt, noise, and even 'social perversions'[56] which befitted an area already identified with the city's Arab past and with its uncleanness. In fact, of course, their location only contributed to the area's ongoing deterioration. The Old City was becoming

---

54   *Ibid.*
55   Deborah Bernstein, *Women on the Margins: Gender and Nationalism in Mandate Tel Aviv* (Jerusalem, 2008)[in Hebrew], Chapter 2.
56   Chovav, *Ramle-Ha'ir Ha'atika: Seker Chevrati* (1968), p. 43.

more and more segregated, despite being part of the town's urban mould.[57] It was seen as a thorn in Ramla's side, and its 'real' incorporation by modern Ramla could have been possible only if it were to give up its latter-day characteristics and be purified, transformed and modernised.[58]

Demolition and Rehabilitation

So-called 'hazardous' or 'unstable' houses in the Old City became an issue that 'disturb[ed] the town elders' peace of mind' over the 1950s and 1960s, and was made synonymous with the Old City's negative image.[59] Legal residence and squatting in old Arab houses, which started collapsing in 1949–50, triggered the establishment of a committee that disqualified hazardous buildings.[60] The harsh winter of 1951, in which dozens of Old City houses collapsed, made matters even more urgent.[61] Demolition proceedings could be initiated by the municipality, Amidar or the tenants themselves, if one of four conditions obtained: the house lacked ventilation, repairing it was deemed more costly than the compensation to the vacated tenants, it had serious cracks, or it was in danger of immediate collapse.[62] Things were not so simple though, since,

57 In her report of 1968, Hagit Chovav suggested treating the Old City not as a separate ecological unit, but as an integral part of the general urban structure. Chovav, *Ramla—Ha'ir Ha'atika*, p. 2.
58 See also Kalush and Lu-Yon, 'Habayit Haleumi Veha'bayit Ha'ishi: Tafkid Hashikun Hatziburi Be'itzuv Hamerchav', in *Space, Land, Home*, Yehouda Shenhav (ed.)(Jerusalem, 2003), pp. 166–198 (p. 176).
59 *Mehana'asa Ba'ir*, p. 5. See also various municipal and national discussions on this issue, for example: Report of the Committee for Evacuation of Dilapidated Houses in Ramla, 20 December 1951, ISA, 56//2211/20–gimel; Minutes of Town Council Meeting hosting the Minister of the Interior, 31 May 1957, ISA, 50//2024/26–gimel; Minutes of Town Council Meeting, 20 August 1959, ISA, 50//2033/6–gimel; Minutes of Town Council Meeting, 31 August 1964, ISA, 50//2632/8– gimel.
60 *Iryat Ramla: Sikum Pe'ulot Ha'irya*, p. 20.
61 *Yediot Ramla* (Ramla, 1958), p. 5; *Iryat Ramla: Sikum Pe'ulot Ha'irya*, p. 20; *Haaretz*, 16 December 1951; *Haaretz*, 21 December 1951.
62 Frank, *Proyekt Shituf Toshavim*, pp. 27–28.

on the one hand, residents of hazardous houses refused to be evacuated to the *ma'abara* unless a more permanent housing option was offered, and, on the other hand, houses were seldom demolished following the municipality's initiative since it was struggling to provide permanent housing to potential evacuees.[63]

Returning to Douglas' ideas on impurity, defilement needs to be separated, demarcated and cleansed for society to deal with it successfully. The designation of Ramla's Old City as dirty and primitive had another aspect—that of the national and municipal drive to purify it, and, at some point in the future, re-incorporate it into town. Symbolically, purification meant the disappearance of Arab presence in Ramla; since that was obviously not a viable option, another possible solution was partial evasion of Arab architecture, at least that perceived as old, derelict, primitive and hazardous. What complicated matters even further, of course, was the presence of Oriental Jews in the Old City. They were also seen as requiring 'purification', which was supposed to eradicate Arab elements in their existence and transform them into 'real' Jews, 'shake away' their primitiveness in order to fit them into the Israeli-Jewish (read Ashkenazi) society.[64] In light of the difficulty to be rid of the Arabness of the Old City inhabitants (whether Jews or non-Jews), planners had to settle with fighting Arab architecture. David Harvey termed the process of 'forced devaluation or destruction of past assets in order to make way for the new' *creative destruction*:

> The image of 'creative destruction' is very important to understanding modernity precisely because it derived from practical dilemmas that forced the implementation of the modernist project. How could a new world be created, after all, without destroying much that had gone before? You simply cannot make an omelette without

---

63 *Ibid.*, p. 30.
64 See Beni Nurieli's article on the Mizrachi Jews in Lydda's Old City. 'Hayehudim Ha'aravim Baghetto BeLod, 1950–1959', *Theoriya Uvikoret* 26 (2005), pp. 13–42.

breaking eggs, as a whole line of modernist thinkers from Goethe to Mao have noted.[65]

The idea of creative destruction fitted well Zionism's modernist utopias; to these was added, as noted above, an urge to purify and de-Arabise the living space of mixed cities.

Plans to demolish and then rebuild parts of Ramla's Old City were made, particularly in the aftermath of the 1965 enactment of a law, which established an inter-departmental authority whose role was to initiate and plan the evacuation, rebuilding and rehabilitation of slums and poor neighbourhoods; it received the title *Pinuy-Binuy* or 'Evacuation-Construction'. In a way, this term euphemized the process it encapsulated, refraining from including any wording pointing at destruction of existing housing units in the process; it denoted instead an almost magical transformation—straightforward and sterile—while skipping the more destructive stages of actual implementation *in situ*.

Surveys were conducted in Ramla in the late 1960s at the request of the Ministry of Housing, in order to evaluate the current situation and suggest ways to rehabilitate this part of town; also, *Pinuy-Binuy* informed Ramla's municipality in September 1969 of its intention to declare the Old City a rehabilitation area.[66] It was clear that the old and dirty 'Other' Ramla needed to give way to the new Ramla, metamorphose in order to survive. The national renewal project, as Gila Menahem has suggested, acted as an ideological declaration, aiming at Israelising the communities that were part of it, and reflecting, in effect, the Jewish-Arab core conflict.[67]

These rehabilitation plans had more than just a symbolic

---

65 David Harvey, *The Condition of Postmodernity* (Cambridge, Mass., 1990), pp. 230, 16.

66 Physical and social surveys such as *Ramla: Seker Likrat Shikum* (1970); Chovav, *Ramla—Ha'ir Ha'atika* (1968); Pinchas Frank, *Proyekt Shituf Toshavim* (1970–71[?]), esp. p. 45.

67 Gila Menahem, 'Arab Citizens in an Israeli City: Action and Discourse in Public Programmes', *Ethnic and Racial Studies* 21:3 (1998), pp. 545–557.

motivation: the land on which the Old City stood, which most of
it was nationalised after 1948,[68] was valuable. Rehabilitation in
the framework of a *Pinuy-Binuy* project would have entailed the
construction of high-standard private and public flats, and inflated
land values.[69] In effect, despite much concern and probably some
good intentions, neither the municipality nor the Ministry of
Housing materialised any of the comprehensive rehabilitation
plans, and no budget was allocated.[70]

Ramla's Old City rehabilitation drive had also social welfare
motivations. In 1967 the area was populated by about 1,700 Jewish
families (among them 81% immigrants from Arab countries
and only 19% from Europe), and 300 Arab families (about 200
Christian, the rest Muslim).[71] 'The problem of demolishing the
derelict buildings in the Old City', argued Yehuda Stein, Ramla's
Mayor in 1967, 'is very serious: the residents of the slums need
to be relieved of their distress, and freed of misery and feelings
of deprivation, bitterness and despair [...]'.[72] Many of the Old
City families were indeed poor, and the envisioned *Pinuy-Binuy*
project intended 'to take some of the problematic families out
of the area so that in the future a neighbourhood with a more
balanced structure could be planned'.[73]

Plans to transfer Old City evacuees into permanent housing
projects, however, were almost exclusively intended for Jews; like
in Jaffa, the Old City's Arabs were not allocated flats in the new
neighbourhoods. Similarly on the national level, government
housing policies from 1948 to the late 1970s were not aimed
at the Arab population; the state did not invest in improving

---

68 Amidar was the owner of 493 dunum; 78.5 dunum were public; the *Waqf* held
    35.5 dunum, and another 230 dunum were held by private owners. Chovav,
    Ramla—Ha'ir Ha'atika, p. 5.
69 *Seker Likrat Shikum* (part I), pp. 41–42; *Ramla: Ha'ir Ha'atika—Seker Kalkali
    Le'shikum Rova* (March 1968), pp. 15–16.
70 Frank, *Proyekt Shituf Toshavim*, pp. 43–47. For later plans concerning the Old
    City see Yuval Tamari, *Seker Tichnuni Bashchunot Ha'araviyot Ba'ir* (Jerusalem,
    2005), p. 31.
71 *Ramla: Seker Likrat Shikum* (part II), p. 1.
72 *Ramla: Bita'on Iryat Ramla* 3 (Ramla, April 1967), p. 4.
73 *Ramla—Seker Likrat Shikum* (part I), p. 10.

living conditions in Arab neighbourhoods, nor in building new ones.[74] As in other Arab residential pockets in mixed towns, living conditions for the residing Arab population only worsened gradually. This deterioration was enhanced by the buildings' old age, and by crowdedness, triggered by both natural increase and absence of alternative housing solutions. Although never formally excluded, Israel's Arab citizens have been practically blocked from receiving 'entitlement' (*zaka'ut*) for public housing, since they were not new immigrants nor did they serve in the army.[75] Ramla's Old City thus remained in its derelict state, its low-income Jewish and Arab residents living amidst growing piles of rubble, hazardous houses, and empty lots,[76] with little hope to extricate themselves from the area.

This widening gap between the city's newer and older areas, between north-west and south-east, clean and dirty, peaceful and noisy, was manifested also in the resources allotted by the municipality. As its residents could not invest money of their own, development was much slower in the Old City area, where 'the only landlord was the CAP' which was not too eager to invest in improving existing housing facilities, and where the only sponsor was therefore Ramla's municipality.[77] Although Neve David neighbourhood was still not connected to the central sewage system in 1959 (despite having been completed in the second half of the 1950s), the Old City and public housing projects in its vicinity suffered the most, with the latter quickly deteriorating into slums due to lack of roads, drainage and sewage systems.[78]

This situation was acknowledged by the municipality, although not all its members shared a similar sense of responsibility. In a Town Council meeting in 1958, for example, Maki's representative

74 Lu-Yon and Kalush, *Diyur BeIsrael* (1994), pp. 10–11, 18.
75 Rosenhek, *The Housing Policy*, pp. 11–15.
76 As described in *Seker Likrat Shikum* (part II), p. 9.
77 *Ramla Bevinyana Uvehitpatchuta*, p. 21; Minutes of Town Council meeting, 30 October 1958, ISA, 50//2028/13–gimel.
78 Minutes of Town Council meetings, 30 October 1958 and 30 March 1959, ISA, 50//2028/13–gimel. Chovav, *Ramla—Ha'ir Ha'atika*, p. 11; *Ramla: Seker Likrat Shikum* (part II), p. 8.

recognised the wrongs that had been done over the years: 'we allowed the city to split socially by neglecting some parts of town and leaving them as they were while improving other parts'. His claim was disputed by a Mapai representative, who denied any discrimination and concluded that 'we take care of all of the town's interests.'[79]

Despite several Town Council resolutions to redirect resources to the development of the Old City, it seems that not enough was actually done. In March 1961, Maki's representative vehemently criticised the disparity between the 'Arab neighbourhood' and other parts of town. He protested against the fact that no street was repaired nor renovated there, lack of any sewage system and playgrounds, as well as the annoying presence of litter, especially in comparison with other areas of town; he called on the council to allocate resources to the neighbourhood, 'so that they don't have the feeling we had in other places'.[80]

Ramla's Old City suffered an ongoing neglect, but in other towns similar 'old cities' were straightforwardly destroyed. This was the case in Haifa which saw, during the last weeks of July 1948, its Old City being torn down during 'Operation Shikmona'; Tiberias' Old City was annihilated in three consecutive stages during 1948 and 1949.[81] In other towns the ruination of the old Arab city was a longer process: in Ramla's neighbouring town of Lydda most of the Old City was destroyed by the early 1970s.[82] In Beer Sheva, on the other hand, the Ottoman town was not actively destroyed, but deliberately left to deteriorate; as in

79 *Yediot Ramla* (Ramla, 1958), p. 10.
80 Minutes of Town Council Meeting, 19 March 1961, ISA, 50//1909/12–gimel. See also *Ramla Bevinyana Uvehitpatchuta*, p. 21; Minutes of Town Council Meeting, 30 October 1958, ISA, 50//2028/13–gimel; and 28 January 1960, ISA, 50//2033/6–gimel.
81 Weiss, *Confiscated Memory*, p. 33; Golan, *Wartime Spatial Changes*, pp. 163–166; M. Abbasi, 'The War on the Mixed Cities: The Depopulation of Arab Tiberias and the destruction of Its Old "Sacred" City (1948–1949)', *Holy Land Studies* 7 (2008), pp. 45–80.
82 Haim Yacobi, 'Urban Iconoclasm: The Case of the "Mixed City" of Lod', in *Constructing A Sense of Place: Architecture and the Zionist Discourse*, Haim Yacobi (ed.)(Aldershot, 2004), pp. 165–191 (pp. 180–182).

Ramla, governmental and municipal funds were directed towards new housing projects away from the town's Old City. Against all odds (similarly to Ramla) this did not deter from the economic importance of the older area, which kept functioning as the town's business centre until the 1980s.[83]

In one sphere only was Ramla's earlier incarnation completely erased: street names.[84] The 'ostensibly visible, quintessentially mundane, and seemingly obvious'[85] street names of Ramla testify to the complex process of Israelisation which the town has undergone. In pre-1948 Ramle, street signs marked the town's identity with names such as Deir El Latin (the Catholic monastery), Suleiman Ibn Abed al-Malik (after Ramle's founder), Omar Ibn Abed al-Khatab (the second Sunni Caliph), and Malik Feisal (the British-appointed king of Iraq).[86] Arab leaders and other geographical and ethnic markers were thus used to signify urban space.

The Israeli act of naming and renaming Ramla's streets in the war's aftermath had much more to it than practical concerns. It was a manifestation of new administrative and political authority and an expression of symbolic appropriation. Ramle's conquest instantly wiped out a long-standing geo-historical reality and imposed a new one in its stead. The (re)naming of streets was thus

83 Hadas Shadar, 'Beer Sheva—a Model of the Development of Public Housing in Israel', in *Beer Sheva: The Growth of a City: A Model of the Development of Public Housing in Israel* (Beer Sheva, 2008), pp. 102–78 (sic.); Eitan Cohen, *Beer Sheva: The Fourth City* (Jerusalem, 2006)[in Hebrew], p. 21.

84 Amit Pinchevski and Efraim Torgovnik have studied street names in Ramla from the British Mandate period until today, as part of a research into street names in four Israeli cities. 'Signifying Passages: The Sign of Change in Israeli Street Names', *Media, Culture and Society* 24 (2002), pp. 365–388 (esp. pp. 370–375). For an updated categorization of Ramla's street names see Table 2 in Yoram Bar-Gal, 'Political Symbolization of an Urban Space: Street Naming in Israel', *Horizons in Geography* 33–34 (1992), pp. 119–132 (p. 129)[in Hebrew].

85 Maoz Azaryahu, 'The Power of Commemorative Street Names', *Environment and Planning D: Society and Space* 14:3 (1996), pp. 311–330 (p. 311).

86 Ze'ev Vilna'i, *Ramla: Hove Ve'avar* (Ramla, 1961), pp. 41–46.

'a celebration of triumph and a mechanism for settling scores with the vanquished regime'.[87]

On the ground, this was accomplished in two stages. The first involved marking the streets in Hebrew letters. As in Jaffa, where numbers temporarily replaced the Arab street-names,[88] this was an intermediate stage towards the complete nationalisation of the formerly Arab urban space. These letters were random and meaningless. Thus, for example, Omar Ibn Abed al-Khatab St. was marked with the Hebrew letter *Tav*. Hitherto nameless streets were also marked that way. The second stage, giving proper names, was slower and fraught with deliberate signification. Ramla's municipality accepted the challenge enthusiastically: by October 1950, there had already been six meetings of the Street Names Committee.[89] This committee named and renamed streets after Jewish and Israeli milestones, people and concepts; mostly linked to Zionism, the nation, or Labour ideology, representing the municipality's leftist orientation. Thus, for instance, Deir al-Latin St., later temporarily *Tav Yod Dalet* St., was finally named Bialik after Israel's national poet; Suleiman Ibn Abed al-Malik St., later *Tav Alef*, was named Jan Masaryk, after the Czech leader and friend of the Jewish nation.

In the early 1950s, only one central street in town had a name with right-wing connotation. Omar Ibn Abed al-Khatab was renamed Jabotinsky, after the leader of Revisionist Zionism. However, after the death in August 1952 of Yitzhak Sadeh of the Haganah, many wished to rename it after him. An attempt was apparently made ('a contemptible conspiracy of Labour representatives', as reported the right-wing *Herut* newspaper) to physically replace street signs accordingly.[90]

---

87 Azaryahu, 'The Power of Commemorative Street Names', pp. 313, 318; Maoz Azarayhu and Arnon Golan, '(Re)naming the Landscape: The Formation of the Hebrew Map of Israel 1949–1960', *Journal of Historical Geography* 27:2 (2001), pp. 178–195 (p. 181).

88 Monterescu, 'Estranged Natives'.

89 *Iryat Ramla: Sikum Pe'iluyot Ha'irya* (Ramla, 1950), p. 9.

90 *Al Hamishmar*, 4 September 1952; *Herut*, 11 June 1953.

Only in the 1960s, with the newly gained power of right-wing factions in Ramla's municipality, did street names become more associated with right-wing ideology, though this was often preceded by heated disputes, another evidence, if you will, for the importance of the national street-naming project to Zionist ideology. One such dispute that erupted in a town council meeting in 1963 around the renaming of Shimshon Hagibor St. (after biblical Samson) as Etzel St. (after the *Irgun* underground movement) illustrates the growing complexity and politicisation of street naming in town, even when negotiated in a nationally-homogenous context, from which Arabs were virtually excluded.[91]

In the aftermath of the 1948 War Ramle's Arab street names were erased off the urban map; moreover, no street has since been given a name linked to Arab culture or history, not even in areas of significant Arab concentrations such as the Old City. One single street named after an Arab personality is that of Shafiq 'Adas, an affluent Jewish businessman publicly executed in Iraq in 1948 for supplying weapons to Israel. In a way, this brought to a full circle the relations between Arabs and Iraqi Jews in Ramla, discussed in Chapter Two. The appropriation of the Old City's Arab space by Iraqi Jews was completed through commemoration and glorification of the persecution and death of a businessman from the Jewish community in Iraq; it represented past commercial success and downfall for Jews in Iraq, and its resurrection (through this street name) and final victory in Israelised Ramla. 'Adas's symbolic presence in the Old City reinforced Israeli-Jewish and especially Iraqi-Jewish physical presence there. Ironically, however, the Arab-sounding street name has been mistaken by many (including Ramla's current mayor) for a Muslim or Christian Arab name.[92] Although naming a street after 'Adas was a meaningful achievement for the Jewish-Iraqi community, another

91 Minutes of Town Council Meeting, 28 November 1963. Ramla's Municipal Archive.

92 See Yossi Alfi, "Osim Tzchok Mehahistoria", *Yediot Aharonot* online, 21 May 2008 (http://www.ynet.co.il/Ext/Comp/ArticleLayout/CdaArticlePrintPrevie w/1,2506,L-3545179,00.html). Accessed on 16 July 2013.

important group in Ramla—those of the Muslim and Christian
Arab communities—has yet to be represented on Ramla's map
and street signs.[93]

Segregation and Discrimination

Whereas Henri Lefebvre claimed that segregation is not a coherent
and consistent strategy designed by institutions or leaders, Iris
Marion Young (among others) sees segregation as reproduced and
maintained by both legal and illegal means, public and private
institutions, as well as individuals.[94] Was there a deliberate
strategy of segregating the Old City and its residents from the
rest of town, or were they segregated in a series of separate acts
that suited the intentions of local and national decision-makers at
certain moments?

A call for segregation was indeed heard, both in the Jewish
public opinion and in professional circles. Some of the violent
episodes between Arabs and Jews in the early 1950s (see Chapter
Two) raised the issue of the problematic proximity of these two
populations (especially Jews from Arab countries and Muslim and
Christian Arabs), and called for physical separation.[95] Separation
was also recommended by the team that surveyed Ramla in 1967:
'Jews and Arabs should not be housed on the same street', it was
argued, particularly Arabs and Jews of Oriental descent. However,

---

93 See a remark from 1961 by a Maki representative in a town council meeting,
    protesting against the ease with which streets were named in town. He believed
    that the chosen names should reflect the town's social and national makeup.
    Minutes of Town Council Meeting, 15 January 1961, ISA, 50//1909/12–
    gimel.
94 Henri Lefebvre, *Writings on Cities*, E. Kofman and E. Lebas (trans. and ed.)
    (Oxford, 1996), p. 140; Iris Marion Young, 'Residential Segregation and
    Differentiated Citizenship, *Citizenship Studies* 3:2 (1999), pp. 237–252 (p.
    239).
95 See, for example, in 1952: Minutes 1 of Subcommittee on Ramla Affairs, 4
    August 1952, ISA, 60//89/15–kaf.

the surveyors did not recommend providing separate institutional and secondary services to the two communities.[96]

Others criticised this attempted segregation. In the early 1970s, Pinchas Frank of the Tel Aviv University Social Work School wrote a report on Ramla's Old City for the Ministry of Housing, in which he interpreted segregation as discrimination, and saw the municipality as the deliberate designer of separation and inequality:

> [C]onsiderable effort is made here in Ramla [by the municipality] so that the Old City residents remain in their crumbling houses, [and] so that they will not be emancipated but remain in their low-low status.[97]

Yet the growing socio-economic gap, which also had visible manifestations, was clearly not the municipality's sole responsibility. Those responsible included the Ministry of Housing (which commissioned Frank's report) and the CAP. Frustrated with the CAP's lack of cooperation concerning sanitation in the Old City, for example, the municipality contemplated (in a 1952 meeting) publicly denunciating this institution.[98] Similarly, the municipality resented having to pay the CAP for the ongoing leasing of land in the Old City, on which it built temporary huts for evacuees of dilapidated houses, especially since these hazardous houses were officially under Amidar's (and the CAP's) responsibility.[99] Likewise, the Ministry of Housing agreed to cooperate with the municipality in paving a certain road only under considerable pressure.[100] More generally, as Hubert Lu-Yon and Rachel Kaluss commented, the state was responsible

---

96 *Ramla: Seker Likrat Shikum* (part I), p. 12; (part II), p. 81; Chovav, *Ramla-Ha'ir Ha'atika*, p. 48.
97 Frank, *Proyekt Shituf Toshavim*, p. 107.
98 Minutes of Town Council Meeting, 18 May 1952, ISA, 59//13616/9–gimel-lamed.
99 Minutes of Town Council Meeting, 31 May 1957, ISA, 50//2024/26–gimel.
100 *Ramla: Bita'on 'Iryat Ramla* (Ramla, 1966), p. 6.

for inequality in housing options as a direct result of its control over land and its uses. Through its acts, the state perpetuated the link between housing and status, and promoted some sectors at the expense of others.[101] Hierarchy was clear: at the top stood Ashkenazi veteran settlers and exempted soldiers; underneath them stood other sectors (proletarian and religious, for example); Mizrachi Jews were allocated an even lower standing on this ladder linking housing and status, whereas Arab populations and their housing needs were most of the time ignored.

Market demand and real estate prices also limited freedom of choice and contributed to growing socio-economic gaps in the country as a whole.[102] Obviously, there were many who could not afford to buy a flat, even with flexible funding terms. Many Old City inhabitants complained they could hardly repay their grocery debt, let alone buy a flat.[103] For some even renting was out of the question. People remained in dilapidated houses in the Old City and in the *ma'abara* because they could not afford higher rents, even in one of the public housing projects, even if their present living conditions were poor.[104] Yet due to hazardous living conditions, the municipality pressured national institutions such as Amidar, the Ministry of Housing or the Jewish Agency to lower rents in their housing projects; at the same time, it also demanded that these institutions build more housing projects for lower-income families.[105]

Cultural differences and personal preferences also influenced Ramla's growing segregation in the 1950s and 1960s. Proximity to friends, family and workplace affected some of the Jewish residents' reluctance to be vacated from the Old City. However, it was especially the desire to live in a central location (near the marketplace and its nearby cafés) and fear of change that made

101 Lu-Yon and Kaluss, *Diyur Beisrael*, p. 2–5.
102 Young, 'Residential Segregation', p. 240.
103 Immanuel Porat, 'Ramla Sheme'ever Le-"Chalon Hara'ava"', *Maariv*, 18 August 1959.
104 Chovav, *Ramla—Ha'ir Ha'atika*, p. 68.
105 Minutes of Town Council Meeting, 20 August 1959, ISA, 50//2033/6–gimel.

residents in the Old City, particularly the elderly and less educated, insist on staying in their old houses. The fact that most of the Jewish families that remained in the Old City were seen as 'lacking ingenuity and initiative, apathetic and resigned to their fate'[106] implies that what could be seen as a personal preference was in fact only another manifestation of an ongoing process of deprivation, discrimination and neglect on behalf of the authorities.

The Arab population was perceived as content with remaining to live in the area, which offered not only social networks but also services for both Christian and Muslim communities, such as educational and religious institutions.[107] They were seen to willingly reside in a ghetto, and have 'a strong attachment' to the area, despite low living standards.[108] The sociologist who saw the Arab concentration in the area as a 'spontaneous phenomenon' that originated in 'the wish of this minority to live together', emphasised these aspects, rather than highlighting the fact that the Arabs were *forced* to reside in this area in the immediate aftermath of Ramle's occupation.[109]

Evidently, among the three components which shaped the human face of the Old City, personal choice was the most negligible, whereas the other two—institutional planning and action, and market demands—were of more influence. Those who eventually remained to live in the Old City were most of the time incapable of moving out of it to reside in the more peaceful and modern neighbourhoods built on the town's outskirts, creating thus—with the contribution of municipal and national policies and their implementation—a socio-economic and spatial reality which was to persevere for years to come.

---

106 Chovav, *Ramla—Ha'ir Ha'atika*, p. 51.
107 *Ramla: Seker Likrat Shikum* (part I), pp.11– 12, *Ramla: Seker Likrat Shikum* (part II), p. 4.
108 *Seker Likrat Shikum* (part II), p. 84; Chovav, *Ramla—Ha'ir Ha'atika*, p. 84.
109 *Ramla: Seker Likrat Shikum* (part II), p. 41; Chovav, *Ramla—Ha'ir Ha'atika*, p. 72.

Ramla's Expansion—The Village of Jawarish

The need to provide housing for the constantly growing town, offer employment to its newcomers, and obtain funding for both, motivated Ramla's continuous expansion. Pre-1948 Arab Ramle Municipality's jurisdiction covered about 2,000 dunum, which also included agricultural lands (see Chapter Three). In a 1947 map, the town's boundaries are clearly marked, including the farthest neighbourhood in the north-west, Saknat Fanus, but excluding the White Tower area.[110] However, only three years down the line, in a report on the first year of Ramla's Municipality (established in 1950), it was proudly remarked that the town's jurisdiction now stretched to about 8,500 dunum. Israeli Ramla expanded mainly westwards; it also annexed some land to the east, and continued doing so throughout the 1950s.[111] Ramla turned into what Harvey Molotch termed 'a Growth Machine', competing for the distribution of resources in order to further develop at the expense of nearby localities, attempting to accumulate in this process of geographical expansion more wealth and power.[112]

This continuous growth was a consequence of constant negotiation between the municipality and state. Not only Ramla, but also neighbouring settlements wanted to expand, be it Lydda to Ramla's north-east, kibbutz Nezer Sereni, or moshav (cooperative village) Yashresh to the south-west. The state attempted to balance the needs and wishes of the various communities; Ramla's counter-tactic was to come up with plausible reasoning for annexing further land. For example, when in 1958 Ramla sought to annex a nearby industrial area, it explained that workers in the factories

---

110 AA 45 1947 (1:2500), sheets 1 and 2.
111 *Iryat Ramla: Sikum Pe'ulot Ha'Irya* (Ramla, 1950), p. 18. See, for example, the municipality's request for the annexation of an industrial area to the north-east of town. *Al Hamishmar*, 7 December 1958.
112 Harvey Molotch, 'The City as a Growth Machine: Toward a Political Economy of Place', *The American Journal of Sociology* 82:2 (1976), pp. 309–332.

in question were represented by the town's Employment Bureau and Workers' Council.[113]

The Arab village of Jawarish (also pronounced Jarushi or Jarishi) is an interesting case in point, in the sense that it articulated together two of the municipality's ambitions, one covert and only semi-planned, the other more explicit: segregation of the Arab community, and expansion of municipal jurisdiction. How were they to fit together?

The Bedouin *hamula* (extended family or clan) of Jawarish originated in the village of Katra (near Gedera); by 1948 they already lived there for two or three generations after their ancestors had arrived from Libya. The clan had a history of harmonious coexistence with its Jewish neighbours in the *moshava* (semi-collective farming community) of Gedera, working as guards for the Jewish National Foundation. In late January 1949 the *hamula's* members (men, women and children, about a hundred people altogether) were transferred to Jewish-occupied Majdal in order to guarantee their safety; they were allocated accommodation in town. Whereas some were employed as guards in a small police unit of sorts, others worked lands outside Majdal, provided to them by the CAP.[114] They were only one group among an Arab population of refugees who had stayed in Majdal after its Jewish occupation, living under military rule. But they were not there to stay: between June and October 1950 Majdal's Arab population—about 2,460 people altogether—was transferred out of town to Gaza, Ramla, Lydda, and Transjordan.[115]

The arrival of the Jawarish clan in an area south-west of Ramla in July 1950 was orchestrated and funded by the Agriculture

113 *Al Hamishmar*, 7 December 1958.
114 Orna Cohen, 'Majdal's Arabs Under the Israeli Regime, 1948–1950', in *Ashkelon Bride of the South: Studies in the History of Ashkelon from the Middle Ages to the End of the Twentieth Century*, Ze'ev Safrai and Nahum Sagiv (eds.) (Ashkelon, 2002), pp. 185–212 [in Hebrew] (pp. 188, 192); 'Tkufa Israelit Chadasha', in *Ashkelon—4,000 Ve'od Arba'im Shana*, Naftali Arbel (general ed.) (Ashkelon[?], 1990), pp. 36–50 [in Hebrew] (p. 39).
115 Cohen, 'Majdal's Arabs', pp. 206–210.

Ministry.[116] The new settlers were provided land patches for cultivation—10–15 dunum per family; they were likewise given tents, in which they were to reside for the next few years. By 1952 building of houses was completed and the families moved into their new, small (20 square meters), one-bedroom units.[117]

In a way, this was an extraordinary and unusual episode, since the state, as argued above, seldom invested in new housing options for the Arab sector. Until the mid 1970s the building of accommodation for this population was carried out almost exclusively in the private market and was self-financed. In the later part of that decade the state became more attentive to the need to provide the Arab sector with housing solutions, especially due to growing illegal construction.[118] The Jawarish *hamula* was offered permanent accommodation near Ramla for two reasons mainly: first, because the state wished to keep this friendly and co-operative clan safe and content, under its watchful eye. Second, because it served an international interest, of showing the world that Israel treated well its Arab internal refugees.[119] The units' minimal size in Jawarish, however, testify to the fact that new accommodation for Arab families was hardly satisfactory in comparison with building projects aimed at the Jewish population, not only in terms of quantity, but also qualitatively: in 1955 the size of a standard flat built for new immigrants was almost double than that provided in Jawarish—40 square meters; flats for veteran Jews were even bigger—64 square meters.[120]

The speech given by the village's representative on the official festive 'opening' of Jawarish village nevertheless exalted the state's trustworthiness and sense of equality:

116 'From the Decisions of the Authority for the Settlement of Refugees', 31 January 1950, ISA, 102//17038/36—gimel lamed; 'Security Report, signed by Military Governor Yehoshua Verbin, 2 July 1950, IDF Archive, 191–834/1953.

117 'From the Decisions of the Authority for the Settlement of Refugees', 31 January 1950, ISA, 102//17038/36—gimel lamed; Letter from the Aljarushi Muchtar to the Agriculture Ministry, 17 September 1951, ISA 102//17029/23—gimel lamed.

118 Lu-Yon and Kalush, *Diyur Beisrael,* p. 10.

119 Rosenhek, *The Housing Policy,* pp. 23–24.

120 Lu-Yon and Kalush, *Diyur Beisrael,* p. 6; Rosenhek, *The Housing Policy,* p. 19.

Honourable ministers and generous gentlemen, I have
the honour to stand among you on this day, when our
young state is handing us, according to its promise, our
new village. In my name and in the name of my brothers
Arab Al-Jawarish I am grateful from the bottom of my
heart for what our state has done for us, and for the
help provided to us [by the state] with love and special
mercifulness following our tragedy [...] And here we live
today in Ramla, enjoying freedom, complete equality
and justice, allowed to cultivate [our lands] as any Israeli
citizen[;] and the joyful hour has arrived in which our
government kept its promise and did not differ between
an Arab and a Jew, and handed us our village while
thousands of Jewish families [still] live in tents.[121]

A photograph taken in March 1953 by Fritz Cohn, a Berlin-born
photographer who worked as the head of the Government Press
Office,[122] shows one of the village's inhabitants standing next to a
grazing flock of sheep; a small newly-built, quaint-looking house
with a tiled roof provides the backdrop for this serene scenery
(fig. 11). Life in the new village, nonetheless, was hardly as
picturesque: in 1954 the village's representative complained in a
letter to Prime Minister Moshe Sharet that promises that he had
been given were yet to be fulfilled, among these the paving of an
entrance road to the village, establishment of a local school, and
building of a village mosque. Half a year later he wrote again to
Sharet, after finding out that the village's inhabitants were asked
to purchase their houses or pay rent, although they had been
told that accommodation was to be given them for free.[123] A few

121 'Speech of Jarushim Representative in the Opening of the Village in Ramla',
   undated, ISA, 102//17038/36—gimel lamed.
122 Guy Raz, *Photographers of Palestine: Eretz Israel/Israel (1855–2000)*(Tel Aviv,
   2003)[in Hebrew], p. 125.
123 Letter from Al Jarushi Village Muchtar Yousef Muhammad Al Jarushi to Prime
   Minister Moshe Sharet, 4 October 1954, ISA, 102//17029/23—gimel lamed;
   Letter from Jarishi Village Muchtar Yousef Muhammad Al Jarushi to Prime
   Minister Moshe Sharet, 21 April 1955, ISA, 102//17038/36—gimel lamed.

years later still, the people of Jawarish already felt betrayed by the Israeli establishment: their municipal status was unclear, they suffered from unemployment, lands they had been promised were in fact being cultivated by nearby Jewish villages, and there was no regular transport to and from their community.[124] Since they saw themselves as loyal inhabitants of 'our young country', they asked—in a letter to the Prime Minister's Office, the Minister of Agriculture and Yosef Weitz of the Jewish National Fund—not to be discriminated relative to new immigrants.[125]

Fig. 11: Fritz Cohen, The Village of Jawarish, 10 March 1953 (Courtesy of the GPO).

124 Letter from the people in the village of Jawarish to the Advisor on Arab Affairs in the Prime Minister's Office, undated (c. 1957); Letter signed by Yousef Muhammad Jarushi and 'Amar Jarushi, undated; Letter from Jawarish to the the Advisor on Arab Affairs in the Prime Minister's Office, 16 December 1962. All letters in the ISA, 102//17029/23–gimel-lamed.
125 Letter signed by Yousef Jarushi and 'Amar Jarushi, undated. ISA, 102//17029/23–gimel-lamed.

Over the years, Ramla's municipal boundaries crawled towards Jawarish, and from September 1962, the village's annexation was discussed between the Prime Minister's Office and Ramla's Municipality. Whereas the state pressured Ramla to annex the village, the latter was willing to do so only in exchange for government assistance. In these discussions, the Prime Minister Office representative promised to provide government funding for electricity, a family health clinic, a kindergarten and a school, as well as to pave a road to the village.[126] The government clearly wished Jawarish to be part of Ramla's jurisdiction. Things were not so simple in town hall. In a heated council meeting in December 1964, many objected, stating reasons of security, plans for future expansion in other directions, potential cultural and socio-economic problems, the deterioration of the town's image, as well as reluctance to increase the percentage of minority communities in town. Other members, however, urged the municipality to view the suggested annexation as an opportunity to 'express sympathy towards the minorities' who are entitled to be treated as any other citizens.[127]

Perhaps it is not coincidental that Ramla experienced one of its most severe Arab-Jewish clashes around this time. The death of a young Jew of Iraqi origin in August 1965, discussed in the Introduction, triggered violent riots in Ramla. The funeral procession, after which mayhem erupted, was well planned: on its way to the cemetery, it passed through Ramla's high street, and carried around town, setting in the process the fire that was to erupt after the funeral.[128] In the aftermath of the clashes, an

---

126 ISA, 102//17029/23–gimel-lamed; Letter of Agreement [...] in the matter of Kiryat Jawarish, 13 September 1962. Ramla's Municipal Archive.
127 Minutes of Town Council Meeting, 28 December 1964, ISA, 50//2632/8–gimel.
128 *Haaretz, Al Hamishmar, Maariv,* and *Kol Haam*—all of 23 August 1965; *Haolam Haze,* 25 August 1965. Coincidently, two months earlier Acre experienced Jewish-Arab riots, and in the week preceding the clashes in Ramla the famous Watts Riots (11–15 August) brought havoc to the streets of Los Angeles, killing 34 people. *Haaretz,* 24 August 1965; *Haaretz,* 26 August 1965; *Kol Haam,* 27 August 1965; *Maariv,* 24 August 1965.

attempt was made to chill the heated atmosphere in Ramla.[129] A meeting organised by the Society for Understanding and Friendship between Jews and Arabs ended with a call for co-operation towards peaceful co-existence. Jawarish's annexation was brought up by the mayor's deputy, who argued that Ramla's Arabs enjoyed equal rights, and pointed to the upcoming annexation as a proof.[130] Yet, as we have seen, for some people at least this annexation meant undesired proximity between Jews and Arabs. It is conceivable, therefore, that the violence that erupted in Ramla in the summer of 1965 was triggered, among other things, by the Jawarish dispute.

In February 1966, the annexation order was signed by the Ministry of the Interior. Subsequently, Ramla's municipality made increasing efforts to bring the town's Arab and Jewish communities closer together, and encouraged local activities by the Society for Understanding and Friendship.[131] There was no lack of good intentions within the municipality, among religious leaders, as well as among ordinary Jews and Arabs; yet it seems that the annexation of Jawarish only added tension to a town constantly verging on violence. By 1969, three years after the annexation, the municipality had already invested 600,000 Israeli Pounds in the village's development—paving roads, founding a kindergarten and a school, opening facilities for the treatment of mother and child, and connecting the village to electricity.[132] On 8 July 1969—exactly nineteen years after their first arrival in Ramla—*Davar* journalist Yitzhak Yacobi described how the village's younger generation not only frequented regularly Ramla's cinemas but also, during the 1967 War, volunteered in nearby agricultural settlements and even donated to the national blood bank.[133] The inhabitants

129 See, for example, Minutes of Town Council Meeting, 27 August 1965, ISA, 50//3195/7–gimel; internal memo in the Public Information Centre, 24 August 1965, ISA, 102//17009/1–gimel-lamed.
130 *Al Hamishmar*, 26 August 1965.
131 *Ramla: Bita'on Iryat Ramla* (Ramla, 1966), p. 6.
132 *Davar*, 17 December 1968; *Davar*, 8 July 1969.
133 *Davar*, 8 July 1969.

of Jawarish, this article implied, have finally completed their absorption within Israeli society, on both local and national levels. With hindsight, this conclusion seems to be premature, idealistic, and almost naive: in the year 2005 about 2,000 people lived in the Jawarish neighbourhood. Most of its lands were owned by the state, whereas almost all buildings there were illegal. Although a mosque has been built in the neighbourhood in recent years, access roads—or lack thereof—still pose a significant problem for the current residents of Jawarish.[134]

* * *

The analysis offered here of Ramla's residential patterns and spatial dispersion conjures up a gloomy picture, to whose creation was responsible the municipality, as well as capitalist market forces, and the aspirations and interests of individuals. Above all these, however, stand the state's housing policy and its implementation on ground. Hubert Lu-Yon and Rachel Kallus summarised neatly this policy and its consequences, and it seems worthwhile repeating their conclusions here at length:

> Although the state repeatedly declares since its foundation that the right for proper accommodation is reserved to any of its citizens, it makes an unequal use of the housing options it offers. This inequality is an outcome of the link between housing activities and spatial control of the state over the land and its uses. The result is disparity in the quality and level of housing between different groups within the population. Likewise, the government's housing policy perpetuates the association between accommodation and status, because decisions relating to location, planning and settling, bring about processes of socio-economic separation. Moreover, by regulation and

---

134 Yuval Tamari, *Seker Tichnuni Bashchunot Ha'arviyot Ba'ir Ramla* (Jerusalem, 2005), pp. 12–18.

direction of the building market on the one hand, and its
supervision on the other hand, the government triggers
promotion and advancement of certain sectors within the
state, in a way that creates severe discrimination of other
sectors. As a result, wide gaps in accommodation levels
have evolved during the years between Jews and Arabs in
Israel, gaps that grow bigger with time[;] a considerable
inequality in housing levels is also created between
Ashkenazi Jews and Mizrachi Jews.[135]

It has recently been claimed that separation of Arab and Jewish
populations in Israel has been pursued by authorities at both
national and local levels, employing three types of strategies. First,
'purification' of the Arab space by restructuring it (demolishing
the old and building the new). Second, segregation, which leaves
the Other in its backwardness in order to reinforce existing power
relations. Finally, exotication of the space through conservation
and renovation, which creates a romantic façade of 'traditional'
landscape without retaining its initial functions (as done for
example in Acre and Jaffa).[136] Although these policies were not
followed uniformly based on an explicit master preconception,
we find in Ramla a desire to 'purify' and incorporate the Old City,
and segregate it at the same time. We also find, although this is
not discussed here, an attempt at renovation and conservation of
certain Arab architectural elements in town.[137]

In her visit to Ramla in April 1954, Rachel Ben Zvi Yana'it saw

135 Lu-Yon and Kallus, *Diyur BeIsrael,* p. 2.
136 Yitzhak Schnell, 'New Approaches to the Study of Mixed Cities: The Case of
    Israel', in *Together But Apart: Mixed Cities in Israel,* Elie Rekhes (ed.)(Tel Aviv,
    2007), pp. 19–26 (pp. 19–20).
137 See, for example, 'Notes for the Excursion of the Inter-Departmental Committee
    for the Improvement of Historical Sites', 22 June 1950, ISA, 98//4738/49–
    gimel; Letter from Yeivin to Levinson, 4 July 1955, ISA, 95//6173/4–gimel;
    Budget Proposal for 1957/8–1958/9 for Improvement of Historical Sites
    [...]', ISA, 95//6173/4–gimel; Budget Proposal for 1963/4–1966/7, ISA,
    56//2755/1–gimel-lamed. The sites are mostly concentrated in the White Tower
    compound. See also St Helena's Cisterns, opened to the public after renovations
    in 1960. Ze'ev Vilna'i, *Ramla: Hove Ve'avar* (Ramla, 1961), p. 32.

all of its inhabitants as citizens, regardless of their country of origin or place of residence. In Neve David neighbourhood, adorned with flowers and trees, she found new immigrants 'turning into citizens' almost by themselves; the veteran immigrant who ran the *ma'abara* oozed a similar air of citizenship.[138] But did the resident of the Old City, who had lost hope of improving her living conditions, feel like a proud citizen? Did an inhabitant of Jawarish see himself comparable to a resident in the affluent Sprintzak neighbourhood? Even if no coherent plan for segregation and discrimination existed, on the ground we find separation and inequity, manifested in the spatial demarcation of town and in the widely varying living standards typical of each area; these were linked to and were made synonymous with the national, ethnic and socio-economic status of their inhabitants.

138 Rachel Ben Zvi Yana'it, 'Ramla', *Davar*, 9 April 1954.

EPILOGUE

Return Visits and the Uncertain Futures of an Open-Ended City

Pierre Nora termed the phrase *Lieux de Mémoire*—sites of memory—and explained it as the tripartite expression—material, symbolic and functional—of the play between memory and history; 'simple and ambiguous, natural and artificial, at once immediately available in concrete sensual experience and susceptible to the most abstract elaboration'. Sites of memory, he noticed, are created first and foremost by a will to remember: '[t]he most fundamental purpose of the *lieu de mémoire* is to stop time, to block the work of forgetting, to establish a state of things, to immortalise death, to materialise the immaterial [...].[1] For many Palestinians who had lived in Ramle prior to 1948 the town has become such a *lieu de mémoire*, whereas the practice of returning to visit their former hometown has been made into the most refined expression of this mnemonic discourse and the will to remember. Susan Slymovics referred to these visits as 'self-conscious efforts to remember by performing acts of commemoration'.[2]

1   Pierre Nora, 'Between Memory and History: Les Lieux de Mémoire', *Representations* 26 (1989), pp. 7–24 (pp. 18–19).
2   Susan Slymovics, *The Object of Memory: Arab and Jew Narrate the Palestinian Village* (Philadelphia, 1998), p. 21.

[205]

The 1967 War was, like the 1948 War, another defining moment in the histories of both Palestinian and Jewish peoples, making the Arab-dominated areas of the West Bank, Golan Heights, Gaza Strip and Sinai Peninsula into Israeli territory. One of the outcomes in the war's aftermath was the implementation of the Open Bridges policy, which enabled movement of people and goods between Jordan and the recently occupied territories. Once the bridges between Israel and the Hashemite Kingdom were opened, many Palestinians residing in neighbouring Arab countries surged along the ways, coming to see the homes they had left nineteen years earlier. While in exile, many of the refugees dreamt of a triumphant return to their lands; the visits which came to fruition conjured up the understanding that what existed in memories was no longer there in reality, that it was impossible to set the clock back.[3] Homecoming returns were laden with mnemonic significance, but also with hope for a future possibility of reunion of owner and house, of the exiling nation and its homeland. For the tens of thousands of refugees who returned to see their former homes in Jerusalem, Jaffa, Haifa, Lydda, Ramla, Acre, Beer Sheva, Safad and Tiberias, the actual encounter tended to shatter any expectations for real reunion; they usually turned into what Danny Rubinstein referred to as 'a fantastic voyage of delusion'.[4] Moreover, some of these returnees came back with stories of the humiliation they had suffered in these visits, so much so that these homecomings were made into 'some kind of masochism'.[5] Despite this sense of humiliation, perhaps as reaction to it, narration and discussion of return visits have become a central component in the Palestinian discourse of the postwar period.[6] Some of these stories

---

3   Helena Lindhom Schulz, *The Palestinian Diaspora: Formation of Identities and Politics of Homeland* (NY, 2003), pp. 215–216.
4   Danny Rubinstein, *The People of Nowhere: The Palestinian Vision of Home*, trans. Ina Friedman (NY, 1991), p. 62.
5   Bashir El-Hairi, *Letters To A Lemon Tree*, trans. D. Brafman (Jerusalem, 1997) [in Hebrew], p. 17.
6   El-Hairi, *Letters*, pp. 17–18.

were recorded and published, mostly in autobiographies and memoirs.[7]

* * *

One of many to visit their former hometown was Bashir el-Hairi, the great-nephew of Sheikh Mustafa Khairi, Ramle's *muchtar* before the 1948 War (see Appendix).[8] Like many of the town's Arab inhabitants, Bashir's family too had fled Ramle to Ramallah when he was six years old. In late 1948 the el-Hairi family settled in Gaza, only to come back to Ramallah nine years later, in 1957. Ten more years down the line, in 1967, Bashir el-Hairi was a twenty-five-year-old lawyer, specialising in labour matters after graduating from Cairo University Law School, where he had been politically active as student.[9]

On a hot summer day in July 1967 Bashir el-Hairi and his two companions—Abu Jalal, a teacher who had been thirteen-years-old when leaving Ramle, and a lawyer named Abu Faras, eleven-years-old back in 1948—left Ramallah on their way to visit their hometown. Travelling by car from Ramallah to Jerusalem, the three then boarded a bus that brought them to their destination—'the point to which the family memory always returns, despite all the disasters and joys surrounding it'.[10] Throughout the years Ramle became the reference point to which the family's diasporic day-to-day existence kept coming back, in spite of chronological and geographical distance. Put more intimately—in romantic, even

---

7   See, for example, those of Hala Sakakini, *Jerusalem and I: A Personal Record* (Jerusalem, 1990), pp. XI-XV; Serene Husseini Shahid, *Jerusalem Memories*, trans. Mali Baruch (Tel Aviv, 2006)[in Hebrew](orig, 1999), pp. 147–151; *Encounters of Memory* (Jerusalem, 2000)[in Hebrew], pp. 125, 132–133; John M. Tleel, *I am Jerusalem* (Jerusalem, 2000), pp. 202–205.

8   Bashir's father, Ahmad Khairi, was the nephew of Sheikh Mustafa Khairi and his adopted son after his parents had died aged seven. Sandy Tolan, *The Lemon Tree: An Arab, a Jew, and the Heart of the Middle East* (NY, 2006), p. 9.

9   Tolan, The Lemon Tree, pp. 58, 103, 123, 125.

10 El-Hairi, *Letters*, pp. 18–21 (quote on p. 21).

erotic, terms—el-Hairi imagined Ramle as a beautified beloved, and himself as the anxious lover longing for reunion.[11]

Once the three men arrived in town they were confronted with the challenge of orienting themselves geographically in an Israeli city they no longer knew. Both Abu Jalal and Abu Faras were confused by the sights surrounding them: they were attempting to allocate the buildings, streets and shops they saw in their childhood memories; at the same time, they noticed the many new houses built in their long absence.[12] These spatial changes were more than merely architectural; rather, they pointed at the town's new Israeli identity, in which there was no place for these three Palestinian men. The town's new face brought up feelings of alienation and estrangement, contrary to the men's attachment and emotionally deep sense of place: 'they are the foreigners, not us', argued Bashir defiantly, 'this is our town, and it is our right to be joyful to see it [...]'. And yet, as he acknowledged, 'all that I have seen so far was completely foreign to me'.[13]

This disparity between the confidence of home and strangeness of a foreign country was concurrently reflected and explained in the changes the town underwent during nineteen years of absence, but also in the deceitful nature of memory. Time and place blurred: for Bashir, Ramle seemed to be both near and far, geographically and chronologically; Abu Faras felt as if he was gone for two or three days only rather than nineteen long years.[14] The epitome of memory's betrayal, however, was the meeting with Abu Muhammad/Mordechay: Abu Jalal thought to have recognised the short, dark, heavy man of fifty wearing a butcher's apron as Abu Muhammad, the Arab butcher whose family had stayed in Ramle during and after the war. Only after the two hugged and kissed enthusiastically, did the three Palestinian men realise the embarrassing yet symbolic mistake of replacing Abu

---

11   *Ibid.*, pp. 19, 22.
12   *Ibid.*, pp. 23–24; 26–27.
13   *Ibid.*, pp. 24, 26.
14   *Ibid.*, pp. 22, 25, 37.

Muhammad with a Jewish man named Mordechay, who had been allocated Muhammad's shop at some point after 1948.[15]

The idea of 'diachronic neighbours' has been used by Yfaat Weiss in her discussion of Wadi Salib neighbourhood in Haifa to describe its concealed Arab past amidst the Israeli present.[16] The meeting between the Palestinian visiting returnees, whose families had owned houses, and their current dwellers was deemed to be laden with meaning and perhaps somewhat confrontational. In a short discussion when first entering Ramla the three men debated the nature of such possible encounters: whereas Bashir and Abu Faras insisted on their right to take a look at their houses, Abu Jalal claimed that the new tenants may refuse to be reminded of the houses' past.[17] This debate was reflected in the actual encounter between the Palestinian and Jewish 'diachronic neighbours' that summer day of 1967 in Ramla. Bashir el-Hairi was quick to point out to the young Jewish woman who had opened the door to his family home—'I am the son of the owner of this house[...]'. Language played here, as in other Palestinian return narratives, a significant role, acting as the only remaining means left for the original Palestinian owners to reclaim their ownership of the houses. Indeed, Efrat Ben Ze'ev has already noticed that the nostalgic rite of Palestinian return visit tended to turn into 'a minor act of political opposition' by reminding the new Jewish inhabitants of the houses' Palestinian past.[18] Bashir's counterparts, on the other hand, were more apprehensive, declaring only the houses' *past* ownership by their families.[19]

---

15   *Ibid.*, pp. 29–31.

16   Yfaat Weiss, *A Confiscated Memory: Wadi Salib and Haifa's Lost Heritage*, trans. Avner Greenberg (NY, 2011), Chapter 1.

17   El-Hairi, *Letters*, p. 23.

18   *Ibid.*, p. 39. See for example Husseini Shahid, *Jerusalem Memories*, p. 148; *Encounters of Memory*, p.133; *Maariv*, 27 June 1967, p. 17. Efrat Ben Ze'ev, 'The Politics of Taste and Smell: Palestinian Rites of Return', in *The Politics of Food*, Marianne Elizabeth Lien and Brigitte Nerlich (eds.)(Oxford and NY, 2004), pp. 141–160 (p. 144).

19   El-Hairi, *Letters*, pp. 28, 33.

The Israeli-Jewish press contributed to the circulation of narratives on Palestinian return visits in the weeks that followed the war's aftermath; in this manner it raised awareness of such potential occurrences in the mixed or formerly Arab towns.[20] Whether curious or dreadful, many of the Jewish tenants and new owners of 'abandoned' Arab houses were therefore ready for an anticipated knock on their door. The fifty years old woman living in what had used to be Abu Jalal's family home did not even wait for the men to introduce themselves; once she had opened the door and saw them standing there she began screaming, cursing and then even physically attempting to remove the three men from the doorstep. Abu Faras was luckier: his childhood home has transformed into a school, with the head mistress being a kind young lady who spoke English. She had not only allowed him to wander around the premises, but also invited Abu Faras to come again next time he visits town. The twenty-year-old woman who opened the door to Bashir's house, on the eastern outskirts of town, was even more welcoming, cooperative and curious to learn of the Palestinian narrative. She spoke English, offered the visitors coffee and invited them to come again; following that visit Dalia and Bashir developed a friendship that was to last many years.[21] This type of face to face encounter confronted the new Jewish owners with the house's Arab past, and triggered fears of Palestinian claims of its ownership, as of the country's lands more generally. For many of the new immigrants such events also brought back memories of houses they had left behind in the countries they emigrated from, homes they were never to see again.[22] On the other hand, it was an opportunity to meet the threatening Other—the Arab enemy, whose absence-presence was inscribed on the house's walls—giving him a face and a name, relating to his childhood memories and feelings of longing.

---

20 See for example, *Haaretz*, 30 June 1967, pp. 1 and 7; *Yediot Ahronot*, 9 July 1967, p. 11; *Yediot Ahronot*, 15 August 1967, pp. 11 and 14; *Haaretz*, 3 September 1967, p. 7; *Maariv*, 13 September 1967, p. 20; *Maariv*, 27 September, p. 17.

21 El-Hairi, *Letters*, pp. 28, 32–35, 39–43.

22 See for example Sakakini, *Jerusalem and I*, p. XV.

The return visit of Bashir, Abu Jalal and Abu Faras ended on a bitter-sweet note: 'In the same way disasters produce sadness, so they produce joy! We thought that when we will be coming back [to Ramallah], after seeing the houses, we will rejoice, and now we are walking the streets full of sadness'.[23] The three men were left confused, pondering on the possibility of reclaiming ownership over their houses instead of merely visiting them.[24] Yet claims that had been submitted for release of Israeli-held property had been few and far between. One of the reasons for this was practical—most absentees were refugees, residing in enemy states outside Israel, and therefore prevented from filing a lawsuit in an Israeli court or actually appearing in one. Hence, files for release of property were usually filed by non-absentees; these were rarely accepted by the Israeli law system.[25] At the same time, acceptance of compensation from the Israeli government (following legislation from 1953) was considered to be an act of compliance and renunciation of legitimate rights. In addition, monetary compensation offered in the law for the expropriated assets was seen by the original owners as failing to reflect the actual contemporary value of their property.[26]

When Bashir el-Hairi returned to Ramallah his family longed to hear stories of Ramle. The semi-private pilgrimage to the *lieu de mémoire* was made in this manner into a collective ritual of retelling and remembering. The Palestinian house left behind was initially a private and family matter, but it has gradually become a collective national metaphor for the relationship between the Palestinian people and their homeland.[27] The symbol of this association between dispossessed homeowner and his house, refugee and homeland, has become that of a key—the key to

23   El-Hairi, *Letters*, p. 43.
24   *Ibid.*, pp. 43–44.
25   Yifat Holzman-Gazit, *Land Expropriation in Israel: Law, Culture and Society* (Aldershot, 2007), pp. 113–114.
26   Forman and Kedar, 'From Arab Land', pp. 819, 821; Holzman-Gazit, *Land Expropriation*, p. 112.
27   Rubinstein, *The People of Nowhere*, p. 131.

the house left behind in 1948, linking together past, present and future, the personal and the collective, the local and the national.[28]

In 1985 Dalia Eshkenazi—the young woman Bashir el-Hairi had met back in 1967—decided to make the house she had lived in into a *lieu de mémoire* which will encapsulate its two national histories. Once her father had died, she became the legal owner of the house; Dalia could then either move in or sell it, but she felt a moral obligation to share it with the original owners—Bashir and his family. Her idea was to turn the house into a kindergarten for the town's Arab children. In 1991 this dream finally materialised, with the inauguration of the Open House, which functions—to this day—as a centre for Jewish-Arab dialogue.[29] In this manner, the house that had been, until 1948, the property of the el-Hairi family, only to be transferred after the war to the CAP and later sold to Moshe Eshkenazi, came to represent the option of symbolic restitution, offering a possibility for a more authentic bi-national coexistence in a mixed town.[30]

But this has been clearly the exception rather than the rule.[31] Within a single generation, the Arab town of Ramle was made into the Israelised city of Ramla: in terms of real-estate and land ownership, public landscape and lived habitat, spoken language and toponymy, economic and cultural life, the town's former Arab markers have been significantly weakened (or totally obliterated), while Zionist, Hebraic and Jewish traits have mostly taken their place.

28   Laleh Khalili, 'Grass-Roots Commemorations: Remembering the Land in the Camps of Lebanon', *Journal of Palestine Studies* 34:1 (2004), pp. 6–22 (pp. 13–14).

29   Tolan, *The Lemon Tree*, p. 222. For the current activity of the Open House in Ramla see its website: http://www.friendsofopenhouse.co.il/ (accessed 18 July 2013).

30   Tolan, *The Lemon Tree*, pp. 190–191.

31   See for example the case of the Baramki house in Jerusalem. Thomas Abowd, 'The Politics and Poetics of Place: The Baramki House', *Jerusalem Quarterly File* 21 (2004), pp. 49–58.

The process of Israelisation, that 'alchemic change' of sending roots into the ground,[32] took different shapes depending on the locality. The effect of the 1948 war on this process was felt less in Tel Aviv, the first Hebraic city, or in the Jewish colony of Rishon le-Zion (founded 1882), than in the formerly Arab towns of Palestine. Whereas Jewish victory in the war and the founding of the state of Israel did not bring dramatic changes to the already existing Jewish population centres, it made a world of difference to the Arab ones, which had to be 'remade' in order to fit the new political and demographic circumstances; their process of Israelisation included also the attempted (successful to varying degrees) de-Arabisation of landscape and tenure rights. In the mixed cities of Haifa and Jerusalem, where Jews and Arabs had lived side by side (even if mostly in different quarters) already before 1948, these post-war changes may have seemed less clear-cut than in the formerly Arab towns of Ramle, Lydda or Jaffa. Hundreds of villages which were razed to the ground or left to slowly deteriorate did not go through any process of Israelisation; rather, they merely ceased to exist as Palestinian rural habitat.

Arguably, the Israeli-Jewish re-construction of Ramle/Ramla stemmed from a Zionist meta-ideology wishing to materialise a Jewish homeland in Palestine. Yet the process of transformation itself was seldom explicit or straightforward; rather, it was a latent and gradual development which continued over the first decades of statehood. Most of the time, it was proceeded not through the implementation of consistent, preconceived and well-planned strategy, but rather by on-ground dynamics and ad-hoc reactions to enfolding circumstances, following the leadership of certain individuals who acted according to their worldview.

Ramla's Israelisation was fraught with attempted dialogues on the one hand, and violent clashes on the other. We witness cooperation and genuine efforts at making Ramla a town of all

---

32 Benedict Anderson, *Imagined Communities* (London, 1991)[1983], p. 149, note 16.

its inhabitants, at creating a mixed town in the discursive sense,[33] in which no dichotomy exists between its various communities. More often, however, conflict and exclusion were at the core of Ramla's existence in its first decades as an Israeli city: conflict between the army and civilians, among government offices, between municipality and state, between the state and individuals, among factions within the municipality, between members of different ethnicities, and between Jewish and Arab townspeople. Numerous 'circumstantial coalitions'[34] also rose and fell in the history of Ramla's fragmented urban regime.

* * *

Evidence of Ramle's Israelisation is ubiquitous these days: in the town museum building, which housed Ramle's municipality until 1947; in the wedding halls that used to be Arab-owned cafés; in the municipal garden renamed after Israel's first president, where old men still rest in the trees' shade; and in the dismal living condition in the Old City. Yet the fact that we can discuss (and sometimes even see) some relics of the old Ramle proves that it was not totally obliterated in the town's Israelisation process. Despite major upheavals, Ramla nevertheless retained some of its past spatial characteristics and original Arab tenure, though mainly religious rather than private. Many of Ramle's features are apparent in modern day Ramla, albeit camouflaged, renamed or derelict. Certain groups are active in reviving or maintaining the Arab presence in the town's cultural and spatial markers, other groups imagine and remember the town from afar, particularly via the virtual world of the internet.

33 D. Rabinowitz and D. Monterescu, 'Introduction: The Transformation of Urban Mix in Palestine/Israel in the Modern Era', in *Mixed Towns, Trapped Communities: Historical Narratives, Spatial Dynamics, Gender Relations and Cultural Encounters in Palestinian-Israeli Towns*, D. Monterescu and D. Rabinowitz (eds.) (Aldershot, 2007), pp. 1–34 (p. 3)

34 D. Monterescu, 'To Buy or Not to Be: Trespassing the Gated Community', *Public Culture* 21:2 (2009), pp. 403–430.

The arrival of new social elements in town—immigrants from Ethiopia and the former Soviet Union, as well as Palestinian collaborators to Israel's security forces—has added to the complexity of Ramla's urban matrix, redrawing its social map; old conflicts are yet to be resolved while new ones are formed. Another recent change evident on the city's streets has been the new and proactive attitude of Ramla's 'Stand Tall Generation'— young women and men who have been struggling for rights, status and identity both as Israeli citizens *and* as part of the Palestinian people.[35] Although Ramla's Arab residents have continually attempted to assert their identity and defend their property and rights, the present generation is more assertive than ever. In today's Ramla Palestinian protest is voiced through civil activism— rallying against house demolitions, fighting for day-care services, complaining against municipal planning of segragating roads and walls, completing new planning surveys, or attempting to change Old City street names.[36]

The process in which Ramle was symbolically, economically and architecturally nationalised undermined any hope that the town could become a true City of Collective Memory, heterogeneous yet unified.[37] The appropriation of Arab Ramle's original habitat—through business appropriation, street renaming or under-budgeting of certain neighbourhoods—disturbed private and public memory and existence, and acted to forestall future integration.[38] Collective memory constructed in post-1948 Ramla was aimed at the Jewish population while mostly excluding the town's original owners and dwellers.

Even when the Arab past is commemorated in modern-day Ramla—as in the architectural design of the new government

35   Dan Rabinowitz, Khawla Abu Baker, *The Stand Tall Generation: The Palestinian Citizens of Israel Today* (Jerusalem, 2002)[in Hebrew], p. 13.

36   Bothayna Dabit, 'Haproyekt: Ir Me'orevet', *Mitsad Sheni* 6–7 (2004), pp. 28–30; Yuval Tamari, *Seker Tichnuni Bashchunot Ha'arviyot Ba'ir Ramla* (Jerusalem, 2005), pp. 10, 33; *Haaretz*, 3 December 2006.

37   Christine Boyer, *The City of Collective Memory: Its Historical Imagery and Architectural Entertainments* (Cambridge, Mass., 1996).

38   Azaryahu, 'The Power of Commemorative Street Names', p. 317.

services complex on the eastern entrance to town, which mirrors the iconic White Tower to the west—this 'homage' seems more like another Israeli-Jewish symbolic appropriation than genuine commemoration. It is hard to envision the realisation of the current municipal vision statement—'Ramla: discovering the past, seeing the future' (*megalim et he'avar, ro'im et he'atid*)—with this ongoing appropriation on the one hand, and the continuous exclusion of the Arab population and partial eradication of their heritage on the other. After sixty five years of statehood, Ramla's Israelisation seems to be still underway.

APPENDIX

An Abridged Historical Introduction

Ramle, from the Arabic Raml, or sand, was named after the sandy terrain on which the Arab-Muslim Umayyad Caliphate (661–750 A.D.) founded it as a regional political and financial capital.[1] The 1033 earthquake destroyed only half of its buildings, but a stronger earthquake in 1068 devastated the entire town. This was followed by the foundation of a new Ramle by the Seljuk Turks, less than a mile to the west of the original town, in the area now known as the Old City.[2] Ramle's most famous symbol—the White Tower (part of the White Mosque compound)—was apparently erected during the Umayyad period, when it was located in the centre of town. Ramle's relocation repositioned thus the White Mosque compound outside the new Ramle.[3]

Although there is evidence of a Christian minority from as early as Ramle's foundation, it was the arrival of the Crusaders in 1099 that gave the city an important standing in the Christian world. An earlier tradition associating Ramle with Rama (Arimathea)— the birthplace of Saint Joseph and Saint Nicodemus—made it

1   On Ramle's foundation and the origin of its name see S. Gat, 'The City of Ramla in the Middle Ages' (PhD thesis, Bar Ilan University, 2003)[in Hebrew], pp. 10–27; also S. Gat, 'A Flourishing Arab City: The Economy of Medieval Ramla', *Cathedra* 123 (2007), pp. 39–66 [in Hebrew].
2   Gat, 'The City of Ramle', pp. 52–63.
3   A.D. Petersen, 'Preliminary Report on Architectural Survey of Historic Buildings in Ramla', *Levant* 27 (1995), pp. 75–100 (p. 79); Gat, 'The City of Ramla', pp. 89–95.

attractive for pilgrims; it was also made into the seat of a bishop, the Episcopus Ramathensis. Between 1177 and its final conquest by the Muslims in 1204, the city changed hands no less than six times.[4] From this period survives what used to be a great Romanesque church which was later made into a mosque, used to this day as the Great Mosque, Al-Jami' al-Kabir; today it is part of the Old City, located close to the town market.[5] Jews were also part of twelfth-century Ramle. The famous traveller Rabbi Benjamin of Tudela reported on his visit that '[A]bout 300 Jews dwell there'.[6]

Throughout the Mamluk period (1250–1517), Ramle again functioned not only as a pilgrimage destination, but also as a central stop on the way between the important cities of the Levant, as it continued to be in the early Ottoman period (1517–1917). Yet Ramle's prosperity was not to last long: the town was devastated again by the 1546 earthquake, to be slowly rebuilt thereafter. Throughout the seventeenth and eighteenth centuries it is mentioned as both a market town and as a stop on the Christian pilgrims' route to Jerusalem. Napoleon's army arrived in Ramle in 1799 and stationed its headquarters there. Later, in the late 1880s 'a new Hebrew colony' of 31 families was established in Ramle, with the help of the Lema'an Zion (for Zion) organisation, and even opened a hotel there.[7]

The British forces that occupied Ramle in November 1917 were to have a more lasting effect on the town.[8] During British Mandate, Ramle was perceived as strategically valuable and was made into a trading centre. Together with nearby Lydda, it became a service centre for the British army, and received (alongside Jaffa) more governmental aid than any other city: roads and railroads were built to strengthen the town's role as a centre of trade and

4   Gat, 'The City of Ramla', p. vi.
5   Petersen, 'Preliminary Report', p. 79; Gat, 'The City of Ramla', pp. 275–280.
6   *The Itinerary of Benjamin of Tudela*, M.N. Adler (trans.) (London, 1907), p. 27; Gat, 'The City of Ramla', pp. 286–7.
7   Ze'ev Vilna'i, *Ramla: Hove Veavar* (Ramla, 1961), pp. 73–82.
8   B. Maisler and S. Yeivin, *Palestine Guide: For Navy, Army and Air Force* (Tel Aviv, 1940), p. 195.

industry, financial help was provided for agricultural development, and a post office was built.[9] The July 1927 earthquake, in which 32 people died, came therefore as a hard blow to this developing regional centre.[10] In terms of urban planning, however, it was seen as a blessing in disguise: much of the 'grossly overcrowded' town was destroyed and new spacious residential areas could be built.[11] Khalil Sakakini, the Arab educator and nationalist (d. 1953), visited Ramle in early December 1931 and reported back in his diary:

> The weather yesterday and today has been lovely, as if it was spring. And as to Ramle—oh God, how beautiful is Ramle. During the winter season no doubt it is heaven on earth: land and sky are purified, the fields begun to turn green, the air is warm, the wind caresses...No doubt one day people will acknowledge Ramle's value...[12]

But not even the romantic gaze of this visitor from Jerusalem could prevent the town's deterioration, and in the mid 1940s Ramle was again in dire straits: in 1943 its municipal council was blamed for letting the town deteriorate into 'rural slums' through its 'lethargy and incompetence'.[13]

Ramle's mayor throughout the 1920s, 1930s and 1940s was Sheikh Mustafa Khairi, the patriarch of the prominent Khairi clan. In the mid 1930s the Khairi family owned many houses and lands in Ramle, as well as the local cinema. Its head was considered to be a man of much power, who often mediated between his townspeople and British authorities. Whereas British officials saw him as 'the

---

9   Roza I.M. El-Eini, *Mandated Landscape: British Imperial Rule in Palestine, 1929–1948* (London, 2006), p. 390; Gideon Biger, *An Empire in the Holy Land: Historical Geography of the British Administration in Palestine 1917–1929* (Jerusalem, 1994), p. 258.
10 Vilna'i, *Ramla*, pp. 51–83.
11 Michael Assaf, *History of the Arabs in Palestine* (Tel Aviv, 1970)[in Hebrew], p. 304; El-Eini, *Mandated Landscape*, p. 393. For the town's overall planning from the 1920s to the 1940s, see El-Eini, *Mandated Landscape*, pp. 383–387.
12 *"Such Am I, Oh World!": Diaries of Khalil al-Sakakini*, trans. Gideon Shilo (Jerusalem, 1990)[in Hebrew], p. 149.
13 El-Eini, *Mandated Landscape*, p. 387.

very able mayor' of Ramle, he was also well respected by the town's inhabitants.[14] Khairi was the prominent mayor of Ramle for 29 years, and even though he died in Jericho in 1949, after being expelled from Ramle in mid July 1948, he was buried in his hometown.[15]

Before the 1948 War, Ramle numbered between 16,000 and 18,000 inhabitants, with an overwhelmingly Muslim majority and a tiny Christian community; many of its residents owned agricultural land, and hired workers for its cultivation. Ramle's inhabitants, in particular those more well-off, enjoyed electricity and running water, telephone connection, regular mail delivery, and a well-organised education system; cultural life in town also prospered, and the townspeople (especially men) congregated in the local cafés, sports club and the al-Andalus cinema.[16] Its few Jewish inhabitants had left in the beginning of the Arab Revolt (1936–1939).[17]

The unfolding Jewish-Arab conflict was felt in town already in the 1930s, when many of its Muslim inhabitants joined the Arab National Movement, and Jewish travellers through town were harassed.[18] 'Wild Ramle continues the tradition and keeps stoning Jewish vehicles passing on the road', reported *Davar* on 10 November 1936, after the window of a truck loaded with mortar was smashed the day before; two years later a Jewish driver, working for the oil company Socony Vacuum, was injured after his front windowpane was stoned while passing Ramle.[19] After the UN Partition Resolution of 29 November 1947 direct confrontation became inevitable; the

---

14   Sandy Tolan, *The Lemon Tree: An Arab, A Jew, and the Heart of the Middle East* (NY, 2006), p. 9.

15   Tolan, *The Lemon Tree*, p. 99.

16   Interviews with Fawzi al-Basoumi (dated 30 March 2005); Maliha al-Khayri (dated 18 March 2005); Abdel Rahman Abu Hamdeh (dated 30 August 2003). All interviewed as part of the Oral History Project of the Palestine Remembered website (http://www.palestineremembered.com/OralHistory/ Interviews-Listing/Story1151.html#al-Ramla).

17   'Ramla', report dated 2 January, 1949, signed by Shlomo Asherov (Ramla Representative of the Ministry for Minorities Affairs), ISA, 49//297/5–gimel; Vilna'i, *Ramla*, p. 83; Interviews with Fawzi al-Basoumi and Maliha al-Khayri (http://www.palestineremembered.com/OralHistory/Interviews-Listing/ Story1151.html#al-Ramla).

18   Vilna'i, *Ramla*, p. 83.

19   *Davar* 10 November 1936; 7 November 1938; also 12 November 1936.

war that enfolded in mid 1948 turned out to be a watershed in the town's history, when the Israel's 'War of Independence' turned out to be the Palestinians' 'Catastrophe', or Nakba.

From the onset of the war, Ramle and Lydda's importance was acknowledged by the Jewish forces. During May and June of that year, Prime Minister David Ben-Gurion was extremely concerned with the two towns, fearing they might attack nearby Tel Aviv, and repeatedly wrote in his diary the two Arab towns should be destroyed. In cabinet meetings, too, he referred to the need to remove 'the two thorns' (*shney hakotzim*), and even added a comment that was censored, which may have been an explicit call for the expulsion of their inhabitants.[20]

Since Ramle was outside the Partition Plan's Jewish State, and King Abdullah of Transjordan promised to protect it, the town's inhabitants could feel relatively safe.[21] The number of Arab Legion regulars in Ramle and Lydda ('little more than a hundred men')[22], however, testified to a different strategy. The British John Glubb (known as Glubb Pasha), who commanded Transjordan's Arab Legion, later described how already before the Mandate had ended (on 15 May 1948) he 'told both the King and the government that we could not hold Lydda and Ramle [...] and had secured their consent to the principle that Lydda and Ramle would not be defended'.[23] The numerical supremacy of the Jewish forces over those of the Arab Legion translated, in Glubb's strategy, to a decision to concentrate on guarding Latrun and Ramallah (farther east), while sacrificing Ramle and Lydda in the process.

Ramle's defence, therefore, consisted of several groups. One was that of the aforementioned token Arab Legion forces, the

20   David Ben-Gurion, *Yoman ha-Milchama* ([Tel Aviv], 1984), vol. II, entries on 20 May, 24 May, 4 June, 16 June, and 18 June, 1948; B. Morris, *The Birth of the Palestinian Refugee Problem Revisited* (Cambridge, 2004), p. 425 and footnote 62 on p. 452. For an overview of the hostilities in the period leading up to Israel's Declaration of Independence on 15 May, 1948, see *Ibid.*, p. 424.
21   Morris, *The Birth*, p. 425.
22   John Bagot Glubb, *A Soldier with the Arabs* (London, 1957), p. 161.
23   *Ibid.*, pp. 142–143.

5th Independent Infantry Company, positioned in the town's police building.[24] A second group consisted of several hundreds of Bedouins from Transjordan—equipped with old rifles and devoid of military training—who had volunteered and were sent to the Ramle-Lydda area by the Arab Legion.[25] When they first arrived in Ramle, lambs were slain in their honour since they were understood to be the advance guard of a much larger force still to come, however overtime they came to be referred to as the 'barefoot brigade' since many of them wore no shoes.[26] A third group defending Ramle was that of fighters (Mujahadin) from the Jihad al-Mukadas—the Palestinian Army—who consisted of young local peasants, veterans of the British Army, and fighters under the leadership (until his death in April) of Abd al-Qadir al-Hussayni.[27] The fourth and last group was that of a local militia organised by the town's civil leadership. One of them was thirty-six-year-old Dib Abdallah Mustafa from the village of Abu Ghosh, who, by 1948, had been living in Ramle with his family for eight years, employed as a construction worker in British army bases. Unemployment in Ramle had driven him back to his village, but then he heard that Ramle's municipality offered a modest salary for anyone carrying weapon who was interested in defending the town's neighbourhoods. After swapping his house in the village for his cousin's Italian rifle and 160 bullets, he returned with his family to Ramle, where he started working as a night watchman.[28]

During the war's first stages no military governor was appointed to Ramle (nor to Lydda) by the Legion forces as was the case in Hebron, Ramallah, Jerusalem and Nablus, for fear that any loss of the two towns while under the command of a military governor will appear worse than if they were left to organise

---

24   *Ibid.*, p. 143.
25   *Ibid.*, p. 158.
26   According to Khanom Khairi quoted in Tolan, *The Lemon Tree*, p. 47.
27   Yoav Gelber, *Palestine 1948: War, Escape and the Emergence of the Palestinian Refugee Problem* (Brighton, 2001), p. 37.
28   Quoted in A. Kadish, A. Sela and A. Golan, *The Occupation of Lydda 1948* (2000)[in Hebrew], p. 101.

their own civil defence.[29] Still, a military governor named Idris Sultan was appointed to the two towns in the end of June 1948, perhaps in order to weaken the growing affinity between Ramle's inhabitants and the Palestinian Arab High Committee (under the leadership of Hajj Amin al-Husseini, the Mufti of Jerusalem). In this capacity, Idris Sultan strove to achieve cooperation between the various forces operating in the area, and to improve the towns' defence.[30] It was apparently not an easy task, and tensions evolved between the local community and the regular forces present in town: in one instance Ramle's mayor wrote to the military governor, complaining that twelve Arab Legion soldiers attacked a policeman who had intervened after seeing them hit with rifles a local grocer; other incidents involved confiscation of cars.[31]

From May 1948 the town was demoralised as the inhabitants were suffering from air strikes and ground attacks, food shortage, and severe unemployment.[32] Thousands of hungry refugees from Jaffa and other areas already occupied by the Jewish forces (such as the hamlets near Sarafand or nearby Bet Dajan), arrived in town. Some of them were accommodated by Ramle's National Committee[33] in the houses of people who had fled from town; others slept under trees in the orange groves and on the streets.[34]

The Israeli forces emerged from the First Truce (11 June—8 July) reequipped and reorganised. The aim of Operation Dani (9–19 July), called after Dani Mass[35] and planned already in May,

---

29 Glubb, *A Soldier*, p. 143.

30 *Zichronot Abdallah al-Tall*, trans. Y. Chalamish (Tel Aviv, 1960), p. 198; Kadish et al., *The Occupation*, p. 24.

31 Quoted in Kadish et al., *The Occupation*, pp. 112–113, 24.

32 Morris, *The Birth*, pp. 424–5.

33 National committees were founded in all Palestinian towns by the Arab High Committee in 1948, and usually manned by local land owners, merchants and professionals. Spiro Munayyer and Walid Khalidi, 'The Fall of Lydda', *Journal of Palestine Studies* 27:4 (1998), pp. 80–98 (p. 97).

34 Yoav Gelber, *Palestine 1948: War, Escape and the Emergence of the Palestinian Refugee Problem* (Brighton, 2001), p. 112; Tolan, *The Lemon Tree*, p. 54; Interview with Fawzi al-Bousami (http://www.palestineremembered.com/ OralHistory/Interviews-Listing/Story1151.html#al-Ramla).

35 The Palmah commander killed on the way to defend 'Etzion Bloc.

was to occupy Lydda and Ramle in a pincer movement; its wider goal, however, was enabling the passage of vehicles between Tel Aviv and Jerusalem, and controlling the hills between Latrun and Ramallah.[36] The Israeli forces involved in the operation included altogether about 9,000 soldiers. This was the first operation the IDF conducted to have had an operational logic and structure; it also involved several forces assigned with separate missions, operating under one single commander—Yigal Alon.[37] It has been claimed that the IDF overestimated the numbers of the Arab forces in the Ramle-Lydda area (believing there were 1,150–1,500 Legionnaires, while about 150 only were actually present), and attributing them offensive intentions of attacking Tel Aviv.[38] This is exactly the reason why, according to Walid Khalidi, 'the fate of Lydda (and Ramle) was sealed the moment Operation Dani was launched'.[39]

With the end of the First Truce, in the early hours of 10 July, the IDF started moving its forces, conquering Lydda's International Airport, the rural area north of Lydda (the villages of Qula, al-Tira, Rantiya, al-Yahudiya and the Templar colony of Wilhelma), and east of Ramle (the villages of al-Kunaiyisa, 'Innaba, Kharruba, Jimzu, Daniyal, and Khirbet al-Dhuheiriya).[40] On the night of 10–11 July, Lydda and Ramle were bombed from the air.[41] Both towns had asked the Arab Legion's headquarters in Ramallah for help, and were promised the prompt arrival of reinforcement (a platoon which was sent to Lydda from Bet Naballah on 12 July was involved

---

36 On Operation Dani, see Netanel Lorch, *Korot Milchemet Ha'atzma'ut* (Tel Aviv, 1966), pp. 324–30; Morris, *Birth*, p. 423–7; Kadish *et al.*, *The Occupation*, Chapter 2; Morris, *1948*, pp. 286–290. On the operation's various metamorphoses and change of name see Benny Morris, 'Operation Dani and the Palestinian Exodus from Lydda and Ramle in 1948', *Middle East Journal* 40:1 (1986), pp. 82–109 (p. 83).

37 David Tal, *War in Palestine 1948: Strategy and Diplomacy* (London, 2004), p. 305.

38 Gelber, *Palestine 1948*, p. 158; Benny Morris, *1948: A History of the First Arab-Israeli War* (New Haven and London, 2008), p. 286.

39 Munayyer and Khalidi, 'The Fall of Lydda', p. 81.

40 Morris, *1948*, p. 287.

41 Kadish et al., *Occupation,* pp. 27–29; Gelber, *Palestine 1948*, p. 159.

in a short skirmish and promptly retreated).[42] Leaflets dropped on 11 July informed the inhabitants of Ramle 'and all those bearing arms' that they were surrounded with no chance of reinforcement. The leaflets went on to explain: 'Our plan is to conquer the cities only for our protection. We intend no harm to life or property. Whoever tries to resist shall be killed. Whoever chooses life will surrender [....]'.[43] In the leaflets, Ramle's inhabitants were given instructions for submission: a delegation was to arrive to the nearby village of Barriya, bearing a white flag. If they do not surrender by the time indicated, 'war will be upon you and your leaders will be held responsible for your spilt blood and destroyed property'.[44]

Galvanised by the leaflets dropped by the IAF, and by the news on the occupation of Lydda (captured after a fight on the evening of 11 July), a delegation of four of Ramle's notables (including Isma'il Nakhas, Haret Haji, Imada Khouri, and Mustafa Khairi's son Hussam Khairi) arrived in Barriya on the night of 11–12 July and was then taken to Yiftach Brigade's headquarters in kibbutz Na'an.[45] In the early hours of morning, the four Arab representatives signed the official surrender of Ramle. This included the following clauses: (1) surrendering arms to the Israeli army; (2) handing over all foreigners in town (meaning fighters from neighbouring Arab countries); (3) allowing non-military-age residents to leave the city 'should they wish so'; (4) ensuring the inhabitants' safety should their representatives cooperate with the army; and (5) informing the army of the location of any minefields or explosives.[46]

---

42 Gelber, *Palestine 1948*, p. 159.
43 10 July 1948, IDF Archive, 6400/49/46.
44 *Ibid.*; also in Morris, *Birth*, p. 426.
45 Morris, *The Birth*, p. 426; according to a different version Ramle's notables tried to escape but were caught near the village of Barriya and brought to Yiftah's headquarters in Kibbutz Na'an. Morris, 'Operation Dani', p. 87.
46 'Surrender Terms of the City of Ramle', IDF Archive, 922/25/1025; Morris, *Birth*, p. 427; also *Haaretz*, 13 July 1948, and *Haolam Haze*, 15 and 22 July 1948. For the overall similar surrender conditions of Haifa see Yfaat Weiss, *A Confiscated Memory: Wadi Salib and Haifa's Lost Heritage*, trans. Avner Greenberg (NY, 2011), pp. 12–13; for those of Acre see Yehoshua Lurie, *The Walled City: Jews Among Arabs, Arabs Among Jews* (Tel Aviv, 2000)[in Hebrew], pp. 508, 512.

Arab Legion fighters in Ramle had withdrawn already before the town submitted, while the Bedouin irregulars scattered in various directions. The Mujahadin's request for reinforcement from Bethlehem and Jerusalem was not answered.[47]

At half past six in the morning of 12 July Kiryati Brigade's 42nd battalion entered and occupied Ramle without a fight, and curfew was imposed.[48] Young males (over 2,000 in number, according to Abdallah al-Tall's memoir[49]) were rounded in churches and mosques, questioned, and later detained (fig. 12).

Fig. 12: David Eldan, The Surrender of Arab Ramle, 11 July 1948 [?] (Courtesy of the GPO).

47   Gelber, *Palestine 1948*, p. 159.
48   Morris, 'Operation Dani', p. 87.
49   *Zichronot Abdallah al-Tall*, p. 199.

Was Ramle's mass exodus the result of a systematic expulsion or willed departure (though one induced by harsh conditions and a grim outlook for the future)? Obscurity in regards to the responsibility for the issuing of the expulsion order, its implementation on the ground by Kiryati's soldiers, and the extent of willed cooperation of Ramle's inhabitants in leaving their hometown, contribute little to clarify this complex picture.[50] Disagreement exists also as to the number of people who left town on the days between 10 and 14 July 1948. Figures estimating the number of refugees from both Lydda and Ramle (including refugees from nearby villages) move between 30,000 to 80,000, but all those who studied this matter agree that they were mainly women, children, and old people.[51]

Benny Morris claimed that Operation Dani was 'designed to induce civilian panic and flight', both as an end in itself, and as a means of precipitating military collapse of Ramle and Lydda.[52] Yet, as early as the beginning of May 1948, people were already leaving Ramle, while militiamen on its outskirts were trying to prevent young males from getting out of town.[53] The rich families of Ramle, according to the testimony of two original inhabitants of Ramle who still live in town,

> [K]new, before 1948 [meaning before the war started?], that the country will be occupied, and whoever had money emigrated[.] They moved to Amman, rented flats there and opened business and only lost their property in the country, and from the keys of the old flats they made a commemorative exhibition...[54]

---

50 On this matter see Tal, *War in Palestine*, p. 312; Morris, 'Operation Dani', pp. 91–99; Morris, *1948*, pp. 289–291; Kadish et al. *The Occupation*, pp. 46–50; Gelber, *Palestine 1948*, pp. 161–163; Munayyer and Khalidi, 'The Fall of Lydda', pp. 95–96.

51 30,000 according to Glubb, *A Soldier*, p. 162; 50,000 according to Morris, *1948*, p. 290; 80,000 according to Munayyer and Khalidi, 'The Fall of Lydda', p. 82.

52 Morris, *The Birth*, p. 425.

53 *Ibid.*, idem.; Gelber, *Palestine 1948*, p. 112.

54 R.Bidas, A.Moshe, R.al-Nablusi and Y.Tamari, *Zochrot et al-Ramle* ([?], 2004), p.5.

There were others, who left to Ramallah. Khanom Khairi, a former resident of Ramle, described how in mid May her father, Ahmad Khairi (nephew of the mayor), hired two large sedans to take the family to Ramallah, which, as a child, she found quiet, small and green, with nice food and nice people.[55] As the war advanced, there were also families who sent their women away to al-Bira and Ramallah for fear they might be raped.[56] Despite the worsening conditions and Jewish attacks (on the ground and from the air) in the second half of May, most population remained in town even by the end of June.[57]

It is not clear how many of Ramle's residents left town in the days after the beginning of Operation Dani and before its occupation by the IDF (10–11 July), but it seems that the mass exodus that gained momentum during the night of 11–12 July was influenced by the town's surrender, and the retreat of the Arab Legion forces that were positioned there.[58]

Until the end of June the expulsion of Arab civilians as part of the fighting was a common phenomenon, decided upon and implemented by particular IDF's commanders of each conquered area. A general order issued by the Israeli General Staff on 6 July, however, prohibited expulsion and depopulation of Arab inhabitants, unless a specific authorisation has been given by the Minister of Defence (Ben-Gurion).[59] In Ramle's case, already on 10 July an order was issued, calling 'to allow the speedy flight from Ramle of women, old people, and children'.[60] After Ramle surrendered an expulsion order was issued to its inhabitants. It seems to have stemmed from Ben-Gurion's hand gesture when discussing the matter with army leaders Yigal Alon and Yitzhak Rabin in the afternoon of 12 July: while they convened in nearby Yazur, Alon informally asked Ben-Gurion what shall be done with

55   Tolan, *The Lemon Tree*, p. 58.
56   F. Kassem, 'Between Private and Collective Memory: The Case of Palestinian Women from Lydda and Ramleh' (PhD Thesis, Morris, The Birth, 2006)[in Hebrew], p. 175.
57   Morris, *The Birth*
58   *Ibid.*, p. 426.
59   Kadish et al., *The Occupation*, p. 46.
60   Quoted in Morris, *1948*, p. 289.

the inhabitants of Lydda and Ramla. Ben Gurion's energetic hand wave was interpreted, and perhaps also followed by explicit words, as 'expel them' or 'drive them out'. At least one historian, however, discredits this story as 'myth', and instead holds Alon responsible for the expulsion order which followed.[61] Enfolding events in nearby Lydda where civilians were killed no doubt contributed in encouraging Ramle's residents to leave; it also accentuated the new occupiers' need to expel them, for fear of potential insurgence.[62]

On the afternoon of 12 July transportation was arranged to carry Ramle's residents to, or beyond, Arab Legion lines. Confiscated Arab cars and Kiryati Brigade's vehicles were not enough; more means of transportation were asked to be brought to town from Tel Aviv in the night of 12–13 July.[63] That same afternoon (12 July) Minister of Minorities Affairs Bechor Shitrit arrived in Ramle and was stunned to discover that an organised expulsion was about to begin without anyone having notified him or secured the cabinet's approval. After Shitrit confronted Foreign Minister Shertok on the matter, and the latter updated Ben-Gurion, new guidelines instructing how to treat Ramle and Lydda's inhabitants were agreed upon: they allowed whoever wanted to leave to do so; warned that Israeli authorities will not be responsible for whoever stays and will not supply food; prohibited the forced expulsion of women, children and the old; and forbade desecration of monasteries and churches. These guidelines' implementation on ground, in a cable to Operation Dani HQ that was sent that night from General Staff, was slightly different: it emphasised the fact that 'all are free to leave, apart from those who will be detained [meaning adult and young adult males, imprisoned as POW]', instructing to carry searches without vandalism and refrain from robbery.[64]

---

61   On the expulsion order see Morris, *The Birth*, p. 429; Kadish et al., *Occupation*, pp. 47–8; A. Golan, *Wartime Spatial Changes: Former Arab Territories Within the State of Israel, 1948–1950* (Beer Sheva, 2001)[in Hebrew], p. 138; also Gelber, *Palestine 1948*, p. 162.

62   Morris, *The Birth*, p. 428.

63   *Ibid.*, p. 429.

64   Quoted in Morris, *The Birth*, pp. 430–431.

Yet, on 13–14 July Ramle's inhabitants were ordered and 'encouraged' to leave. Many of the remaining town's people were strewn along the main street at the entrance to Ramle, waiting to be transported in vehicles.[65] Ramle's inhabitants were trucked and bussed out of town, to a point not far from the village al-Qubab; from there they walked to Legion-held Latrun and Salbit, where Arab Legion vehicles transported them to Ramallah.[66] 'The Jews brought busses, loaded us, and discarded us in a place I do not know its name', remembered years later a woman from Ramle who witnessed the events.[67] Unlike the people of Lydda, most of Ramle's residents were not forced to walk all the distance from their hometown to the Arab Legion lines in the blazing sun of July.[68] Only a few hundreds of Ramle's original inhabitants remained in town, mainly the old and infirm, as did several Christian families. Over the next months, some expellees managed to return.[69]

Some of the refugees from Ramle arrived at villages in the south that were under the control of the Egyptian army; others managed to cross River Jordan and arrived in Amman; yet most of them walked to the city of Ramallah.[70] The town of Ramallah soon became crowded with about 70,000 refugees from Ramle, Lydda and nearby villages. Once there, hungry and angry, they stoned officers and soldiers of the Arab Legion, blaming them to be traitors and 'worse than Jews'. Also in Amman and Nablus people demonstrated against King Abdallah and the

65 Interview with Fawzi al-Basoumi (http://www.palestineremembered. com/OralHistory/Interviews-Listing/Story1151.html#al-Ramla); Morris, 'Operation Dani', p. 96.

66 Morris, 'Operation Dani', p. 96; Morris, *The Birth*, p. 432; Morris, *1948*, p. 291.

67 Quoted in Kassem, 'Between Private and Collective Memory', p. 76.

68 Morris, *1948*, p. 290; Glubb, *A Soldier*, p. 162; Munayyer and Khalidi, 'The Fall of Lydda', p. 82 (quoting the historian Aref al-Aref, who estimated the number of those who died on the way as 350 individuals).

69 Morris, *The Birth*, pp. 430–34.

70 Gelber, *Palestine 1948*, p. 162.

Arab Legion.[71] The exiling Palestinian refugees were supported by contemporary public opinion. Criticism could be heard also within the army: Abdallah al-Tall, a Jordanian commander in the Arab Legion, for example, blamed Glubb Pasha for handing down Ramle and Lydda to the Israeli forces as part of an Anglo-Jewish conspiracy.[72]

Following Ramle's surrender and expulsion, military administration was promptly established in town, headed by Zusman Jawitz from the Haganah.[73] The remaining Arab population, both Muslims and Christians, was enclosed in a restricted area, between today's Herzl Blvd. and Bialik, Jabotinsky and Hama'apilim streets; this area was then fenced. Since then, the area has been known as the Ghetto, or simply *sakne*, Arabic for compound or habitat. None was allowed to exit this compound without special permission, and night curfew was enforced, initially between 20:00 and 06:00 and later between 22:00 and 05:00.[74] By January 1949, the Arab population, still thus incarcerated, protested against living 'in a limited residential zone behind a barbed wire fence with no freedom of movement in their hometown...'.[75] When Dov Friberg, who had escaped the extermination camp in Sobibor (Poland) and settled in Ramle, saw for the first time the fenced and guarded area in which Arab people were walking, he was astounded to hear it was referred to

---

71 Glubb, *A Soldier*, p. 163; Kadish et al., *The Occupation*, p. 98; Morris, *1948*, 291.

72 *Zichronot Abdallah al-Tall*, pp. 192–201; Kadish et al., *The Occupation*, p. 13.

73 On the military administration see S. Ozacky—Lazar, 'The Military Government as an Apparatus of Control of the Arab Citizens in Israel: The First Decade, 1948–1958', *Mizrah Hehadash* 43 (2002), pp. 103–132.

74 'Survey on the State of Security and Other Governmental Issues in Ramle [...]', undated, IDF Archive, 1860/50/32; 'Monthly Report on the Activities of the Military Governor of Ramle-Lydda [...] for the period 1 September—10 October 1948', IDF Archive 1860/50/31; 'Report on the Activities of the Military Administration in Ramle and Lydda for January 1949', IDF Archive 1860/50/31; 'Report on the Activities of the Military Administration Ramle-Lydda for February 1949', 20 March 1949, IDF Archive, 1860/50/31.

75 'Ramla', report dated to 2 January 1949, signed by Shlomo Asherov, ISA, 49//297/5–gimel. For Jaffa see Golan, *Wartime Spatial Changes*, p. 94; for Majdal see Morris, *The Birth*, p. 528.

as 'the Arab ghetto'. 'The word 'ghetto'[...], here in Israel, hit my
ears as if I had heard something that was impossible.' He was less
bothered by the fact that Arab people were closed and segregated
by barbed wire since he assumed that it was necessary and
justifiable under the circumstances.[76] But there were other, more
sympathetic, reactions, too: a Jewish communist couple—Micko
and Loti—who had arrived in town from Bulgaria in December
1948, shook hands through the fence with Arab communists
named Suhil and Amin, who resided within the compound.[77]
Similar 'ghettos' existed in other occupied Arab towns: in early
August a part of 'Ajami neighbourhood in Jaffa was separated by
barbed wire, following a decision to populate the city with Jews;
most of Haifa's Arabs were instructed to settle at the end of June
in Wadi Nisnas, although initially there had been an intent to
settle there only the city's Christian population; in Majdal, on
the other hand, the Arab population was gradually ghettoised,
a process that began in December 1948 and ended in the first
months of 1950.[78]

In August 1948, the immigration department of the Jewish
Agency (JA) requested the Ministry of Defence to allow settling
of new Jewish immigrants in Ramle. Although Ben-Gurion
was in favour of the idea, Moshe Sharet and Eliezer Kaplan,
the Foreign and Finance Ministers, opposed it: as part of
ongoing peace negotiations, King Abdullah demanded the
settlement of Arab refugees in Ramle and Lydda to be included
in any future agreement. This opposition caused Ben-Gurion
to hesitate for more than two months before finally submitting
the settlement plan to the government's approval.[79] At the
beginning of January 1949, Ben-Gurion instructed the Israeli
delegates in the negotiations with Transjordan to adamantly

76 Dov Friberg, *To Be Like Everyone Else* (Ramla, 1996)[in Hebrew], p. 69.
77 *Zochrot et al-Ramle*, p. 8.
78 *Zochrot et al-Ramle*, p. 8.
79 A. Golan, 'Lydda and Ramle: From Palestinian-Arab to Israeli Towns, 1948–
    67', *Middle Eastern Studies* 39 (2003), pp. 121–139 (pp. 125–126); Ben-
    Gurion, *Yoman Hamilchama*, vol. II, entry 26 August 1948.

refuse any concession with regard to Ramle, and to leave the Lydda question pending.[80]

The Jewish Agency's request to settle Ramle with Jews was finally approved by the government on 5 November 1948. This required the JA to provide municipal services, organise a police force and collect taxes.[81] Nine days later, on 14 November, the first group of 300 immigrants arrived in Ramle, and the end of the military administration in town (30 June 1949) marked another step towards ostensible renormalisation; by March 1949 there were as many as 6000 new Jewish settlers in town.[82]

With this new influx of immigrants, municipal matters required a more thorough approach. In a meeting of the temporary government on 6 March 1949, it was decided to authorise the Minister of the Interior, Chaim-Moshe Shapira, to appoint municipal committees in the towns of Ramla, Lod (Lydd's new Israeli name) and Acre, which will consist of government officials and representatives of the local population, including Arabs. The committees were to prepare at once for the election of a municipal council; this was supposed to materialise within a month's time. In effect, however, elections could not take place prior to the government's decision on the final annexation

---

80   Golan, 'Lydda and Ramle', p. 126; Ben-Gurion, *Yoman Hamilchama*, vol. III, entry 4 January 1949. Nevertheless, until as late as the end of April 1949 King Abdullah was still negotiating for Ramle's future status. In a caricature titled 'fishing', Abdullah was depicted as a *kaffiya*-wearing fisherman who had already managed to catch fish identified as the 'Triangle' and 'Hebron', and was still waiting to catch 'Katamon', 'Lod' and 'Ramle' swimming in the pond. *Maariv*, 29 April 1949.

81   Golan, 'Lydda and Ramle', p. 126; on this same day a letter was sent from Dov Patishi, manager of housing department in the JA, urging the military administration to allow the settlement of about a thousand families of new immigrants in Ramle, dated 5 November 1948, IDF Archive, 1860/50/31.

82   'Report on the Activities of the Military Administration in Ramle and Lydda for the period 10 October—15 November 1948', undated, IDF Archive, 1860/50/31; 'Report on the Activities of the Military Administration in Ramle and Lydda for February 1949', 20 March 1949, IDF Archive 1860/50/31. In other mixed towns, such as Lydda and Jaffa, the military administration was similarly terminated in 1949 (in Acre it ended only in June 1951), unlike its prolongation until the end of 1966 in the Galilee, the 'Triangle' and the Negev. Ozacky-Lazar, 'The Military Government'.

of both Ramla and Lydda.[83] Two months later, on 9 May 1949,
'the Municipality Committee for Ramla' (va'adat ha'irya leRamla)
was appointed by the Minister of the Interior, according to the
1934 Municipalities Order (Pkudat Ha'iryot). Meir Melamed, a
veteran settler of Bulgarian descent, was appointed as its head.[84]
On this appointment, he said years later:

> When a central position in Ramla was offered me, I have
> already lived here for several months and was familiar with
> the place[.] I knew of the chaos that existed here. I told
> to those who imposed the position on me: 'Gentlemen, I
> have no idea of how to run a city, let alone a city like this
> one[;] why, you are sending me into a jungle, a veritable
> jungle!'. I was told, 'well, you are a gymnastics teacher in
> your profession, you were a Haganah man, an officer in
> the army—you'll manage [...].[85]

Melamed was later elected as Ramla's Mayor and remained in this
position for more than a decade.

In July 1949 there were about 1400 Arabs in Ramla, consisting
of Muslims and Christians (Greek-Orthodox, Catholics,
Protestant, Armenian and Coptic), very few compared to the pre-

83 'Decisions: A Meeting of the Temporary Government', 6 March 1949, ISA,
    50//2639/5–gimel; Golan, 'Lydda and Ramle', pp. 127–128.
84 'Order from the Minister of the Interior as to the Appointment of the
    Municipality Committee to Ramle', ISA, 50//2639/5–gimel. On the operation
    of this appointed municipal committee see a leaflet which summarised its
    activity between 1 July 1949 and 30 September 1950: *Iryat Ramla: Sikum
    Pe'ulot Ha'irya* (Ramla, 1950). The appointing of the committee was criticised
    in the Knesset's first session (6 June 1949): Meir Vilner of the Communist
    Party (Maki) directed a parliamentary question to the Minister of the Interior,
    M. Shapira, in protest against the arbitrary and undemocratic appointment of
    municipalities to the cities of Ramla, Lydda and Acre. In his answer, Shapira
    commented that these appointments were made according to the decision
    of the temporary government, which instructed the appointment of these
    committees next to the military governor and under him. Their representatives
    were proposed by the governors after inquiring into the ethnic composition
    and political affiliations of the local population. *Divrey HaKnesset*, vol. I, p. 14.
85 *Ramla 'Iri (Hahebet Hahistori): Mikra'a Lamore*, Ze'ev Ilan (ed.)(Ramla, 1978),
    p. 30.

war population of 18,000 (16,000 Muslims and 2000 Christians).[86] The town's Arab population had changed dramatically as a result of the war. Whereas before the occupation in July 1948, 80% of the town's population were Muslim and the rest Christian, after the war 80% of Ramle's Arab residents was Christian.[87] This is an important point, since Muslims and Christians have had different patterns of political mobilisation and relations with colonial powers, including the Israeli State. The exiling of the Muslim urban elites resulted in the rise of Christian socio-political leaders; indeed, between the 1950s and 1970s Israeli Christians were prominent in contemporary politics, especially within the Communist Party and as representatives in the Arab political parties linked to Ben-Gurion's Mapai Party.[88] Moreover, most of Ramla's Christians after 1948 originated from urban centres (Jaffa and Haifa, but mostly Ramle itself), whereas its smaller Muslim community arrived, after 1948, from nearby abandoned villages.[89] There were hundreds of returnees;[90] there were also new Arab inhabitants in town and on its outskirts: about 400–500 agricultural workers brought from Nazareth around 1948–49 lived around the Arab *sakne*.[91]

When the first municipal elections in Ramla finally took place (symbolically, on 14 November 1950, exactly two years after the first Jewish new immigrants had arrived in town), 6,000 people

---

86 In 1959, Ramla's population included 1230 Christians (850 Greek-Orthodox; 300 Catholic; 35 Protestant; 30 Armenian; and 15 Coptic), and 649 Muslims. Ze'ev Vilna'i, *Ramla: Hove Ve'avar* (Ramla, 1961), pp. 15, 88. The 1931 census mentions 10,400 Arabs. Hagit Chovav, *Ramla—Hair Ha'atika: Seker Chevrati* (1968), p. 70; 'Ramle', 2 January 1949, ISA, 297/5–gimel.

87 'Monthly Report on the Actions of the Military Governor of Ramle-Lydda' (for the period 10 October 1948 to 1 September 1949), IDF Archive, 1860/50//31.

88 Dafna Tsimhoni, 'Hanotzrim BeIsrael: Beyn Dat Lepolitika', in *The Arabs in Israeli Politics: Dilemmas of Identity*, Elie Rekhes (ed.)(Tel Aviv, 1998)[in Hebrew], pp. 63–72.

89 Hagit Chovav, *Ramla—Hair Ha'atika: Seker Chevrati* (1968), p. 70.

90 Morris, *The Birth*, p. 434.

91 'Monthly Report on the Actions of the Military Governor of Ramle-Lydda' (for the period 10 October 1948 to 1 September 1949), IDF Archive, 1860/50//31.

were allowed to vote, among them 688 Arabs.[92] The elected council, with Melamed at its head, consisted of thirteen members, most of them immigrants from Central and Eastern Europe who had arrived in 1948–9; only one member, the Christian Eliya Fanus, represented the town's Arab community.[93]

92 Two Arab parties participated in the elections: 'Unity and Progress', headed by Fanus, who was part of the municipal committee, received 8% of the votes and entered the council; 'The Popular List', headed by the Muslim Isma'il Nachas failed to enter the council, supported by only 3% of the voters. ISA, 50//2639/5–gimel.
93 *Ramla Bevinyana Uvehitpatchuta* (Ramla, 1952), p. 12.

Bibliography

Archives

Archive of the City of Tel Aviv-Jaffa
Central Zionist Archive
The Hagannah Archive
Israel Defense Forces (IDF) Archive
Israel State Archive (ISA)
Lavon Institute for Labour Research
Ramla's Municipal Archive
Ramla's Municipal Museum
State of Israel, National Photo Collection (GPO—Governmental Press
   Office)

Primary Sources

Ben-Gurion, David, *Yoman haMilchama* ([Tel Aviv], 1984)
Bialik, Chaim Nachman, *Poems from the Hebrew*, L.V. Snowman (ed.)
   (London, 1924)
Chovav, Hagit, *Ramla—Hair Ha'atika: Seker Chevrati* (1968)
Dayan, Moshe, *Moshe Dayan: Story of My Life* (NY, 1976)
Divrey HaKnesset
Encounters of Memory (Jerusalem, 2000) [in Hebrew]
Frank, Pinchas, *Proyect Shituf Toshavim Bebinuy Upinuy: Sikum Mechkar
   Pe'ula* (Tel Aviv University, c. 1970–1971?)
Friberg, Dov, *To Be Like Everyone Else* (Ramla, 1996) [in Hebrew]
Glubb, John Bagot, *A Soldier with the Arabs* (London, 1957)

El-Hairi, Bashir, *Letters to A Lemon Tree*, trans. D. Brafman (Jerusalem, 1997)[in Hebrew]

Halewi, Aharon, 'The City Garden "Gan Meir" at Tel Aviv', *Hatteva' Vehaaretz* (Nature and Country) 2 (1933), pp. 105–110

Herzl, Theodor, *Altneuland* (Tel Aviv, 2004)[in Hebrew]

Husseini Shahid, Serene, *Jerusalem Memories*, trans. Mali Baruch (Tel Aviv, 2006)[in Hebrew][1999]

Iryat Ramla: Sikum Pe'ulot Ha'irya (Ramla, 1950)

The Itinerary of Benjamin of Tudela, trans. M.N. Adler (London, 1907)

Kanafani, Ghassan, *Men in the Sun and Other Stories*, trans. Hilary Kilpatrick (Washington, D.C., 1993)

Kaniuk, Yoram, *1948* (Tel Aviv, 2010)[in Hebrew]

Maisler, B. and Yeivin, S., *Palestine Guide: For Navy, Army and Air Force* (Tel Aviv, 1940)

Masterman, E.W.G. and Macalister, R.A.S., *Occasional Papers on the Modern Inhabitants of Palestine: Tales of Welys and Dervishes* (1915)

Matson, Olaf, *The American Colony Palestine Guide* (Jerusalem, 1930)

Mehanaasa Ba'ir: Igeret Le'ezrachey Ramla 1 (Ramla, August 1954)

Mehana'asa Ba'ir: Igeret Le'ezrachey Ramla 3 (Ramla, November 1954)

Mehana'asa Ba'ir: Igeret Le'ezrachey Ramla 4 (Ramla, April 1957)

Mehana'asa Ba'ir: Igeret Le'ezrachey Ramla 5 (Ramla, May 1957)

Mituv Tverya: Dapim Lecheker Tverya, Rephael Yankelevitch (ed.) (Jerusalem, 1988)

Munayyer, Spiro and Khalidi, Walid, 'The Fall of Lydda', *Journal of Palestine Studies* 27:4 (1998), pp. 80–98

Ramla—Seker Likrat Shikum (parts I, II)(April 1970)

Ramla 'Iri (Hahebet Hahistori): Mikra'a Lamore, Ze'ev Ilan (ed.)(Ramla, 1978)

Ramla Bevinyana Uvehitpatchuta (Ramla, 1952)

Ramla: Bita'on Iryat Ramla 1 (Ramla, 1966)

Ramla: *Bita'on Iryat Ramla* 3 (Ramla, April 1967)

Sakakini, Hala, *Jerusalem and I: A Personal Record* (Jerusalem, 1990)

Shafrir, Dov, *Arugat Chaim* (Tel Aviv, 1974/75)

"Such Am I, Oh World!": Diaries of Khalil al-Sakakini, trans. Gideon Shilo (Jerusalem, 1990)[in Hebrew]

Tleel, John M., *I am Jerusalem* (Jerusalem, 2000)

Toren, Bilha, *Sdom Vehamora: Sipurim—Lo Liyladim!* (Tel Aviv, 2004)

Vilna'i, Ze'ev, *Ramla: Hove Veavar* (Ramla, 1961)

Yediot Ramla (Ramla, 1958)

Zichronot Abdallah al-Tall, trans. Y. Chalamish (Tel Aviv, 1960)

Secondary Sources

Abbasi, M., 'The War on the Mixed Cities: The Depopulation of Arab
Tiberias and the Destruction of Its Old "Sacred" City (1948–1949)',
Holy Land Studies 7 (2008), pp. 45–80

—, 'Families of Arab Notables in Acre at the End of Ottoman Rule and
During the Mandate Period: Continuation or Change?', *Cathedra* 130
(2009), pp. 51–74 [in Hebrew]

Abowd, Thomas, 'The Politics and Poetics of Place: The Baramki House',
Jerusalem Quarterly File 21 (2004), pp. 49–58

Abufarha, Nasser, 'Land of Symbols: Cactus, Poppies, Orange and Olive
Trees in Palestine', *Identities* 15 (2008), pp. 343–368

Abu-Lughod, Janet L., 'The Islamic City—Historic Myth, Islamic Essence,
and Contemporary Relevance', *International Journal of Middle East
Studies* 19:2 (1987), pp. 155–176

Acts of Memory: Cultural Recall in the Present, M. Bal, J. Crewe and L. Spitzer
(eds.)(Hanover, NH, 1999)

The Age of Zionism, A. Shapira, J. Reinharz and J. Harris (eds.)(Jerusalem,
2000)[in Hebrew]

*All That Remains: The Palestinian Villages Occupied and Depopulated by Israel
in 1948*, Walid Khalidi (ed.)(Washington, D.C., 1992)

Almog, Oz, *The Sabra—A Profile* (Tel Aviv, 1997)[in Hebrew]

Alon-Mozes, Tal and Amir, Shaul, 'Landscape and Ideology: The Emergence
of Vernacular Gardening in Pre-State Israel', *Landscape Journal* 21:2
(2002), pp. 37–50

Aly, Götz, *Hitler's Beneficiaries: Plunder, Racial War, and the Nazi Welfare
State*, trans. J. Chase (NY, 2006)[2005]

Anderson, Benedict, *Imagined Communities* (London, 1991)[1983]

The Arabs in Israeli Politics: Dilemmas of Identity, Elie Rekhes (ed.)(Tel Aviv,
1998)[in Hebrew]

Arieh-Sapir, Nili, 'Carnival in Tel Aviv: The Purim Festival in the 'First' Hebrew City', *Jerusalem Studies in Jewish Folklore* 22 (2002), pp. 99–121

—, 'The Procession of Lights: Hanukkah as a National Festival in Tel Aviv, 1909–1936', *Cathedra* 103 (2002), pp. 131–150 [in Hebrew]

Ashkelon—4,000 Ve'od Arba'im Shana, Naftali Arbel (ed.)(Ashkelon?, 1990)

Ashkelon Bride of the South: Studies in the History of Ashkelon from the Middle Ages to the End of the Twentieth Century, Z. Safrai and N. Sagiv (eds.) (Ashkelon, 2002)[in Hebrew]

Assaf, Michael, *History of the Arabs in Palestine* (Tel Aviv, 1970)[in Hebrew]

Azaryahu, Maoz, *State Cults: Celebrating Independence and Commemorating the Fallen in Israel 1948–1956* (Beer Sheva, 1995)[in Hebrew]

—, 'The Power of Commemorative Street Names', *Environment and Planning D: Society and Space* 14:3 (1996), pp. 311–330

—, 'The Independence Day Military Parade: A Political History of A Patriotic Ritual', in *The Military and Militarism in Israeli Society*, Edna Lomsky-Feder and Eyal Ben-Ari (eds.)(NY, 1999), pp. 89–116

Azarayhu, Maoz and Golan, Arnon, '(Re)naming the Landscape: The Formation of the Hebrew Map of Israel 1949–1960', *Journal of Historical Geography* 27:2 (2001), pp. 178–195

Bajohr, Frank, *'Aryanisation' in Hamburg: The Economic Exclusion of Jews and the Confiscation of Their Property in Nazi Germany* (NY and Oxford, 2002)

Baker, Alan R.H., 'Introduction: On Ideology and Landscape', in *Ideology and Landscape in Historical Perspective: Essays on the Meanings of Some Places in the Past*, Alan R.H. Baker and Gideon Biger (eds.)(Cambridge, 1992), pp. 1–14

Bardenstein, C., 'Threads of Memory and Discourses of Rootedness: Of Trees, Oranges and the Prickly-Pear Cactus in Israel/Palestine', *Edebiyat* 8 (1998), pp. 1–36 [in Hebrew]

—, 'Trees, Forests, and the Shaping of Palestinian and Israeli Collective Memory', in *Acts of Memory: Cultural Recall in the Present*, M. Bal, J. Crewe and L. Spitzer (eds.) (Hanover, NH, 1999), pp. 148–168

Bar-Gal, Yoram, 'Political Symbolization of an Urban Space: Street Naming in Israel', *Horizons in Geography* 33–34 (1992), pp. 119–132 [in Hebrew]

Barkan, Elazar, *The Guilt of Nations: Restitution and Negotiating Historical Injustices* (Baltimore, 2000)

Beer Sheva: Metropolis in the Making, Y. Gradus and E. Meir-Glitzenstein (eds.)(Jerusalem, 2008)[in Hebrew]

Beer Sheva: The Growth of a City: A Model of the Development of Public Housing in Israel (Beer Sheva, 2008)

Beinin, Joel, *Was the Red Flag Flying There? Marxist Politics and the Arab-Israeli Conflict in Egypt and Israel, 1948–1965* (Berkeley, 1990)

Ben Arav, Joseph, *Gardens and Landscape in Israel* (Tel Aviv, 1981)[in Hebrew]

Ben-Amos, Avner, 'Theatres of Death and Memory: Monuments and Rituals in Israel', in D. Dominey and F. Lebée-Nadav, *Everywhere: Landscape and Memory in Israel*, M. Vigoder (ed.)(Tel Aviv, 2002), pp. 18–20 [in Hebrew]

Ben-Artzi, Yossi, *The Creation of the Carmel as a Segregated Jewish Residential Space in Haifa, 1918–1948* (Jerusalem, 2004)[in Hebrew]

Ben Ze'ev, Efrat, 'The Politics of Taste and Smell: Palestinian Rites of Return', in *The Politics of Food*, Marianne Elizabeth Lien and Brigitte Nerlich (eds.)(Oxford and NY, 2004), pp. 141–160

Benvenisti, M., *Sacred Landscape: The Buried History of the Holy Land since 1948*, trans. M. Kaufman-Lacusta (Berkeley, 2000)

Ben-Zaken, Avner, *Communism as Cultural Imperialism: The Affinities between Eretz-Israeli Communism and Arab Communism 1919–1948* (Tel Aviv, 2006)[in Hebrew]

Bernstein, Deborah, *Women on the Margins: Gender and Nationalism in Mandate Tel Aviv* (Jerusalem, 2008)[in Hebrew]

Bernstein, D. and Hasisi, B., '"Buy and Promote the National Cause": Consumption, Class Formation and Nationalism in Mandate Palestinian Society', *Nations and Nationalism* 14:1 (2008), pp. 127–150

Bestor, Theodore C., *Tsukiji: The Fish Market at the Center of the World* (Berkeley and LA, 2004)

Bickford, Susan, 'Constructing Inequality: City Spaces and the Architecture of Citizenship', *Political Theory* 28:3 (2000), pp. 355–376

Bidas, R., Moshe, A., al-Nablusi, R., and Tamari, Y., *Zochrot et al-Ramle* ([?], 2004)

Biger, Gideon, *An Empire in the Holy Land: Historical Geography of the British Administration in Palestine 1917–1929* (Jerusalem, 1994)

—, 'Unit 3: Regulative Planning in Towns in Palestine During the Period of British Mandatory Rule', in *Settlement Geography of Israel: Spatial Experiments* (Tel Aviv, 1996), pp. 208–211 [in Hebrew]

Birshut Harabim: Mechva leganan ha'ir Tel Aviv, Avraham Karavan, Ya'el Moriya and Sigal Bar Nir (eds.)(Tel Aviv, 2003)

Boal, F.W., 'From Undivided Cities to Undivided Cities: Assimilation to Ethnic Cleansing', *Housing Studies* 14:5 (1999), pp. 585–600

Bonner, M., *The Majesty of the State: Triumphal Progresses of Foreign Sovereigns in Renaissance Italy 1494–1600* (Florence, 1986)

Boyer, Christine, *The City of Collective Memory: Its Historical Imagery and Architectural Entertainments* (Cambridge, Mass., 1994)

Boymal, Yair, 'Ekronot Mediniyut Ha'aflaya Klapey Ha'aravim BeIsrael', in *Iyunim Bitkumat Israel: Studies in Zionism, the Yishuv and the State of Israel* 16 (2006), pp. 391–410

Brace, Catherine, 'Landscape and Identity', in *Studying Cultural Landscapes*, I. Robertson and P. Richards (eds.)(London, 2003), pp. 121–140

Braverman, Irus, *Planted Flags: Trees, Land, and Law in Israel/ Palestine* (Cambridge, 2009)

Brener, Mussa, *Asara Mi Yode'a? (Aseret Mefakdey Hahagannah Shel Ha'ir Tel Aviv)* (Tel Aviv, 1988)

Brooks, John, *Gardens of Paradise: The History and Design of the Great Islamic Gardens* (London, 1987)

Brown, Andrew, *Civic Ceremony and Religion in Medieval Bruges c. 1300–1520* (Cambridge, 2011)

de Certeau, Michel, *The Practice of Everyday Life*, trans. S. Rendall (Berkeley and LA, 1984)[1980]

Chatuka, Tali, 'Parallel Realities: Gan Hakovshim and its Surroundings, Tel Aviv 2003', in *Birshut Harabim: Mechva leganan ha'ir Tel Aviv, Avraham Karavan*, Ya'el Moriya and Sigal Bar Nir (eds.)(Tel Aviv, 2003), pp. 68–77

Chetrit, Sami Shalom, *The Mizrahi Struggle in Israel Between Oppression and Liberation, Identification and Alternative 1948–2003* (Tel Aviv, 2006) [in Hebrew]

Clark, Emma, *The Art of the Islamic Garden* (Marlborough, Wiltshire, 2004)

Clarke, John and Critcher, Chas, 'Leisure and Inequality', in *Sociology of Leisure: A Reader*, C. Critcher, P. Braham and A. Tomlinson (eds.) (London and NY, 1995), pp. 247–255

Cohen, Aharon, *The Arab Worker's Movement (in Egypt, Palestine, Lebanon, Syria, Iraq): History, Summaries, Problems* (Haifa, 1947)[in Hebrew]

Cohen, Eitan, *Beer Sheva: The Fourth City* (Jerusalem, 2006)[in Hebrew]

Cohen, Erik, 'The City in Zionist Ideology', in *Towns in Israel: A Reader*, A. Shachar, D. Weintraub, E. Cohen and L. Shelach (eds.)(Jerusalem, 1973), pp. 5–10 [in Hebrew]

Cohen, Orna, Majdal's Arabs under the Israeli Regime, 1948–1950', in *Ashkelon Bride of the South: Studies in the History of Ashkelon from the Middle Ages to the End of the Twentieth Century*, Z. Safrai and N. Sagiv (eds.)(Ashkelon, 2002), pp. 185–212 [in Hebrew]

Cohen, Shaul Ephraim, *The Politics of Planting: Israeli-Palestinian Competition for Control of Land in the Jerusalem Periphery* (Chicago, 1993)

Constructing A Sense of Place: Architecture and the Zionist Discourse, Haim Yacobi (ed.)(Aldershot, 2004)

Da Matta, Roberto, 'Constraint and License: A Preliminary Study of Two Brazilian National Rituals', in *Secular Ritual*, S.F. Moore and B.G. Myerhoff (eds.)(Amsterdam, 1977), pp. 244–264

Dabit, Bothayna, 'Haproyekt: Ir Me'orevet', *Mitsad Sheni* 6–7 (2004), pp. 28–30

Dancho, Arnon, 'Nabi Mussa Rituals', *National Geographic* 34 (2001)(no page number)[in Hebrew]

Davies, Douglas, 'The Evocative Symbolism of Trees', in *The Iconography of Landscape: Essays on the Symbolic Representation, Design and Use of Past Environments*, D. Cosgrove and S. Daniels (eds.)(Cambridge, 1988), pp. 32–42

Davis, Susan G., *Parades and Power: Street Theatre in Nineteenth-Century Philadelphia* (Berkeley and London, 1986)

Dean, Martin, *Robbing the Jews: The Confiscation of Jewish Property in the Holocaust, 1933–1945* (Cambridge, 2008)

Diner, Dan, 'Memory and Restitution: The Second World War as a Foundational Event in a Uniting Europe', in *Restitution and Memory: Material Restoration in Europe*, D. Diner and G. Wunberg (eds.)(NY, 2007), pp. 9–23

Dominey, D. and Lebée-Nadav, F., *Everywhere: Landscape and Memory in Israel*, M. Vigoder (ed.)(Tel Aviv, 2002)[in Hebrew]

Domínguez, Virginia R., *People as Subject, People as Object: Selfhood and Peoplehood in Contemporary Israel* (Madison, Wis., 1989)

Donner, Batya, 'Shkifut Hakoach Hanir'e', in *Hod Vehadar: Tiksey Haribonut Hayisraelit, 1948–1958* (Tel Aviv, 2001), pp. 8–61

Don-Yehiya, Eliezer, 'Festivals and Political Culture: The Celebrations of Independence Day in the Early Years of Statehood', in *State, Government and International Relations* 23 (1984), pp. 5–28

Doron, Dov, 'Ha'ayara Majdal VeSvivata BeMilchemet HaKomemiyut', in *Ashkelon—4,000 Ve'od Arba'im Shana*, Naftali Arbel (eds.)(Ashkelon?, 1990), pp. 26–35

Drori, Yosef, 'Nabi Salah', *Moreshet Derech* 10 (1985), pp. 18–19

Duncan, James S., *The City as Text: The Politics of Landscape Interpretation in the Kandyan Kingdom* (Cambridge, 1990)

Durkheim, Émile, *The Elementary Forms of Religious Life*, trans. Carol Cosman (Oxford, 2001)

Edgar, Andrew, *The Philosophy of Habermas* (Chesham, Bucks., UK, 2005)

—, *Habermas: The Key Concepts* (NY, 2006)

El-Eini, Roza I.M., *Mandated Landscape: British Imperial Rule in Palestine, 1929–1948* (London, 2006)

Ellisséeff, Nikita, 'Physical Lay-Out', in *The Islamic City*, R.B. Serjeant (ed.) (Paris, 1980), pp. 90–103

Enis, Ruth, *Documentation of Three Gardens in Israel (1935–1950)*(Haifa, 1988)[in Hebrew]

—, 'Historical Gardens in Eretz-Israel and their Pioneer Designers', in *Point of View: Four Approaches to Landscape Architecture in Israel*, Lipa Yahalom *et al.* (eds.)(Tel Aviv, 1996), pp. 7–18 [in Hebrew]

Escher, Anton, 'Construction of the Public Sphere in the Middle Eastern Medina During the First Half of the 20th Century', in *Middle Eastern Cities 1900–1950: Public Places and Public Spheres in Transformation*, Hans Chr. Korsholm Nielsen and Jacob Skovgaard-Petersen (eds.) (Aarhus, 2001), pp. 164–175

Fairchild Ruggles, D., *Islamic Gardens and Landscapes* (Philadelphia, 2008)

Falah, Ghazi, 'Living Together Apart: Residential Segregation in Mixed Arab-Jewish Cities in Israel', *Urban Studies* 33:6 (1996), pp. 823–857

'Feasts, Celebrations and Pilgrimage to Saints' Tombs', in *Religion and Ritual and Tombs of Muslim Saints in Eretz Yisrael*, Eli Shiller (ed.)(also referred to as *Ariel* 117–118 (1996), pp. 190–191 [in Hebrew]

Fischbach, Michael R., *Records of Dispossession: Palestinian Refugee Property and the Arab-Israeli Conflict* (NY, 2003)

Forman, G. and Kedar, A., 'From Arab Land to "Israel Lands": The Legal Dispossession of the Palestinians Displaced by Israel in the Wake of 1948', *Environment and Planning D: Society and Space* 22 (2004), pp. 809–830

Fuchs, Ron, 'The Planning of the British War Cemeteries in Mandatory Palestine', *Cathedra* 79 (1996), pp. 114–139 [in Hebrew]

—, 'The Palestinian Arab House Reconsidered: Part 1: The Pre-Industrial Vernacular', *Cathedra* 89 (1998) pp. 83–126 [in Hebrew]

—, 'The Palestinian House Reconsidered: Part 2: Domestic Architecture in the 19th Century', *Cathedra* 90 (1989), pp. 53–86 [in Hebrew]

Gal (Gale), N., 'From Rural to Urban Center: Ashkelon as a Case Study of Israeli Socio-Regional Changes from the Establishment of the State of Israel to the Mid-Ninetees' in *Ashkelon Bride of the South: Studies in the History of Ashkelon from the Middle Ages to the End of the Twentieth Century*, Z. Safrai and N. Sagiv (eds.)(Ashkelon, 2002), pp. 213–232

Gat, Moshe, *A Jewish Community in Crisis: The Exodus from Iraq, 1948–1951* (Jerusalem, 1989)[in Hebrew]

Gat, Shimon, 'A Flourishing Arab City: The Economy of Medieval Ramla', *Cathedra* 123 (2007), pp. 39–66 [in Hebrew]

Geertz, Clifford, 'Suq: The Bazaar Economy in Sefrou', in *Meaning and Order in Moroccan Society: Three Essays in Cultural Analysis* (Cambridge, 1979), pp. 123–313

Gelber, Yoav, *Palestine 1948: War, Escape and the Emergence of the Palestinian Refugee Problem* (Brighton, 2001)

George, Alan, 'Making the Desert Bloom: A Myth Examined', *Journal of Palestine Studies* 8:2 (1979), pp. 88–100

Golan, A., *Wartime Spatial Changes: Former Arab Territories Within the State of Israel, 1948–1950* (Beer Sheva, 2001)[in Hebrew]

—, 'Lydda and Ramle: From Palestinian-Arab to Israeli Towns, 1948–67', *Middle Eastern Studies* 39 (2003), pp. 121–139

Gonen, Amiram, *Between City and Suburb: Urban Residential Patterns and Processes in Israel* (Aldershot, Hants., 1995)

Goren, Tamir, *Mitlut Lehishtaltut* (Haifa, 1996)

Gosewinkel, Dieter, and Meyer, Stefan, 'Citizenship, Property Rights and Dispossession in Postwar Poland (1918 and 1945), *European Review of History* 16:4 (2009), pp. 575–595

Haim, Sylvia G., 'Aspects of Jewish Life in Baghdad under the Monarchy', *Middle Eastern Studies* 12:2 (1976), pp. 188–208

Haine, W. Scott, *The World of the Paris Café: Sociability among the French Working Class, 1789–1914* (Baltimore and London, 1996)

Hakim, Besim Selim, *Arabic-Islamic Cities: Building and Planning Principles* (London, 1986)

Handelman, Don, *Models and Mirrors: Towards an Anthropology of Public Events* (Cambridge, 1990)

Harvey, David, *The Condition of Postmodernity* (Cambridge, Mass., 1990)

Hasan, Manar, 'The Destruction of the City and the War on the Collective Memory: The Victorious and the Defeated', *Theory and Criticism* 27 (2005), pp. 197–207 [in Hebrew]

Haskell, Guy H., *From Sofia to Jaffa: The Jews of Bulgaria in Israel* (Detroit, 1994)

Hattox, Ralph S., *Coffee and Coffeehouses: The Origins of a Social Beverage in the Medieval Near East* (Seattle, 1985)

Helman, Anat, *Urban Culture in 1920s and 1930s Tel Aviv* (Jerusalem, 2007)[in Hebrew]

Helphand, Kenneth, *Dreaming Gardens: Landscape Architecture and the Making of Modern Israel* (Santa Fe, NM, 2002)

Holzman-Gazit, Yifat, *Land Expropriation in Israel: Law, Culture and Society* (Aldershot, 2007)

The Iconography of Landscape: Essays on the Symbolic Representation, Design and Use of Past Environments, D. Cosgrove and S. Daniels (eds.) (Cambridge, 1988)

Ideology and Landscape in Historical Perspective: Essays on the Meanings of Some Places in the Past, Alan R.H. Baker and Gideon Biger (eds.) (Cambridge, 1992)

Inbar, Zvi, *The Sclaes of Justice and the Sword* (Tel Aviv, 2005)[in Hebrew]

Isin, Engin F. and Siemiatycki, Myer, 'Fate and Faith: Claiming Urban Citizenship in Immigrant Toronto', CERIS Working Paper Series, Working Paper no. 8 (June 1999), pp. 1–30

Isin, Engin, 'Who is the New Citizen? Towards a Genealogy', *Citizenship Studies* 1:1 (1997), pp. 115–131

The Islamic City, R.B. Serjeant (ed.)(Paris, 1980)

Israeli Society: Critical Perspectives, Uri Ram (ed.)(Tel Aviv, 1993)[in Hebrew]

Jarman, N., *Material Conflicts: Parades and Visual Displays in Northern Ireland* (Oxford and NY, 1997)

Jews among Arabs: Contacts and Boundaries, M.R. Cohen and A.L. Udovitch (eds.)(NJ, 1989)

Jiryis, Sabri, 'Domination by Law', *Journal of Palestine Studies* 11:1 (1981), pp. 67–92

Kadish, A., Sela, A. and Golan, A., *The Occupation of Lydda 1948* ([Tel Aviv], 2000)[in Hebrew]

Kagan, Michael, 'Destructive Ambiguity: Enemy Nationals and the Legal Enabling of Ethnic Conflict in the Middle East', *Columbia Human Rights Law Review* 38 (2007), pp. 263–319

Kalush, R., and Lu-Yon, H., 'Habayit Haleumi Veha'bayit Ha'ishi: Tafkid Hashikun Hatziburi Be'itzuv Hamerchav', in *Space, Land, Home*, Yehouda Shenhav (ed.)(Jerusalem, 2003), pp. 166–198

Kaplan, J., 'Excavations at the White Mosque in Ramla', *Atiqot* 2 (1959), pp. 106–115

Kassem, Fatmeh, 'Language, History and Women: Palestinian Women in Israel Describe the *Nakba*', *Theory and Criticism* 29 (2006), pp. 59–80 [in Hebrew]

Kazzaz, Nissim, *The Jews in Iraq in the Twentieth Century* (Jerusalem, 1991) [in Hebrew]

Kedourie, Elie, 'The Break between Muslims and Jews in Iraq', in *Jews among Arabs: Contacts and Boundaries*, M.R. Cohen and A.L. Udovitch (eds.)(NJ, 1989), pp. 21–63

Kelly, John R., *Leisure Identities and Interactions* (London, 1983)

Keshavarzian, Arang, *Bazaar and State in Iran: The Policies of Tehran Marketplace* (Cambridge, 2007)

Khalidi, Rashid, *Palestinian Identity: The Construction of Modern National Consciousness* (NY, 1997)

Khalidi, Walid, *Before Their Diaspora: A Photographic History of The Palestinians 1876–1948* (Washington D.C., 1984)

Khazzoom, Aziza, 'The Great Chain of Orientalism: Jewish Identity, Stigma Management, and Ethnic Exclusion in Israel', *American Sociological Review* 68:4 (2003), pp. 481–510

—, 'Did the Israeli State Engineer Segregation? On the Placement of Jewish Immigrants in Development Towns in the 1950s', *Social Forces* 84:1 (2005), pp. 115–134

Kliot, Nurit, 'Ideology and Afforestation in Israel: Man-Made Forest of the Jewish National Fund', *Studies in the Geography of Israel* 13 (1992), pp. 87–106 [in Hebrew]

Korn, Alina, 'Good Intentions: The short History of the Minority Affairs Ministry, 14 May 1948—1 July 1949', *Cathedra* 127 (2008), pp. 141–168 [in Hebrew]

Kupferschmidt, Uri M., *The Supreme Muslim Council: Islam Under the British Mandate for Palestine* (Leiden, 1987)

Lancaster, Michael, 'Public Parks', in *The Oxford Companion to Gardens* (Oxford, 1991), pp. 456–461

Landscape and Power, W.J.T. Mitchell (ed.)(Chicago and London, 2002) 2nd ed.

Lang, Sharon, '*Sulha* Peacemaking and the Politics of Persuasion', *Journal of Palestine Studies* 31 :3 (2002), pp. 52–66

Lefebvre, Henri, *Writings on Cities*, E. Kofman and E. Lebas (trans. and eds.)(Oxford, 1996)

Levin, Itamar, *Locked Doors: The Seizure of Jewish Property in Arab Countries*, trans. Rachel Neiman (Westport, Conn., 2001)

Levine, Mark, 'Planning to Conquer: Modernity and Its Antinomies in the "New-Old Jaffa"', in *Constructing A Sense of Place: Architecture and the Zionist Discourse*, Haim Yacobi (ed.)(Aldershot, 2004), pp. 192–224

Lindholm Schulz, Helena, *The Palestinian Diaspora: Formation of Identities and Politics of Homeland* (NY, 2003)

Liphschitz, Nili and Biger, Gideon, 'Afforestation Policy of the Zionist Movement in Palestine 1895–1948', *Cathedra* 80 (1996), pp. 88–108 [in Hebrew]

—, *Green Dress for a Country: The Afforestation in Eretz-Israel, The First Hundred Years 1850–1950* (Jerusalem, 2000)[in Hebrew]

Lissak, Moshe, *The Mass Immigration in the Fiftees: The Failure of the Melting Pot Policy* (Jerusalem, 1999)[in Hebrew]

Lockman, Zachary, *Comrades and Enemies: Arab and Jewish Workers in Palestine, 1906–1948* (Berkeley, 1996)

Lorch, N., *Korot Milchemet Ha'atzma'ut* (Tel Aviv, 1966)

Lu-Yon, H., and Kaluss, R., *Diyur BeIsrael: Mediniyut Ve'i- shivyon* (Tel Aviv, 1994)

Ludi, Regula, *Reparations for Nazi Victims in Postwar Europe* (Cambridge, 2012)

Lurie, Yehoshua, *The Walled City: Jews Among Arabs, Arabs Among Jews* (Tel Aviv, 2000)[in Hebrew]

Luz, N., 'Umayyad Ramle', *Cathedra* 79 (1996), pp. 22–52 [in Hebrew]

—, 'The Re-making of Beersheba: Winds of Modernization in Late Ottoman Sultanate', in *Ottoman Reforms and Muslim Regeneration: Studies in Honor of Prof. Butrus Abu Manneh*, I. Weissman , F. Zachs (eds.)(London and NY, 2005), pp. 187–210

Maier, Charles S., 'Overcoming the Past? Narrative and Negotiation, Remembering, and Reparation: Issues at the Interface of History and the Law', in *Politics and the Past: On Repairing Historical Injustices*, John Torpey (ed.)(Lanham, Md., 2003), pp. 295–304

Malkin, Ahuvia, *Ha'activist: Sipur Chayav shel Eliyahu Golomb* (Tel Aviv, 2007)

Margalit, Haim, 'Enactment of a Nationality Law in Israel', *The American Journal of Comparative Law* 2:1 (1953), pp. 63–66

Marin, L., 'Notes on a Semiotic Approach to *Parade, Cortege*, and *Procession*', in *Time Out of Time: Essays on the Festival*, Alessandro Falassi (ed.)(Albuquerque, 1987), pp. 220–228

McCormick, M., *Eternal Victory: Triumphal Rulership in Late Antiquity: Byzantium, and the Early Medieval West* (Cambridge, 1986)

Meir-Glizerstein, Esther, 'The Absorption of Iraqi Jews in Israel', in *The Age of Zionism*, A. Shapira, J. Reinharz and J. Harris (eds.)(Jerusalem, 2000), pp. 271–295 [in Hebrew]

Memory and Violence in the Middle East and North Africa, Ussama Makdisi and Paul A. Silverstein (eds.)(Bloomington, 2006)

Menahem, Gila, 'Arab Citizens in an Israeli City: Action and Discourse in Public Programmes', *Ethnic and Racial Studies* 21:3 (1998), pp. 545–557

Middle Eastern Cities 1900–1950: Public Places and Public Spheres in Transformation, Hans Chr. Korsholm Nielsen and Jacob Skovgaard-Petersen (eds.)(Aarhus, 2001)

The Military and Militarism in Israeli Society, Edna Lomsky-Feder and Eyal Ben-Ari (eds.)(NY, 1999)

Mishori, Alec, *Lo and Behold: Zionist Icons and Visual Symbols in Israeli Culture* (Tel Aviv, 2000)[in Hebrew]

Mitchell, W.J.T., 'Introduction', in *Landscape and Power*, W.J.T. Mitchell (ed.)(Chicago and London, 2002) 2nd ed., pp. 1–4

Mituv Tverya: Dapim Lecheker Tverya, Rephael Yankelevitch (ed.) (Jerusalem, 1988)

Mixed Towns, Trapped Communities: Historical Narratives, Spatial Dynamics, Gender Relations and Cultural Encounters in Palestinian-Israeli Towns, D. Monterescu and D. Rabinowitz (eds.)(Aldershot, 2007)

Molotch, Harvey, 'The City as a Growth Machine: Toward a Political Economy of Place', *The American Journal of Sociology* 82:2 (1976), pp. 309–332

Monterescu, Daniel, 'To Buy or Not to Be: Trespassing the Gated Community', *Public Culture* 21:2 (2009), pp. 403–430

—, 'Estranged Natives and Indigenized Immigrants: A Relational Anthropology of Ethnically Mixed Towns in Israel', *World Development* 39:2 (2011), pp. 270–281

Morris, B., 'Operation Dani and the Palestinian Exodus from Lydda and Ramle in 1948', *Middle East Journal* 40:1 (1986), pp. 82–109

—, *Israel's Border Wars, 1949–1956: Arab Infiltration, Israeli Retaliation and the Countdown to the Suez War* (Tel Aviv, 1996)[in Hebrew]

—, *The Birth of the Palestinian Refugee Problem Revisited* (Cambridge, 2004)

—, *1948: A History of the First Arab-Israeli War* (New Haven and London, 2008)

Mossek, Moshe, 'Kulanu Bulgarim', in *The Tribes –Evidence of Israel: Exile, Immigrations, Absorption, Contribution and Integration*, A. Mizrahi and A. Ben-David (eds.)(Netanya, 2001), pp. 238–258 [in Hebrew]

Munayyer, Spiro, 'The Fall of Lydda', *Journal of Palestine Studies* 27:4 (1998), pp. 80–98

Newman, Simon P., *Parades and the Politics of the Street: Festive Culture in the Early American Republic* (Philadelphia, 1997)

Nora, Pierre, 'Between Memory and History: Les Lieux de Mémoire', *Representations* 26 (1989), pp. 7–24

Nurieli, Beni, 'Hayehudim Ha'aravim Baghetto BeLod, 1950–1959', *Theory and Criticism* 26 (2005), pp. 13–42

Ozacky—Lazar, S., 'The Military Government as an Apparatus of Control of the Arab Citizens in Israel: The First Decade, 1948–1958', *Hamizrah Hehadash* 43 (2002), pp. 103–132

The Oxford Companion to Gardens (Oxford, 1991)

Petersen, A.D., 'Preliminary Report on Architectural Survey of Historic Buildings in Ramla', *Levant* 27 (1995), pp. 75–100

Petrovsky-Shtern, Y., 'The Marketplace in Balta: Aspects of Economic and Cultural Life', *East European Jewish Affairs* 37:3 (2007), pp. 277–298

Pinchevski, Amit and Torgovnik, Efraim, 'Signifying Passages: The Sign of Change in Israeli Street Names', *Media, Culture and Society* 24 (2002), pp. 365–388

Point of View: Four Approaches to Landscape Architecture in Israel, Lipa Yahalom *et al.* (eds.)(Tel Aviv, 1996)[in Hebrew]

Politics and the Past: On Repairing Historical Injustices, John Torpey (ed.) (Lanham, Md., 2003)

The Politics of Food, eds. Marianne Elizabeth Lien and Brigitte Nerlich (Oxford and NY, 2004)

Pratt, L.M., 'Arts of the Contact Zone', in *Ways of Reading*, D. Bartholomae and A. Petroksky (eds.)(NY, 1999)

Rabinowitz, D., 'Oriental Nostalgia: How the Palestinians Became "Israel's Arabs"', *Theory and Criticism* 4 (1993), pp. 141–152 [in Hebrew]

Rabinowitz, D. and Monterescu, D., 'Introduction: The Transformation of Urban Mix in Palestine/Israel in the Modern Era', in *Mixed Towns, Trapped Communities: Historical Narratives, Spatial Dynamics, Gender Relations and Cultural Encounters in Palestinian-Israeli Towns*, D. Monterescu and D. Rabinowitz (eds.)(Aldershot, 2007), pp. 1–34

Rabinowitz, Dan, Abu Baker, Khawla, *The Stand Tall Generation: The Palestinian Citizens of Israel Today* (Jerusalem, 2002)[in Hebrew]

Raz, Guy, *Photographers of Palestine: Eretz Israel/ Israel (1855–2000)*(Tel Aviv, 2003)[in Hebrew]

Re-Naming the Landscape, Jurgen Kleist and Bruce A. Butterfield (eds.)(NY, 1994)

Restitution and Memory: Material Restoration in Europe, Dan Diner and Gotthard Wunberg (eds.)(NY, 2007)

Rivlin, Gershon and Aliza, *The Stranger Cannot Understand: Code-Names in the Jewish Underground in Palestine* (Tel Aviv, 1988)[in Hebrew]

Robbery and Restitution: The Conflict Over Jewish Property in Europe, Martin Dean, Constantin Goschler and Philipp Ther (eds.)(NY, 2007)

Robertson, I. and Richards, P., 'Introduction', in *Studying Cultural Landscapes*, I. Robertson and P. Richards (eds.)(London, 2003), pp. 1–18

Rose, Norman A., *Chaim Weizmann: A Biography*, trans. Karmit Guy (Jerusalem, 1986) [in Hebrew]

Rosen-Ayalon, M., 'The First Century of Ramla', *Arabica* 43 (1996), pp. 251–263

—, 'The First Mosaic Discovered in Ramla', *Israel Exploration Journal* 26 (1976), pp. 104–119

Rosenhek, Zeev, *The Housing Policy Toward the Arabs in Israel in the 1950s-1970s* (Jerusalem, 1996)[in Hebrew]

Rouse, Joseph, 'Power/Knowledge', in *The Cambridge Companion to Foucault*, G. Gutting (ed.)(Cambridge, 1994), pp. 92–114

Rozen, Shay, 'A Tour around the British Cemetery in Ramla', *Ariel* 175 (2006), pp. 90–107 [in Hebrew]

Rubin, M., *Corpus Christi: The Eucharist in Late Medieval Culture* (Cambridge, 1991)

Rubinstein, Danny, *The People of Nowhere: The Palestinian Vision of Home*, trans. Ina Friedman (NY, 1991)

Safed: A Walk Through Time: A Waling-Tour Guide with Yad Ben-Zvi, Eyal Meron (ed.) (Jerusalem, 2006)[in Hebrew]

Said, Edward W., *Orientalism* (London, 1985)[1978]

Sassatelli, Roberta, *Consumer Culture: History, Theory and Politics* (London, 2007)

Sasson, Avi, 'The Ziyara of Nabi Rubin in the Late Ottoman and Mandate Period', *Hamizrah Hehadash* 45 (2005), pp. 209–218 [in Hebrew]

Schnell, Yitzhak, 'New Approaches to the Study of Mixed Cities: The Case of Israel', in *Together But Apart: Mixed Cities in Israel*, Elie Rekhes (ed.) (Tel Aviv, 2007), pp. 19–26 [in Hebrew]

Secular Ritual, S.F. Moore and B.G. Myerhoff (eds.)(Amsterdam, 1977)

Segev, Tom, *Palestine under the British* (Jerusalem, 1999)[in Hebrew]

Sela, Rona, *Photography in Palestine in the 1930s—1940s* ([Tel Aviv], 2001)
[in Hebrew]

Shadar, Hadas, 'Beer Sheva—a Model of the Development of Public
Housing in Israel', in *Beer Sheva: The Growth of a City: A Model of the
Development of Public Housing in Israel* (Beer Sheva, 2008), pp. 102–78.

Samy, Shahira, *Reparations to Palestinian Refugees: A Comparative Perspective*
(London and NY, 2010)

Shammas, Anton, 'Autocartography: The Case of Palestine, Michigan', *The
Threepenny Review* 63 (1995), pp. 7–9

Shapir, Gershon, 'Land, Work and Population in the Zionist Colonization:
General and Unique Perspectives', in *Israeli Society: Critical Perspectives*,
Uri Ram (ed.)(Tel Aviv, 1993), pp. 104–119 [in Hebrew]

Sharaby, Rachel, 'May Day Ceremonies in the State of Israel's First Decade:
From a Sectorial to a National Holiday', *Megamot* 44 (2005), pp. 106–
136 [in Hebrew]

Shenhav, Yehouda, 'The Jews of Iraq: Zionist Ideology, and the Property of
the Palestinian Refugees of 1948: An Anomaly of National Accounting',
International Journal of Middle East Studies 31:4 (1999), pp. 605–630

—, 'Ethnicity and National Memory: The World Organization of Jews from
Arab Countries (WOJAC) in the Context of the Palestinian National
Struggle', *British Journal of Middle Eastern Studies* 29:1 (2002), pp.
27–56

Shiler, Eli, 'The British Cemeteries in Eretz Israel', *Ariel* 171–172 (2005),
pp. 196–223 [in Hebrew]

Shor, Nissan, *Dancing with Tears in Our Eyes: History of Club and Discotheque
Culture in Israel* (Tel Aviv, 2008)[in Hebrew]

Sibley, David, *Geographies of Exclusion* (London, 1995)

Slymovics, Susan, *The Object of Memory: Arab and Jew Narrate the Palestinian
Village* (Philadelphia, 1998)

Smoli, Eliezer, 'Letoldot Chag Haneti'ot', *Teva Va'aretz* 9 (1966), pp. 70–72

Sociology of Leisure: A Reader, C. Critcher, P. Braham and A. Tomlinson
(eds.)(London and NY, 1995)

Sofer,Gili, 'Siach Brook in Haifa: The Bustan', *Masa Acher* 180 (September
2006), pp. 104–106.[in Hebrew]

Space, Land, Home, Yehouda Shenhav (ed.)(Jerusalem, 2003)[in Hebrew]

Stern, Anat, 'Is the Army Authorized to Prosecute Civilians? Trial of Civilian Looting by the IDF in 1948', in *Citizens at War: Studies on the Civilian Society During the Israeli War of Independence,* M. Bar-On and M. Chazan (eds.)(Jerusalem, 2010)[in Hebrew], pp. 465–493

Sternhell, Zeev, *The Founding Myths of Israel: Nationalism, Socialism, and the Making of the Jewish State* (Princeton, 1998)

Stowe, David W., 'The Politics of Café Society', *Journal of American History* 84:4 (1998), pp. 1384–1406

Studying Cultural Landscapes, I. Robertson and P. Richards (eds.)(London, 2003)

Taking Wrongs Seriously: Apologies and Reconciliation, Elazar Barkan and Alexander Karn (eds.)(Stanford, Calf., 2006)

Tal, David, *War in Palestine 1948: Strategy and Diplomacy* (London, 2004)

Talmor, Sharon, 'Back to Nabi Mussa', *Eretz ve'Teva* 99 (2005), 60–66

Tamari, Yuval, *Seker Tichnuni Bashchunot Ha'arviyot Ba'ir Ramla* (Jerusalem, 2005)

Time Out of Time: Essays on the Festival, Alessandro Falassi (ed.)(Albuquerque, 1987)

Together But Apart: Mixed Cities in Israel, Elie Rekhes (ed.)(Tel Aviv, 2007) [in Hebrew]

Tolan, Sandy, *The Lemon Tree: An Arab, A Jew, and the Heart of the Middle East* (NY, 2006)

Torpey, John, *Making Whole What Has Been Smashed: On Reparations Politics* (Cambridge, Mass., 2006)

Totah, Faedah M., 'Return to the Origin: Negotiating the Modern and the Unmodern in the Old City of Damascus', *City & Society* 21:1 (2009), pp. 58–81

Towns in Israel: A Reader, A.Sachar, D. Weintraub, E.Cohen and L. Shelach (eds.)(Jerusalem, 1973)[in Hebrew]

The Tribes –Evidence of Israel: Exile, Immigrations, Absorption, Contribution and Integration, A. Mizrahi and A. Ben-David (eds.)(Netanya, 2001) [in Hebrew]

Tsimhoni, Dafna, 'Hanotzrim BeIsrael: Beyn Dat Lepolitika', in *The Arabs in Israeli Politics: Dilemmas of Identity,* Elie Rekhes (ed.)(Tel Aviv, 1998), pp. 63–72 [in Hebrew]

Turner, Victor, *The Forest of Symbols: Aspects of Ndembu Ritual* (NY, 1967)

—, *The Ritual Process: Structure and Anti-Structure* (London, 1969)

Vekart, Ora, *Lod: Geografia Historit* (Tel Aviv, 1977)

de Vries, David, 'Cross-National Collective Action in Palestine's Mixed Towns: The 1946 Civil Servants Strike', in *Mixed Towns, Trapped Communities: Historical Narratives, Spatial Dynamics, Gender Relations and Cultural Encounters in Palestinian-Israeli Towns,* D. Monterescu and D. Rabinowitz (eds.)(Aldershot, 2007), pp. 85–112

Weiss, M., 'Bereavement, Commemoration and Collective Identity in Contemporary Israeli Society', *Anthropological Quarterly* 70:2 (1997), pp. 91–101

Weiss, Yfaat, *A Confiscated Memory: Wadi Salib and Haifa's Lost Heritage,* trans. Avner Greenberg (NY, 2011)

Wiesen, S. Jonathan, *Creating the Nazi Marketplace: Commerce and Consumption in the Third Reich* (Cambridge, 2011)

Yacobi, Haim, 'Urban Iconoclasm: The Case of the "Mixed City" of Lod', in *Constructing A Sense of Place: Architecture and the Zionist Discourse,* Haim Yacobi (ed.)(Aldershot, 2004), pp. 165–191

—, 'Planning, Control and Spatial Protest: The Case of the Jewish-Arab Town of Lydd/Lod', in *Mixed Towns, Trapped Communities: Historical Narratives, Spatial Dynamics, Gender Relations and Cultural Encounters in Palestinian-Israeli Towns,* D. Monterescu and D. Rabinowitz (eds.) (Aldershot, 2007), pp. 135–155

Yahav, Dan, *Gardens and Gardening in Tel Aviv-Jaffa* (Azur, 2006)[in Hebrew]

Yang, Anand A., *Bazaar India: Markets, Society, and the Colonial State in Gangetic Bihar* (Berkeley and LA, 1998)

Yiftachel, Oren and Roded, Batya, 'To be Your Prisoner of Love: Judaizing Space in Israel/Palestine', *Motar* 11 (2003), pp. 35–44

Young, Iris Marion, 'Residential Segregation and Differentiated Citizenship', *Citizenship Studies* 3:2 (1999), pp. 237–252

Zerubavel, Yael, 'Patriotic Sacrifice and the Burden of Memory in Israeli Secular National Hebrew Culture', in *Memory and Violence in the Middle East and North Africa,* Ussama Makdisi and Paul A. Silverstein (eds.)(Bloomington, 2006), pp. 73–100

Zilberman, Ifrah, 'The Renewal of the Pilgrimage to Nabi Musa', in *Sacred Space in Israel and Palestine: Religion and Politics,* Marshall J. Breger,

Yitzhak Reiterad and Leonard Hammer (eds.)(London and NY, 2012), pp. 103–115

Unpublished Works

Bar Nisan, N., 'Ramla's Museum' (work submitted to the Department of Geography at the Hebrew University, 2004)[in Hebrew]

Gat, S., 'The City of Ramla in the Middle Ages' (PhD thesis, Bar Ilan University, 2003)[in Hebrew]

Kassem, F., 'Between Private and Collective Memory: The Case of Palestinian Women from Lod and Ramleh' (PhD Thesis, Ben Gurion University of the Negev, 2006)[in Hebrew]

Keren-Steinmetz, Hila, 'The Location and Place of Ramle's Old Market' (work submitted to Geography Department, Bar Ilan University, 2010) [in Hebrew]

Mesika, Natali, 'Archaeology in Ramla: Findings Report and Bibliography' (1996)[in Hebrew]

Electronic Resources

Palestine Remembered—The Oral History Project:
http://www.palestineremembered.com/OralHistory/Interviews-Listing/Story1151.html#al-Ramla

Ramla's Municipality Website:
http://www.ramla.muni.il

Index

Abdullah, King of Transjordan 221, 232, 233 n. 80
absentees/present-absentees 39, 40 n. 51, 42, 43, 51, 53, 54, 211
Abu Ghosh, village of 222
Abudi, Avraham 71-73, 74, 78
Acre 25, 71 n. 36, 132, 199 n. 128, 202, 206, 225 n. 46, 233, 233 n. 82, 234 n. 84
'Adas, Shafiq 189
afforestation 105, 114, 128
Afif, Anton 66, 67
al-Bira, village of 228
al-Husseini, Musa Kazim 135
al-Husseini, Haj Amin 159
al-Khayri, Maliha 65 n. 15, 79 n. 60, 115, 119 n. 64, 220 n. 16 and 17
al-Nachas, Isma'il 50, 80, 236 n. 92
al-Qadir al-Hussayni, Abd 222
al-Qubab, village of 230
al-Rauf, Abed 52-53
al-Tall, Abdallah 226, 231
al-Wahab, Nicola Azar 43
Allenby, Edmund 131
Alon, Yigal 30, 224, 228-229
Altman, Aryeh 83, 88
Altneuland 104
Amasyas, 'Adel 73, 78
Amidar 70, 174, 175, 181, 184 n. 68, 191, 192
appropriation 15, 17, 19, 20, 25, 26, 45, 46, 53, 60, 61, 62, 71, 78, 83, 89, 90, 93, 94, 105, 109, 117, 121, 126, 132, 133, 134, 137, 165, 187, 189, 215, 216
Arab High Committee 223
Arab Legion 221-231
Arab National Movement 220
Arab Revolt, the (1936-1939) 81, 158, 220
Arab Workers' Congress (AWC) 149
archaeology 18, 160
Ashkenazi Jews 20, 89, 96, 172, 173, 176, 177, 178, 182, 192, 202
Australia 106
Austria 23
Azar, George 71

Balta 63
Barriya, village of 225
Bastuni, Rostam 80, 82
Bat-Yam 178
Baysan/Beit Shean 25
Beersheba/Beer Sheva 25, 69, 131, 139, 186, 206
Ben-Gurion, David 30-31, 122 n. 78, 221, 228-229, 232, 235
Benjamin of Tudela, Rabbi 218
Berlin 66, 116, 151 n. 65, 197
Berman, Etka 66, 67
Bet Dajan 223
Bet Naballah 224
Bethlehem 226
Beyt Chanan 159
Bialik, Chaim N. 117 n. 63, 126, 173, 188, 231
Bible, the 28-29, 110
Bishara, Eliya 54
Black Panthers, the 89
Bonaparte, Napoleon 218
Bonné, Alfred 68
British Mandate 18, 43, 56, 61, 64, 75, 81, 102, 103, 109, 111, 116, 120, 124, 151, 180, 187 n. 84, 218, 221
Bulgaria 34, 85, 86-87, 139, 149, 232, 234

cafés 75, 77, 78-79, 180 see also Ramle/ Ramla, cafés in
Cairo 78, 207
Chicago 147
citizenship 167-168, 203
Cohen, Yidov 83
Cohn, Fritz 176, 197, 198
Committee of Inquiry into Property Claims in Ramla and Lydda (1949) 51, 53
Commonwealth War Graves Commission (CWGC) 129
Communism 147-150
compensation 23, 24, 40 n. 51, 46, 49, 53, 92, 93, 94, 96, 181, 211
conservation 103 n. 14, 202
consumption 61, 62
contact zones 16, 179, 180

crusaders 156, 158, 217
Custodian of Abandoned Property *see*
   Custodian of Absentees Property
Custodian of Absentees Property (CAP) 30
   n. 19, 31, 39, 40 n. 51, 41-44, 46-48, 49,
   50, 51, 52, 53, 55, 87, 92, 93, 94, 185,
   191, 195, 212

Dabit, Samir 10, 73 n. 42, 74 n. 46, 75 n.
   48, 79, 124 n. 85
Damascus 63
Darazi, Yitzhak 12
Dayan, Moshe 163
Diaspora 95, 101, 136, 167, 207
Dib Abdallah Mustafa 222
dispossession 23, 25-27, 31, 35, 38, 39, 41,
   44, 50, 53, 78, 79, 82, 83, 90, 91, 94, 95,
   96, 211
Dori, Yaacov 30
Douglas, Mary 169, 182
Durkheim, Émile 134

Easter 135, 155
Ekron 158
el-Hairi, Bashir 207-212
Erem, Moshe 44, 47 n. 73 and n. 74, 83
   n. 76
Eshkenazi, Dalia 210, 212
Eshkenazi, Moshe 212
Eshkol, Levi 11
Ethiopia 215
Etzel 11 n. 3, 189

Fanus, Eliya 44, 50 n. 85, 52, 236
farhud, the (1941) 85-86
Fauzi, Mahmood 12
Foucault, Michel 134
France 137
Friberg, Dov 33, 231

gardens 102-105, 107, 111, 113, 114, 115,
   116, 127, 131-132 *see also* Ramle/Ramle,
   gardens in
Gaza 63, 65, 163, 195, 206, 207
Gedera 195
Geneva Regulations, the 40
Germany 23, 38, 61, 95, 116, 121
Glazer, Yisrael 49
Glubb, Johan (Glubb Pasha) 221, 231
Golomb, Eliyahu 125
Great Britain 41, 55
Gvirtz, Yitzhak 30

Haganah, the 30 n. 19, 46, 125, 126, 188,
   231, 234
Hague Regulations, the 28, 40
Haifa 16, 25, 32 n. 27, 34 n. 35, 36, 45, 75,
   89, 103, 121, 131, 138, 144 n. 39, 163,
   169, 178, 186, 206, 209, 213, 225 n. 46,
   232, 235
Haji, Haret 225
Halewi, Aharon 107
Hallak, Hana Zakaria 71-73, 77, 78, 80,
   83, 87, 88, 177
Hallak, William 71
Hamburg 116
Hanukkah 136
Haymarket Affair (1886) 147
Hebron 163, 222, 233 n. 80
Herzl, Theodor (Benjamin Ze'ev) 104, 105
Histadrut, the 148, 150, 153
Holocaust, the 86
Holon 178

identity 13, 14, 15, 21, 62, 96, 99, 101,
   106, 117, 122, 123, 127, 129, 134, 141,
   156, 158, 164, 169, 179, 187, 208, 215
Independence Day 68, 122, 123, 127-128,
   132, 137-138, 139-140, 141, 142
India 61-128
infiltration 45, 54-55, 161
internationalism 147-148, 152
Intifada, the first 163
Iraq 24, 38, 70, 84, 85, 86, 88, 89, 90, 91,
   92, 93, 94, 139, 174, 187, 189 *see also*
   Ramle/Ramle, population of, Iraqui-Jews
Israel, State of 13, 21, 24, 25, 27, 28, 33, 35,
   38, 39, 40, 42, 44, 46, 48, 49, 53, 54, 55,
   56, 59, 60, 62, 70, 80, 89, 90, 93, 94, 106,
   110, 116, 119, 127, 136, 139, 140, 145,
   147, 154, 172, 175, 177, 184, 191, 194,
   196, 197, 199, 201, 202, 213, 214, 235
   Arab minority in 17, 46, 48, 80, 94, 96,
      142, 144, 168
   Development Authority 36 n. 40, 40 n.
      51
   High Court of Justice 53
   housing policy of 172, 175, 184-185,
      201-202
   Israel Lands Administration 59
   Knesset, the 71 n. 37, 80, 91, 92, 94,
      123, 149, 150 n. 61, 168, 234 n. 84
   Ministry of Agriculture 39, 46, 51, 195-
      196, 198
   Ministry of Defence 36, 228, 232

Ministry of Finance   41, 46, 47, 56, 58, 59 n. 111, 232

Ministry of Housing   183, 184, 191, 192

Ministry of Justice   43

Ministry of Labour   149, 175

Ministry of Minorities Affairs   30 n. 19, 43, 44, 45, 46, 47, 48, 49, 50, 51, 82, 83 n. 76, 229

Ministry of the Police   43, 50, 82, 94

Ministry of Religious Affairs   160, 161-162

Ministry of the Interior   43, 52, 53, 74, 80, 82, 112 n. 46, 114, 139, 200, 233, 234

police   12, 18, 19, 36, 43, 49, 54, 55, 59, 72, 73, 74, 75, 78, 79, 80, 81, 84, 149, 154, 159, 161, 162 n. 100, 163, 173, 195, 222, 223, 233

political parties in –
Herut   83, 88, 150 n. 61
Maki   83, 148, 150, 154, 178, 185, 186, 190 n. 93, 234 n. 84
Mapam   80 n. 66, 83, 148, 150, 152
Progressive   83
State Comptroller   56, 59

Israel Defence Forces (IDF)   18, 27, 29, 30, 41, 110, 125, 138, 139, 137-146, 224, 228

Israelisation   12, 13, 15, 17, 19, 90, 96, 114, 119, 131, 165, 183, 187, 213, 214, 216

Istanbul   78

Italy   133

Jaffa   16, 25, 28, 32, 35, 42, 43, 48, 63, 75, 91, 100, 104, 113, 119 n. 66, 121, 136, 144, 150, 161, 169, 173, 178, 180, 184, 188, 202, 206, 213, 218, 223, 232, 233 n. 82, 235

Jamal, Khalil   52

Jawitz, Zusman   30, 32, 33, 36, 42, 43, 45-46, 47, 48, 49, 52, 125-126, 149, 160-161, 231

Jericho   135, 220

Jerusalem   11, 25, 32, 36, 48, 63, 73 n. 42, 78, 89, 111, 135, 138, 139, 142, 143, 144, 145, 150, 159, 163, 171, 173, 206, 207, 213, 218, 219, 222, 223, 224, 226

Jewish Agency (JA)   10, 35, 48, 49, 122 n. 78, 192, 232, 233

Jewish National Fund (JNF)   40 n. 51, 105, 128, 151, 198

Jihad al-Mukades   222

Jordan/Transjordan   52, 54, 66 n. 18, 141,

195, 206, 221, 222, 231, 232

Judaisation   12 n. 9, 91, 96

Kaduri, Na'im   73, 74, 78

Kaduri, Zvi   71-73, 74, 78

Kaniuk, Yoram   33

Kaplan, Eliezer   41, 232

Katra, village of   195

key, as symbol   211-212, 227

key money   36

Khairi, Ahmad   207 n. 8, 228

Khairi, Hussam   225

Khairi, Khanom   222 n. 26, 228

Khairi, Mustafa   207, 219, 225

Kheiri family   100, 111

Khouri, Imada   225

KKL *see* Jewish National Fund

Kluger, Zoltan   151-152

Koran, the   102, 155

Kovner, Abba   29

Kudkha, Amin   153

landscape   13, 15, 20, 24, 33, 45, 60, 62, 91, 99-107, 108, 114, 115, 116, 121, 122, 128, 132, 134, 151, 169, 202, 212, 213

Latrun   221, 224, 230

Lebanon   105

legislation   38, 39-40, 53, 60, 62, 92-93, 96, 103-104, 167-168, 211, 234

leisure   16, 75, 115, 132, 178

Lema'an Zion   218

Lev, Pesach   139

Levant, the   218

Libya   195

liminality   75, 96, 130, 134, 179

Livne, Eliezer   123

looting *see* plunder

Loudon, John Claudius   116

Lydda   17, 25, 30, 32, 41, 42, 46, 48, 51, 63, 131, 139, 145, 150, 160, 161, 170, 182 n. 64, 186, 194, 195, 206, 213, 218, 221, 222, 224, 225, 227, 229, 230, 231, 232, 233, 234

ma'abarot   72, 77, 84, 85, 87, 88, 8, 174-175, 182, 192, 203 *see also* Ramle/Ramle, *ma'abarot* in

Majdal/Ashkelon   25, 45, 175, 195, 232

Malban   70

maps   13, 14, 18, 59, 62, 111, 120, 124, 145, 156, 175, 189, 190, 194, 215

markets   61, 63, 64, 68, 69 *see also* Ramle/

Ramla, markets in

Marxism   147, 148

Mass, Dani   223

Meir, Golda   34 n. 35

Melamed, Meir   58, 72, 167, 169, 234, 236

Memorial Day   127-128

memory   16, 17, 35, 100, 101, 102, 114,
   119, 121, 122, 125, 126, 127, 128, 129,
   132, 137, 145, 146, 147, 189, 205, 206,
   207, 208, 210, 215, 216, 227

Mendelson, Hugo   66, 67

Micko and Loti   34, 149, 232

Mikve Israel   121

Miller, Zvi   121, 125

Mishmarot, Kibbutz   33

mixed city   13, 15-16, 20, 89, 132, 138,
   139, 151, 164, 177, 183, 185, 210, 212,
   213, 214 *see also* Ramle/Ramle, as a mixed
   town

Mizrachi Jews   20, 75, 89, 90, 96, 172, 177,
   178, 179, 190, 192, 202

Mohamed, the Prophet   155

Na'an, Kibbutz   51 n. 88, 225

Nabi Mussa   135, 158, 159

Nabi Rubin   158, 159

Nabi Salah   20, 154, 155-164, 165

Nablus   163, 222, 230

Nakba *see* War, 1948

Nakhas, Isma'il *see* al-Nachas, Isma'il

naming/renaming   13-14, 15, 17, 19, 20,
   66, 71, 121-122, 124-125, 128, 177-178,
   187-190, 214, 215

nationalisation   24, 38, 93, 153, 184, 188,
   215

nationalism   14, 19, 20, 21, 62, 80, 91, 96,
   99, 101, 105, 108-109, 110, 114, 117,
   122, 123, 124, 127, 129, 133, 137, 141,
   145, 147-148, 152, 153, 154, 163, 164,
   165, 189, 219

Nazareth   25, 148-149, 163, 168, 235

Nazism   23, 38, 41, 61, 95

Netanya   32, 33

Nezer Sereni, Kibbutz   194

nostalgia   101, 114, 209

Operation Dani   30, 223-224, 227, 228,
   229

Operation Shikmona   186

Orientalism   69, 96-97, 177

Ottoman period   69, 131, 186 *see also*
   Ramle/Ramla, during Ottoman period

Palestine Labour League (PLL)   148, 153

Palestinian-Israeli conflict   24, 40, 183, 220

Palm Sunday   135

Palmach, the   30, 31

Paris Congress of the Second International
   (1889)   147

Pasha, Jamal   131

pinuy-binuy   183-184

plunder   26-33, 41, 42, 53, 92

Po'aley Zion   147, 148

Poland   9, 38, 41, 46, 66, 95, 231

pollution/cleanliness   68 n. 25, 169-171

population exchange   91, 94

prickly pear   15 n. 16, 108

private/public sphere   27, 75, 77, 90, 102,
   134

property   9, 15, 41, 74, 77, 182, 215, 225
   absentees and 'abandoned' Arab   19, 24-
      60, 70, 89-90, 91-94, 96, 119, 211, 212,
      227
   in Arab countries, Jewish   24, 85, 91-94,
      96
   in Europe, Jewish   38, 94-95
   waqf   23, 70, 112

Purim   136

Rabin, Yizhak   228

rallies   82, 123, 135, 147, 162 n. 101, 215

Ramallah   54, 55, 100, 163, 207, 211, 221,
   222, 224, 228, 230

Ramle Platform   148

Ramle/Ramle
   as a mixed town   13, 15-16, 20, 77, 89,
      138, 139, 151, 164, 185, 212, 213-214
   as Rama (Arimathea)   217
   cafés in   12, 19, 20, 55, 62, 71-82, 83,
      87, 91, 95, 96, 120, 177, 179, 180, 192,
      214, 220
   cemeteries in   111, 112, 118, 129-131,
      132, 155, 199
   central bus station in   150, 180
   churches in   226, 229
      Anglican   52
      Armenian   64, 70
      Greek Orthodox   43, 70
   cinemas in   200, 219, 220
   clubs in   179-180
   demographics   184, 220, 234-235
   dilapidated houses in   138, 171, 175,
      181, 191-192
   during British Mandate   18, 43, 56, 64,

111, 120, 124, 187 n. 84, 218
during the 1948 War 18, 19, 25, 26, 27-34, 36-37, 41-43, 44, 46-47, 48-51, 54, 55, 60, 65, 90, 114, 160-161, 162 n. 100, 221-235
during Mamluk period 158, 218
during the Middle Ages 17-18, 63, 112, 155
during Ottoman period 64, 218
earthquakes in 217, 218, 219
expansion of 194-201
gardens in 19, 20, 100, 111, 112-113, 114, 116-117, 118, 131, 132, 146, 175, 178
  British War Memorial Cemetery 118, 129-131, 132
  Gan Hahaganah 118, 124-129, 132
  Municipal Garden, the/Gan Hanasi 64, 111, 112, 118, 119-124, 131, 132, 214
Jewish settlement of 15, 32, 33, 36, 49, 65, 78, 86, 87, 114, 117, 139, 144, 149, 152, 167, 170, 173, 176, 177, 184, 196, 203, 232-233, 235, 236
ma'abarot in 72, 84, 85, 87, 88, 89, 174, 175, 182, 192, 203
markets in 19, 20, 62, 63-71, 76, 77, 87, 91, 96, 150, 155, 159, 179, 180, 192, 218
mayor of *see* Melamed, Meir *and* Stein, Yehuda
military administration in 18, 30, 32, 36, 45, 51, 125, 149, 151, 153, 160-161, 231
mosques in 160, 161, 201, 226
  al-Zaytune 52
  Great Mosque (al-Jami al-Kabir, Jami al-Umari) 64, 65, 155, 156, 162, 179, 218
  White Mosque (al-Jami al-Abyad) 155, 156, 160, 217
municipality of 10, 14, 18, 43, 44, 45, 49, 55-59, 62, 63, 64, 66, 68, 70, 79, 82, 84, 86-87, 89, 90, 111, 112, 113, 114, 116, 117-118, 119-124, 125, 128, 131, 150, 150, 167, 168, 170, 174, 175, 178, 181, 182, 183, 184, 185, 187, 188, 189, 191, 192, 194, 195, 200, 201, 214, 219, 222, 233-234, 235
museum of 10, 56, 122, 214
name of 13-14
neighbourhoods in

Agaf Hashikun 175
Bilu 175
El Mufti 111
Jawarish 20, 194-201, 203
Old City, the 20, 71, 73, 74, 79, 90, 91, 117, 123, 155, 168, 170, 171, 172-203
Neve David 117, 175, 178, 185, 203
Saknat Fanus 194
sakne (the Arab neighbourhood, *ghetto*) 11, 36, 42, 43, 45, 66, 72, 78, 79, 87, 89, 90, 117, 123, 124, 128, 131, 149, 151, 154, 168, 173, 185, 186, 193, 231-232, 235
Sprinzak 177, 176
Taf-Zain 175
olive industry in 14, 109, 112, 113, 114, 176
population of –
  Bulgarian Jews 34, 85, 86-87, 139, 149, 232, 234
  Christian Arabs 21, 54, 70, 71, 84, 131, 178, 184, 190, 193, 217, 220, 230, 231, 234-235, 236
  Iraqui Jews 20, 21, 70-71, 73-75, 78, 79, 82-97, 139, 174, 177, 189, 199
  Muslim Arabs 50, 70, 80, 131, 132, 142, 155, 156, 158, 161, 162, 164, 178, 184, 190, 193, 220, 231, 234-235, 236 n. 92
processions in
  May Day 20, 124 n. 85, 136, 147-154, 164, 165
  military parade (1954) 20, 136, 137-147, 164, 165
  Nabi Salah parade 20, 154, 155-164, 165
Society for Understanding and Friendship between Jews and Arabs in 200
St Helena's Cisterns 117, 202 n. 137
streets in 12, 19, 20, 26, 30, 33, 34, 64, 65, 66, 71, 74, 79, 117, 118, 119, 124-125, 128, 137, 138, 143, 144, 146, 150, 151, 152, 153, 154, 155, 157, 162, 164, 165, 170, 171, 173, 178, 186, 187, 188-190, 199, 208, 211, 215, 223, 230, 231
strikes in 72, 81
symbol of 14-15, 114
violence in
  1949 36-37
  1950 153-154
  1952 73-74, 79-80, 81, 82, 84, 88,

91, 95
  1956 71-73, 79, 80-84, 88, 95
  1959 154
  1965 11-12
  White Tower 117, 156, 159, 194, 202, n.
    137, 216, 217
refugees, Palestinian 24, 25, 26, 48, 54, 55,
  92, 101, 121, 161, 195, 196, 206, 211,
  223, 227, 230-231, 232
Rehovot 145, 158
Reichart, Ezra 28
reparation politics 23, 24
return visits 19, 20, 54, 205-214
returnees, Palestinian 33, 39, 45, 54, 206,
  230, 235
Rishon LeZion 158, 213
ritual 13, 122, 125, 134, 137, 145, 159, 211
rootedness *see sumud*

sabra and *sabres see* prickly pear
Safad 25, 32, 69, 127, 206
Said, Edward 69
Sakakini, Khalil 219
Salbit, village of 230
Sarafand *see* Tzrifin
Sefrou (Morocco) 63, 64
segregation 16, 20, 75, 90, 131, 153, 169,
  173, 177, 178, 181, 190-193, 195, 202,
  203, 232
Shafrir, Dov 41-42, 43, 47
Shapira, Chaim-Moshe 233, 234 n. 84
Shar'abi, Yisrael 95
Sharet (Shertok), Moshe 92, 197, 229, 232
Shitrit, Bechor 50, 82, 83, 94, 229
shuk see markets
Simchat Torah 122-123
Six Days War *see* War, 1967
South Africa 106
Soviet Union 136, 215
squatting 35-37, 49, 181
St Joseph 217
St Nicodemus 217
Star of David, symbol of 14, 114
Stein, Yehuda 184
structure/anti-structure 134, 145, 146, 169
Subcommittee on Ramla Affairs (1952) 74-
  75, 82-83, 84, 88, 91, 94, 95
Sultan, Idris 223
suq see markets
sumud 109
Syria 65, 105, 131, 141
Taji, Muhammad 10, 17 n. 23, 65, 163
Tehran 63

Tel Aviv 11, 41, 46, 52, 68, 75, 107, 113,
  116, 119 n. 66, 126, 136, 138, 139, 144,
  145, 146, 150, 169, 170, 171, 178, 180,
  213, 221, 224, 229
Tiberias 25, 139, 174, 186, 206
Tokyo 63
Toren (née Elchalal), Bilha 69, 130
trees 100-104, 107, 108, 109, 110, 111, 112,
  113, 115, 117, 118, 120, 124, 125, 126,
  128, 129, 132, 146, 171, 203, 214, 223
  citrus 100-101, 111, 101 n. 5, 108, 112,
    113, 223
  cypress 128, 129
  eucalyptus 108
  olive 14, 20, 44, 52, 108-111, 112, 113,
    114, 128, 176
  palm 104, 120, 128
  pine 108, 128
  planting of 105, 109, 112, 115-117, 124,
    125, 127, 128, 146
  uprooting of 44, 52, 112 n. 46, 114, 116
Tu Bishvat 125-126
Tzriffin 142

UN Partition Resolution (1947) 220, 221
United Kingdom *see* Great Britain
United States 106

War of Independence *see* War, 1948
Watts Riots, the (1965) 199
Weinberg, Shlomo 107, 127
Weitz, Yosef 198
Weizmann, Haim 121-122
World Organisation for Jews from Arab
  Countries (WOJAC) 93
War, 1948 12, 18, 19, 25, 26, 28, 56, 65,
  114, 119, 121, 137, 143, 144, 189, 206,
  213, 221-233
  1967 200, 206
  First World 41, 109, 128, 129, 132
  Second World 38, 41, 129

Yana'it Ben Zvi, Rachel 178, 202
Yashresh, moshav 194
Yazur, village of 228
Yizhak, Rina 34-35

Zidan, Abdullah 31
Zionism 12 n. 9, 14, 20, 66, 83, 85, 86, 93,
  101, 104, 105-107, 108, 113, 114, 116,
  117-118, 119, 122, 123, 125-126, 128,
  129, 136, 147, 148, 151, 159, 167, 168,
  183, 188, 189, 212, 213

Ramle, when most of the
r material and symbolic
ose who remained in or
came a minority in their

on that the city of Ramle/
s differential implications
ges the town experienced
Piroyansky thoroughly
s and practices linked to
rban landscape redesign,
here in three different yet
national.

book—those of property
rban spatial practices—
t is first and foremost
aphical, anthropological,
s and terminologies to
h.

historian of medieval
her PhD doctorate at
n (2005). She has since
l text books, as well as
g the fascinating inter-
e, religion and politics in
th a focus on the creation
rtyrs in fourteenth and
d (*Martyrs in the Making:*
e Macmillan, 2008).
re, Piroyansky took up a
rly studying the cultural
as so far authored a few
nding at the heart of the
isation of an Arab Town
investigation. Piroyansky
quently referred to as the

Danna Piroyansky **Ramle Remade**

Danna Piroyansk

RAMLE I

The Israelisation of
1948–1967

π

www.ingramcontent.com/pod-product-compliance
Lightning Source LLC
Chambersburg PA
CBHW051821040426
42447CB00006B/312